THE
SOCIAL CONTRACT

THE
SOCIAL CONTRACT

A Critical Study of its Development

BY

J. W. GOUGH
FELLOW OF ORIEL COLLEGE

SECOND EDITION

GREENWOOD PRESS, PUBLISHERS
WESTPORT, CONNECTICUT

65050

Library of Congress Cataloging in Publication Data

Gough, John Wiedhofft.
    The social contract.

    Reprint of the 1957 ed. published by Clarendon
Press, Oxford.
    Includes bibliographical references and index.
    1. Social contract.   I.   Title.
[JC336.G6   1978]   320.1'1   78-6099
ISBN 0-313-20494-2

First edition 1936

This reprint has been authorized by the Clarendon Press Oxford

Reprinted in 1978 by Greenwood Press, Inc.,
51 Riverside Avenue, Westport, CT. 06880

Printed in the United States of America

10 9 8 7 6 5 4 3 2 1

PREFACE TO SECOND EDITION

DURING the twenty years since this book was first published I have been working on only a relatively small part of the very long stretch of time it covers. Some chapters, therefore, seemed to me to need a good deal of revision, but the other chapters, though they probably needed revising just as much, did not strike me in that way. The result, I must admit, is something of a patchwork. There is a new paragraph towards the end of Chapter IV, but otherwise the chapters on the Ancient World and the Middle Ages are reprinted largely as they stood, except for the correction of some minor errors, and a number of places where I have tried to clarify or otherwise improve the phraseology. In Chapters V–IX, on the other hand, the alterations are more substantial, and there are some pages which had to be rewritten altogether. Chapter X is another that contains only very slight changes, but a section that seemed to call for fairly drastic revision was the discussion of Rousseau in Chapter XI. At the end of this chapter I have added a few paragraphs on Hegel's attack on the contract theory, and Chapter XII has also been expanded and altered somewhat. A kindly review of the first edition by Professor Keith Feiling impelled me to insert two or three pages on Coleridge (whose significance I had overlooked) at the beginning of Chapter XIII. I have also revised and enlarged the final chapter, which in its original form made a very inadequate conclusion.

When the book first appeared, some critics said that it was too much concerned with theory, and did not pay enough attention to the actual events and situations which gave rise to the theory. This is a criticism to which any history of thought must be liable to some degree. I had had it in mind (cf. my original preface), and alterations in the present edition go some way, I hope, to meet it, but to meet it fully would have meant writing a different and much longer book. Perhaps the most serious risk in writing the history of an idea is that by following its appearances in a succession of writers, especially when each writer admits his indebtedness by quotations from and references to his predecessors, one may give an appearance of continuity which is really misleading. On the other hand it would be a mistake to concentrate entirely on the practical utility of the contract theory. Many of its exponents were professors and scholars whose interests were mainly academic, and whose main concern with it was as an element in the construction of a systematic political philosophy. Nevertheless, the contract theory did not develop entirely by the force of its own inner logic. It was evoked at different times and in different places by historical circumstances, usually as a means of attacking some existing régime, and then men went to the books to find and adapt and refurbish the arguments that suited them. Maybe it was only when men of action with a cause at heart borrowed the theory as a weapon to do battle with that the contract affected the history of the world. Yet without the thinkers the theory would not have been so readily, if at all, available.

I have sometimes been asked what I meant by the statement, in the preface to the first edition, that the distinction between truth and falsehood, good and evil, is 'a question which history alone is powerless to answer'. I shall not attempt an explanation here, because I should now express myself rather differently. But I still believe that some kinds of political behaviour are admirable and others detestable, that some political theories are tenable and others not, and I am not shaken by historical evidence that other men in other ages or in other places have thought otherwise.

J. W. G.

Oriel College, Oxford
24 September 1956

PREFACE TO FIRST EDITION

My object in this book has been first to discover the various ideas which combined to give birth to the theory of the social contract, and then to trace its history as it was developed and adapted to meet fresh situations and fresh criticisms. I have not attempted to construct a system of political philosophy of my own, but I have sought throughout to discuss the general tenability of the theories I have described, and to point out where and why I consider them to be sound or unsound. The general standpoint from which I have done so will become clear as the reader proceeds, and is briefly indicated in my concluding chapter. Those who have read Mr. E. F. Carritt's recently published book, *Morals and Politics* (Oxford, 1935), will observe that I find myself in substantial agreement with his general position, though I do not entirely accept his interpretation of certain particular questions, and I should like to take this opportunity of acknowledging my indebtedness to his work.

I am aware that the danger of surveying a set of ideas with such a long history as this in the light of general principles is that the whole treatment may become too abstract, and that it is equally necessary to understand the political conditions of time and place by which a particular theory was affected. To do this thoroughly would involve a general history of political thought; but I have endeavoured not to lose sight of the importance of judging a political theory in the light of its circumstances. At the same time, though it is undoubtedly true that one cannot prescribe a single political doctrine for all peoples and places (this was an illusion of nineteenth-century liberalism, from the consequences of which many countries are suffering today), I should maintain that in politics as much as in any other branch of philosophy there is an absolute and not merely a relative distinction between truth and falsehood, good and evil, and that that is a question which history alone is powerless to answer.

As the social contract theory developed, it constantly reached out and affected the evolution of affiliated groups of ideas, such as those of federalism, international law, and so on. Many of these I have been obliged either to omit altogether or to mention only in passing. Even on the central theme of the social contract—the relationship of citizens and government within the state—there is such a quantity of literature that anything like completeness of treatment would make the book impossibly long; but I hope that my selection of authorities has omitted none whose influence was vital to the development of the theory.

I am much indebted to several of my colleagues at Oriel, and I should specially like to thank the Provost, Professor F. M. Powicke, and Mr. W. G. Maclagan, who have read some of my chapters in manuscript and made a number of helpful criticisms and suggestions. I also owe a debt of gratitude to my wife for her encouragement and her valuable assistance in transcribing and verifying numerous quotations and references.

J. W. G.

Oriel College, Oxford
26 May 1936

CONTENTS

I

INTRODUCTORY

IN these days, when the liberal principles which a century ago were the hope of progressive political opinion are openly despised and rejected in many parts of the world, it may seem a vain thing to write a book about the social contract; for of all the accoutrements of liberty, it may be said, this is perhaps the most outworn, the most derided by critics, the least likely to serve it today in its struggle for existence. Yet while the contest of individual liberty against absolutism is still a live one, it will not be a waste of time if we study anew the part played by the social contract in the struggle for freedom. Apart from their plight under the dictatorships, the rights of individuals are none too secure even in the Western democracies, and certainly cannot be left to take care of themselves. The whole trend of modern economic organization inevitably spells more 'planning', which means more direction and control, and the demands of military security are not easily reconciled with freedom. This being so, those who care for liberty of thought and expression, and the values of individual personality, cannot afford to relax their vigilance. Different arguments are needed today from those which carried weight against despotism in the seventeenth and eighteenth centuries, but we may find, amid much that was erroneous or untenable, that beneath the outward form of contractarian theory there lay a vital principle, of the importance of which the modern world, it may be hoped, has not irrevocably lost sight.

The seventeenth and eighteenth centuries were, indeed, the heyday of the social contract. They were an age of monarchy, and often of absolute monarchy, firmly rooted in the divine right of kings. That theory, too, has an antiquated sound today, for the philosophical justification of modern dictatorships owes more to the inspiration of Hegel and Karl Marx than to the older faith in dynasties embodying the will of God. Yet, as Figgis has shown,[1] the divine right of kings also contained some elements of truth, veiled beneath an outward form peculiar to its own age. Partisan-

---

[1] J. N. Figgis, *The Divine Right of Kings* (Cambridge, 2nd edn., 1914), esp. pp. 250 ff.

B

ship has often blinded men to everything but what suited their own point of view, and thereby betrayed them into overstatements which invited the attacks of their opponents; but we may learn much from having the whole controversy before us, and may perhaps hope to discern more completely what was then concealed, except in part, from either side.

It is well known that the divine right of kings, while essentially a theory of the post-Renaissance age, sprang from roots far older. It sprang from the divine right of Emperors in their medieval struggle with the Papacy, and that in turn reached back to biblical texts and maxims enjoining obedience to 'the powers that be' or 'the Lord's anointed', to the sway of the deified Roman Caesars, and the earlier despotisms of the successors of Alexander of Macedon. So it was, too, with the social contract. Popularized, like its great rival, in the age of the Renaissance despots, and to a great extent, in fact, a protest against the overweening powers they claimed to hold, it grew from ideas already current in the Middle Ages, which can be traced back to that very Investiture Contest between Popes and Emperors which also brought the claims of divine right into prominence. Behind that we are led again to biblical origins on the one hand, and on the other, through Roman Law, and the Stoic philosophers, to the political speculations of ancient Greece.

Here, then, we must begin; but first of all let us make clear exactly what we are to discuss. For the name social contract (or original contract) often covers two different kinds of contract, and although the distinction between them is not rigid, for we can find numerous examples of contracts which do not fit exactly into either category, it is useful in tracing the history of the contract theory. Both kinds were current in the seventeenth century, and both can be discovered also in Greek political thought. The first of these, in logical order, is the social contract proper—the *Gesellschaftsvertrag*, or *pacte d'association*—which supposes that a number of individuals, living in a 'state of nature', agreed together to form an organized society. A good example of men translating this theory into practice is in the often-quoted covenant of the Pilgrim Fathers, who, when they landed from the *Mayflower* in November 1620, resolved: 'We do solemnly and mutually, in the presence of God and of one another, covenant and combine ourselves together into a civil body politic.' This is a theory, then, of the origin of the state; it is commonly, though not necessarily, associated with the doctrine of 'natural rights', which belonged to individual men as such, and of which they agreed by the contract to surrender some, in return for a guarantee of the remainder.

The second form of the social contract may more accurately be called the contract of government or the contract of submission— *Herrschaftsvertrag* or *Unterwerfungsvertrag*, or *pacte de gouvernement*. A well-known example of this is that 'original contract between king and people' which James II was said to have broken. Properly this has nothing to do with the foundation of the state, but, presupposing a state already in existence, it purports to define the terms on which it is to be governed: the people have made a contract with their ruler which determines their relations with him. They promise him obedience, and he promises them protection and good government. While he keeps his part of the bargain they must keep theirs, but if he misgoverns the contract is broken and allegiance is at an end. Sometimes, however, this form of contract (as was implied in calling it 'original') was not only a definition of the conditions of government but also an account of its inauguration, and in this respect it would resemble the social contract proper.

In historical development (leaving aside the first occurrences of these theories in antiquity) the logical order was reversed, and the contract of government was the first to make its appearance; for it was this theory which in a monarchical age was of obvious value (e.g. to oppressed minorities) in suggesting a limit to the powers of the monarch. The social contract proper, which, in essence, at any rate, was more purely speculative, became prominent somewhat later. It was, in fact, largely a development from the earlier governmental contract, and its emergence was marked by transitional forms like that mentioned above. When a complete system of political science came to be constructed on the basis of contract, both contracts were used, the first to bring the state into existence, the second to regulate its government. Sometimes the formation of society itself was attributed to the first or social contract, and in that case the second contract was supposed to have both established and defined the powers of the government. A political theory of this type did not necessarily stand for popular rights, though it often imposed limitations on the powers of monarchy. In course of time, with the development of more radical ideas, the contract of government tended to disappear, leaving the social contract proper in possession of the field, until we reach the culminating position in Rousseau, where the relation of people to ruler is no longer one of contract, but the government is merely the servant of the will of the sovereign people.

It may be well before proceeding farther to mention a particular line of criticism that has been directed against the contract theory in both its forms. The whole historical school, from Blackstone[1] and Paley to Maine and his followers, have pointed out, what is now obvious and undeniable, that in actual historical fact states and governments were not deliberately established by contract, but developed naturally from more primitive groupings and loyalties, such as that of the family or the clan. In that respect, it is true, there is more to be said for the argument of Filmer's *Patriarcha* than for Locke's *Treatise of Civil Government*. We shall return to this historical argument later; suffice it to say for the moment that in so far as the social contract theory is really an attempt at analysing the logical presuppositions rather than the historical antecedents of the state, the argument is beside the mark. We may pause a moment, however, at a particular variety of the historical criticism of the contract theory, associated specially with Maine's celebrated dictum that the development of society has been 'from status to contract'.

This line of criticism fastens especially on the word 'contract'. Contract, it is argued, is a legal category which not only is of relatively late appearance in the history of the evolution of human society, but also presupposes a developed legal system within which alone it can exist. It is therefore not only historically absurd to suppose that primitive men in the state of nature could make a contract, but it is also a logical inversion to derive the institution of government, and so of law, from contract, which itself is really the creature of law. We must remember, however, that to contractarian writers law did not mean only the positive law enforced in a particular state by a particular government. To them natural law was as real as positive law, and in terms of natural law there is no logical absurdity in basing government and the state on contract. Natural law does not necessarily imply a 'state of nature', but in order to avoid its unhistorical associations some writers have preferred to express the fundamental ideas that underlie the contract theory in other words, such as 'covenant', 'pact', or 'com-

---

[1] More than a century before this the social contract had been attacked on historical grounds by the Dutch jurist Horn (1620–70?): see Gierke (tr. Barker), *Natural Law and the Theory of Society* (Cambridge, 1934), i. 111; ii. 304.

pact'. Yet, as Ritchie pointed out,[1] there is nothing to be gained by this; Hobbes and Rousseau both used 'contract' for what Locke called 'compact', and the difference is really only one of words. Political theory has always, and naturally, borrowed much of its phraseology from law, and seeing that the essence of both the social contract and the ordinary civil contract consists in there being mutual and reciprocal agreements between two (or more) parties, with rights and obligations on both sides, an easily intelligible analogy led to the word 'contract' being used for its political counterpart. Whether we call it compact or contract makes no real difference to the theory behind the phrase, or to its implications.

This, surely, is also the attitude we may reasonably adopt towards the arguments put forward by Professor R. W. Lee in his little book on *The Social Compact*.[2] Here he charges contractarian thinkers with 'the indiscriminate use of two words *compact* (or *contract*) and *obligation*, which were confused respectively with the words *consent* and *duty*'. Compact, he tells us, means 'a mutual expression of intention and a mutual expression of expectation. Compact is a narrower term than consent. There can be consent without compact. Contract is a narrower term than either of them. A contract is a compact enforceable at law.'[3] Similarly, we read, 'by duty is meant liability to law; if to positive law, it is legal duty; if to moral law, it is moral duty. By obligation is meant a certain kind of legal duties arising from contract and in certain other ways. . . . Obligation is a narrower term than duty and contractual obligation is narrower still.'[4]

'That Society implies or requires consent' he is prepared to admit; in fact, he says, it 'had been a political truism ever since the time of Aristotle'. Also, he holds, 'that Society implies or requires rights and duties is undeniable. That Society implies or requires a reciprocity of rights and duties between rulers and ruled is generally, if not universally admitted.' The fault of the contract theory is that it narrowed 'consent into compact and compact into contract; . . . duty into obligation and obligation into obligation *ex contractu*'.[5]

Now for purposes of strict legal definition Professor Lee's distinctions between the meanings of compact and contract, duty and

---

[1] D. G. Ritchie, *Darwin and Hegel* (1893), p. 210 note; cf. E. C. Clark, *Practical Jurisprudence* (Cambridge, 1883), p. 144.
[2] Oxford, 1898. [3] *The Social Compact*, p. 5.
[4] Ibid. pp. 8–9. [5] Ibid.

obligation, are valuable enough; but there is more to be said than
that, both for and against the contract theory, and the real crux of
the question lies farther back, behind the narrowing process of
which he complains. We may well agree that 'a reciprocity of rights
and duties between rulers and ruled' is essential in any ethically
tolerable form of government, but when this is expressed in the
language of contract a question of principle is involved, and not
merely a question of terms. It is not only a question whether the
duty of allegiance has been wrongly narrowed down to a contractual obligation, but whether the real reason in the last resort why
it is our duty to obey the government is that we have consented or
agreed in any way to do so. I shall discuss this question more fully
later;[1] but in the meantime I should say that to express political
obligation in the legal terminology of contract is to use a legal
analogy, and perhaps in some ways an unfortunate analogy; but
whether we write of agreement or covenant, compact or contract
as the basis of the state, the essence of the theory is the same, and
the real question is not so much that of the exact terms in which
the analogy is expressed as whether the analogy itself is justifiable.

I should not wish to deny the importance of strictly defining
one's terms in political theory as much as in every other branch of
study; and it is true that many of the political writers who used the
social contract theory were jurists and professors of law, who may
be supposed to have chosen their language with care. But many
were not lawyers but men of letters, or frankly pamphleteers, and
we need not suppose that they always used their terms in the
strictest legal senses. In ordinary speech these words compact and
contract, duty and obligation, are to a great extent synonymous, as
every one must be aware from his own use of them, and as is borne
out by reference to a dictionary.[2]

The truth is that when we read of the state, or of government,
owing its origin to any kind of mutual arrangement between individuals, however much the supposed terms of that arrangement
or agreement may vary, and whatever be the precise terminology
used to describe it, we are moving in a world of political ideas that
are essentially those of the social contract. It is interesting to
discover when and by whom these ideas first found expression in

---

[1] See Chapters XIII and XV.
[2] Cf. e.g., the definitions in the *O.E.D.* of such words as *compact, contract,
covenant, duty, obligation*. Remembering, too, that much of the relevant literature is in Latin, cf. the meanings of the words *foedus, pactum,* and *pactio* as given
in Lewis and Short.

terms of contract, but in a sense their expression in those terms is merely incidental, albeit fruitful of important practical consequences. For of deeper importance than this question of terms, or even than that of the truth or falsehood of the contract theory itself, is the principle which contractarians were ultimately striving to uphold.

In some of its forms the contract theory was the expression of an exaggerated individualism which recognized no ultimate reality but force, and no higher end for it to serve than man's natural appetites. We shall meet this type of theory among the earliest manifestations of the contract in ancient Greece. The inadequacy of such a theory as an explanation either of society or of human nature is obvious, and the realization of this led many thinkers to reject the contractarian outlook altogether, and to insist instead on the naturally social character of man. Government is, then, not the artificial product of agreement between individuals, but the natural, historical outcome of organized social existence. Yet here too exaggeration can do harm, and lead to the exaltation of the state as the highest embodiment of power as an end in itself. In this totalitarian guise the cult of force is even more odious, and far more dangerous, than in the hands of individuals. We need not, however, judge a theory exclusively by the way in which it is open to exaggeration or abuse. In the course of history the outstanding service of the contractarians has been to defend the values of human personality by insisting that the authority of government is derived from and exists for the benefit of individuals. Of course this or that individual cannot have everything his own way, but it does not follow that all individual liberty is illusory. In the last resort the important question is whether the state exists to secure the fullest development of individual personality, or whether the absolute, totalitarian state is the one omnipotent real 'person', to whose pattern individuals are to be moulded, and whose ends alone they must serve.

II

THE SOCIAL CONTRACT IN THE
ANCIENT WORLD

THE physical speculations of the early Greek philosophers of the Ionian school (Thales and his successors) were inspired by a belief in some uniform natural principle which underlay and somehow accounted for the varying phenomena of the physical world. The Ionian philosophers themselves do not seem to have paid much attention to ethical or political matters, but when physical science came to Athens in the fifth century B.C. with Anaxagoras and his disciples, a contrast began to be drawn between the supposed uniformity of physical nature and the instability and changeableness of the ways of men. Hence arose the distinction between φύσις and νόμος, nature and convention, which is frequently met with in Greek literature.

Most early peoples accept their own laws and customs unquestioningly as unalterable, if not divine, but fifth-century Athens had far outgrown this child-like credulity, and inquiring minds were ready to question all things. A critical attitude might well be suggested, for instance, by the travels and stories of the historian Herodotus, who described the strange habits of distant peoples, often emphasizing the differences between them and the ways of the Greeks at home. Readers of Herodotus will remember his anecdote about the Persian king Darius and the burial customs of the Greeks and the Indians. Darius asked some Greeks at his court

'What he should pay them to eat the bodies of their fathers when they died?' To which they answered, that there was no sum that would tempt them to do such a thing. He then sent for certain Indians, of the race called Callatians, men who eat their fathers, and asked them, while the Greeks stood by, . . . 'What he should give them to burn the bodies of their fathers at their decease?' The Indians exclaimed aloud, and bade him forbear such language. Such is men's wont herein; and Pindar was right, in my judgment, when he said, 'Law is the king o'er all'.[1]

The moral which Herodotus found in this story was that 'if one

[1] Herodotus, iii. 38 (Rawlinson's translation). Herodotus rather misinterprets Pindar here, who was really referring to a 'natural law' that the stronger should rule the weaker: cf. Plato, *Gorgias*, 484 B.

were to offer men to choose out of all the customs of the world such as seemed to them the best, they would examine the whole number and end by preferring their own'; but the implication certainly is that if customs be compared, and accepted or rejected, no one custom can be unalterably rooted in the nature of things. Actually, we are told, it was Archelaus of Athens, a follower of Anaxagoras, who first drew 'the famous distinction between φύσις and νόμος in the world of human affairs, and taught that the noble and the base exist by convention (νόμῳ) and not by nature (φύσει)'.[1]

The same Greek word, νόμος, which meant custom, or convention, also meant law, and an obvious result of this distinction would be to throw doubt on the duty of obedience to the law. In one direction this led to the growth of the idea of a law of nature, sometimes conceived of as divine in origin, binding on all men, and of higher moral validity than the merely local positive laws of any particular state, so that if the higher and the lower laws conflicted, man's duty was to obey the higher at the expense of the lower. This is the situation that lies at the centre of Sophocles' tragedy *Antigone*. King Creon has ordered that the body of his son Polyneices, who has come with an army against his city, is to lie unburied; but Antigone disregards his orders in obedience to what she believes to be the superior claim of her duty as a kinswoman to give her brother the rites of burial. When Creon demands an explanation of her conduct, she replies that his proclamations, the orders of a mortal, cannot override the unwritten, changeless, and eternal laws of the gods.[2]

In the hands of some of the sophists, however, the contrast of nature and convention led to a radically individualistic standpoint. The idea of a state of nature, in which individual men moved freely in pursuit of their own ends, was contrasted with civil society, in which man's natural freedom was hampered by the laws. This state of nature might be portrayed as a poetical golden age in the distant past, from which man had fallen, but more usually it was regarded as a state of war (like the state of nature in Hobbes) in which every one was in competition and potential conflict with every one else. From this conception it was but a short step to the social contract. Every one in the state of nature was in danger of being injured by his neighbours, and therefore men made a contract or bargain (συνθήκη, or ὁμολογία, are the Greek words most

---

[1] See E. Barker, *Greek Political Theory, Plato and his Predecessors* (1918), p. 53.　　[2] Sophocles, *Antigone*, 446 ff.; cf. *Oedipus Tyrannus*, 863 ff.

often used) with one another, by which each man undertook to refrain from injuring his neighbour, provided that his neighbour in return would refrain from injuring him. Thus laws were made, based on this convention between individuals, and with them came the idea of justice and the difference between right and wrong. By nature moral considerations have no existence; what every man thinks most desirable is to have the maximum power of hurting others, with the minimum risk to himself;[1] what he most wishes to avoid is to be injured by others without being able to take vengeance. Justice, arising from this mutual agreement to refrain from mutual injury, is accepted as something midway between the two extremes which for each individual would be ideally most and least desirable.

Here we have the theory as it is put into the mouth of Glaucon in the well-known passage in the second book of Plato's *Republic*.[2] Glaucon, we may reasonably suppose, was here voicing a theory current among the sophists of his day, like the theory expressed by Thrasymachus in the previous book, that justice is 'the interest of the stronger'. This theory, though it does not contain any contractual element, rests on the same basic disbelief in the validity of anything but force in the 'state of nature'. Thrasymachus holds that while every man naturally acts for himself and gets what he can, the strongest man will be the most successful, and will institute a rule over his weaker neighbours in order to exploit them for his own interests.[3] There is the same lawless individualism in both theories, but while Thrasymachus treats the institution of government from the point of view of the strong man, Glaucon looks at the other side of the picture, and imagines the relatively weak banding themselves together to avoid being exploited.

Not all the sophists held these extreme views on ethics and politics. Some were mainly interested in grammar and the origins of language, others in logic, others again in rhetoric and the art of dialectic and public disputation. Some of the greater sophists who discussed political questions did not seek in this way to overthrow the foundations of ordinary morality. Protagoras, for example, gave an account of the origin of the state which begins with men living apart from one another in a kind of state of nature, open to

---

[1] This is how he would behave if a magic ring of Gyges enables him to make himself invisible (Plato, *Republic*, 359–61).   [2] *Rep.* 358 E–359 B.

[3] *Rep.* 338 C ff. Cf. the theory in Plato's *Gorgias*, 492 C, where Callicles rejects all law as mere συνθήματα made by the weak to prevent the strong from getting what they are naturally entitled to.

the attacks of wild beasts and creatures stronger than themselves. Accordingly they sought to congregate together and find safety in the foundation of cities; but when they had come together they wronged one another because they had not yet learnt the art of politics. But Protagoras' conclusion is not that they drew up conventional rules based on a contract, but that justice and a moral sense are divine: Zeus sent Hermes to them, bringing them shame and justice, to govern their cities and bind them together in friendship.[1]

Nevertheless, there is evidence that views such as those put into the mouths of Thrasymachus and Glaucon were widely current in Athens in the fifth and fourth centuries. A theory almost exactly corresponding to that of Glaucon was expressed by the sophist Antiphon in a work *On Truth*, of which some fragments have survived among the papyri from Oxyrhynchus.[2]

Justice [we read here] consists in not transgressing . . . any of the legal rules (νόμιμα) of the state in which one lives as a citizen. A man therefore would practise justice in the way most advantageous to himself if, in the presence of witnesses, he held the laws in high esteem, but in the absence of witnesses, and when he was by himself, he held in high esteem the rules of nature. For the rules of the laws are adventitious (ἐπίθετα), while the rules of nature are inevitable (ἀναγκαῖα); and again the rules of the laws are created by covenant and not produced by nature (ὁμολογηθέντα οὐ φύντα ἐστίν), while the rules of nature are exactly the reverse. A man, therefore, who transgresses legal rules, is free from shame and punishment whenever he is unobserved by those who made the covenant (τοὺς ὁμολογήσαντας), and is subject to shame and punishment only when he is observed. It is otherwise with transgression of the rules which are innate in nature. If any man strains any of these rules beyond what it can bear, the evil consequences are none the less, if he is entirely unobserved, and none the greater, if he is seen of all men; for the injury that he incurs is not due to men's opinion but to the facts of the case (οὐ γὰρ διὰ δόξαν βλάπτεται ἀλλὰ δι' ἀλήθειαν).

It is not clear exactly what are the rules of nature which, according to Antiphon, cannot be broken with impunity, but the main tendency of the argument is plain—it is to discredit the ordinary ideas of justice and the duty of obeying the laws, in favour of a crudely materialistic individualism which regards political institutions as an arbitrary and conventional interference with the natural bent of the individual. Other instances could be given to show

[1] Plato, *Protagoras*, 322 B–C; cf. Barker, *Gk. Pol. Theory, Plato*, p. 63.
[2] *Oxyrhynchus Papyri*, xi, no. 1364, pp. 92–104. See Barker, op. cit., pp. 66–69, 83–85.

that notions of this kind, varying no doubt in the lengths to which their holders were prepared to go, were widely held, and were associated with the teaching of the sophists. The sophist Lycophron, for example, held that the law was simply a contract and a means of securing mutual justice;[1] again, the school of Diogenes and the Cynics, while much of their conduct may be legendary, clearly represented in an extreme (and at the same time practical) form the revolt not only against the state but also against all the accompaniments of civilization as contrary to 'nature'.[2]

Several considerations may have helped to make the Greek world a receptive audience for the propagation of such views. Greek political experience was familiar with στάσις and revolution which often led to radical alterations in the laws of a city, while many, if not most cities, held that they had been founded at some definite date in the past, and that their laws had then or subsequently been framed by a νομοθέτης, or lawgiver. Not only so, but the Greeks could often see the foundation of cities and the creation of new constitutions taking place before their eyes. Colonies, offshoots from the mother-city, whether military or trading stations, or new homes for bands of emigrants, were being founded all over the Mediterranean world, and each would form a new city-state, equipped with a new constitution, and often with a new code of laws specially drawn up for it. All this experience would tend to deepen the impression that laws are man-made, and that what man can make he can also unmake; that laws, in fact, are conventional.[3]

---

[1] Aristotle, *Politics*, iii. 1280ᵇ10: . . . καὶ ὁ νόμος συνθήκη καί, καθάπερ ἔφη Λυκόφρων ὁ σοφιστής, ἐγγυητὴς ἀλλήλοις τῶν δικαίων, ἀλλ' οὐχ οἷος ποιεῖν ἀγαθοὺς καὶ δικαίους τοὺς πολίτας. Another reference to the materialistic theory that laws originated in contract and that justice has no place in the 'natural' scheme of things occurs in Plato, *Laws*, 889 E:

Ἀθ. Θεούς, ὦ μακάριε, εἶναι πρῶτόν φασιν οὗτοι τέχνῃ, οὐ φύσει, ἀλλά τισιν νόμοις, καὶ τούτους ἄλλους ἄλλῃ, ὅπῃ ἕκαστοι ἑαυτοῖσι συνωμολόγησαν νομοθετούμενοι· καὶ δὴ καὶ τὰ καλὰ φύσει μὲν ἄλλα εἶναι, νόμῳ δὲ ἕτερα, τὰ δὲ δὴ δίκαια οὐδ' εἶναι τὸ παράπαν φύσει, ἀλλ' ἀμφισβητοῦντας διατελεῖν ἀλλήλοις καὶ μετατιθεμένους ἀεὶ ταῦτα, ἃ δ' ἂν μετάθωνται καὶ ὅταν, τότε κύρια ἕκαστα εἶναι, γιγνόμενα τέχνῃ καὶ τοῖς νόμοις ἀλλ' οὐ δή τινι φύσει.

[2] The Cynics seem to have anticipated the fallacy of the 'noble savage' and the early views of Rousseau. The radical sophists, it will be observed, carried their views much farther than the contractarians of the seventeenth and eighteenth centuries, for they derived not only the state but also the whole of morality from convention, whereas the latter's theories, with few exceptions, were *naturrechtlich*, judging the state and its rules by a criterion beyond its scope.

[3] Cf. the remarks of the sophist Hippias in Xenophon, *Mem.* IV. iv. 14:

Νόμους δ', ἔφη, ὦ Σώκρατες, πῶς ἄν τις ἡγήσαιτο σπουδαῖον πρᾶγμα εἶναι, ἢ τὸ πείθεσθαι αὐτοῖς, οὕς γε πολλάκις αὐτοὶ οἱ θέμενοι ἀποδοκιμάσαντες μετατίθενται;

Much of the political philosophy of Plato and Aristotle was designed to combat these subversive opinions. Instead of the picture of the natural man striving for his own ends, Plato presents us with an account of an organized society in which every man has his 'station and its duties', with the implication that it is only in such a life that the nature of man can find its fullest expression. Aristotle's refutation of the sophists is essentially similar. He will not allow the distinction between φύσις and νόμος to be applied to the state, but holds that man is 'by nature a political animal', and that it is therefore not contrary to, but in the fullest accordance with, his nature for him to live in an organized political society. The state is not, he urges, a mere living together in one place for the sake of mutual protection and the exchange of goods; it is a moral association, to develop man's highest faculties, and enable him to live the good life.[1] Man's nature, in other words, is not what he has in common with the lower animals, to be contrasted with the conventional (and supposedly unnatural) restrictions of civilized political life; it is rather what is peculiarly human, what differentiates him from the lower animals—the sense of right and wrong which makes him a moral being, and necessitates political life.

This is the essence of Aristotle's reply to sophistic teaching, and he was not concerned, any more than Plato was, to treat the social contract theory as untrue to historical fact, or to counter it by an alternative description of how the state grew into existence. It is true that the *Politics* opens with a brief account of households growing into villages, and villages being united to form a state; but Aristotle's real answer to the sophists lies in his contention that the state, when it did come into existence, was something different in kind from any society at a less complete stage of its development,[2] and that the state alone could fully satisfy the potentialities of man's nature. As Sir Ernest Barker has pointed out,[3] Aristotle,

like all the Greeks, who thought of politics as a sphere of conscious making, would appear to believe in a creation of the state. 'By nature there is an impulse in all men to such society; but the first man to *construct* it was the author of the greatest of benefits.'[4] There is no contradiction [he continues] in such a sentence; for there is no con-

[1] *Politics*, iii. 1280ᵇ29.
[2] Here he disagreed with Plato, who had stated in the *Politicus* that the science of the state was not essentially different from that of the family or smaller groups. Aristotle attacks this idea at the outset of his *Politics*.
[3] *Cambridge Ancient History*, vi. 521.   [4] *Politics*, i. 1253ᵃ29.

tradiction between the immanent impulses of human nature and the conscious act, which is, after all, a part of the same nature.

The sophists themselves, in fact, were not much interested in the historical aspect of the contract theory—less so, certainly, than some of the contractarians of the Renaissance age; their real object was a logical analysis of the implications of the state, and therefore they did not trouble to present a fully worked out account of its foundation in contract.[1] Their aim rather was to expose the flimsiness, as they conceived it, of ordinary morality and the basis of government, with its apparatus of legal rules and punishments, and their contract theory is only sketched in lightly and incidentally. But different though their conclusions were, there is the same philosophy behind the theories expressed by Antiphon and Glaucon as there is behind that of Hobbes.

While there can be no question that both Plato and Aristotle were firmly opposed to this whole school of thought, it is nevertheless true that phrases and sentences can be found in the works of Aristotle which appear to suggest a contractarian theory of the state. Thus in the course of a discussion of various kinds of friendships (φιλίαι) in the *Nicomachean Ethics*, he refers to πολιτικαὶ φιλίαι in a list together with other kinds, and remarks that they all appear to rest on a kind of agreement (καθ' ὁμολογίαν τινὰ φαίνονται εἶναι);[2] but a casual sentence like this can hardly be weighed against his whole philosophy as expounded in the *Politics*. There is also an interesting passage in the *Rhetoric*, where he appears at first sight to say that law is a contract (καὶ ὅλως αὐτὸς ὁ νόμος συνθήκη τις ἐστίν); but it is clear from closer inspection that what he is really emphasizing is the need to respect the sanctity of contracts, which bind those who have entered into them; disregard of contracts, he urges, leads to disregard of the laws themselves.[3]

If we really wish to find Aristotle at fault, we can do so most justifiably in his economic theory. Here, indeed, he seems to have

---

[1] Cf. W. L. Newman, Introduction to his edition of the *Politics*, i. 26; 'Those who claimed that the State is not φύσει but νόμῳ did not necessarily imply that it owes its existence to a compact, though the two ideas do not lie far apart: they might mean only that its claims rest on general acceptance—that it is the traditional, received thing—that its authority is artificial, not based on Nature, but "of man's devising", and that it need not have existed, if men had not chosen that it should.'   [2] *N. Ethics*, viii. 1161ᵇ13.

[3] *Rhetoric*, i. 1376ᵇ10: ἡ γὰρ συνθήκη νόμος ἐστὶν ἴδιος καὶ κατὰ μέρος, καὶ αἱ μὲν συνθῆκαι οὐ ποιοῦσι τὸν νόμον κύριον, οἱ δὲ νόμοι τὰς κατὰ τὸν νόμον συνθήκας. καὶ ὅλως αὐτὸς ὁ νόμος συνθήκη τις ἐστίν, ὥστε ὅς τις ἀπιστεῖ ἢ ἀναιρεῖ συνθήκην, τοὺς νόμους ἀναιρεῖ.

been betrayed by the etymological affinity between νόμος (law, custom, convention) and νόμισμα (money) into the very fallacy that he repudiated in the sphere of politics. Holding, quite rightly, that money is an artificial and conventional medium of exchange, he proceeds to argue that it is unnatural and valueless in itself.[1] In this belief, and in his well-known theory about the immorality of usury which flows from it, Aristotle seems to have forgotten the meaning he gave to 'nature' in his account of man's place in the state, and to relapse into the Cynical identification of the natural with the primitive and undeveloped.

Already in Aristotle's lifetime the city-state, which for him was the focus of all political philosophy, was collapsing before the advance of the Macedonian monarchy, and the Hellenistic age which followed was at the same time more cosmopolitan and more individualistic. Of the two great schools of philosophy which dominated this epoch, one, Stoicism, reverted from the attitude of Plato and Aristotle to a point of view more akin, in its individualism, to that of the sophists, though it stopped short of the sophists' attack on morality. The great Stoic maxim was 'Live according to Nature', but by this they did not mean, as Plato and Aristotle would have done, the life of an active citizen. Like Plato and Aristotle, indeed, they found man's nature not in his animal nature but in his reason, but they made of this a guide to individual conduct rather than an argument for positive citizenship. With this notion of nature or reason as man's guide, and a cosmopolitan belief in the equality and brotherhood of all men, the Stoics developed a theory of a universal law of nature, which was a law of reason; and this was ultimately, through its reception into Roman Law, to become a legacy of the greatest importance to subsequent political thought. But the Stoics themselves were less interested in political questions than in personal ethics, and, in the bad days of the Roman Empire, at any rate, the main function of their philosophy lay in its consolation to the individual just man, who could strive by its guidance to keep his soul pure and uncorrupt.

In Epicurus, on the other hand, the leader of the second chief school of post-Aristotelian philosophy, the contract theory reappears in its old sophistic form. Justice, according to Epicurus, is a mere mark of expediency to prevent men from injuring and being injured by one another (τὸ τῆς φύσεως δίκαιον, ἐστὶ σύμβο-

[1] N. Ethics, v. 1133ᵃ29; the same point of view is expressed in a more extreme form in Pol. i. 1257ᵇ10.

λον τοῦ συμφέροντος, εἰς τὸ μὴ βλάπτειν ἀλλήλους, μηδὲ βλάπτεσθαι).
There is no such thing as absolute justice (οὐκ ἦν τι καθ' ἑαυτὸ
δικαιοσύνη); justice and injustice arose from the need men felt,
when they came to live together, to make a contract (συνθήκη
τις) to secure each other from mutual harm.[1]

Sir Ernest Barker gives some reasons for believing that Epicurus
may have inherited his theory of contract from the fifth-century
contemporary of Socrates, Democritus of Abdera, whose follower
he was in many other respects.

Democritus, like Epicurus, professed a theory of hedonism, and such
a theory, emphasizing as it does the individual, is naturally allied with
a political theory which finds the origin of the State in a contract of
individuals. Again, we know that Democritus believed in the conventional and artificial origin of language; and we are told that he
attributed secondary qualities like colour and taste to 'convention'.
What he believed with regard to language and secondary qualities may
well have been his belief with regard to the State.[2]

However that may be, it certainly became and remained a tenet of
the Epicurean school, and an echo of it can be found in Lucretius.[3]

So far we have dealt entirely with the social contract proper,
which explains the origin, or the causation, of organized society.
The other form of contract—the governmental contract, between
a people and its ruler—plays a much less important part in Greek
political thought, though some traces of it are to be found there.
One of these is in the *Laws* of Plato, where the Athenian Stranger
alludes to certain oaths which were made in the three Dorian
kingdoms by the kings and their peoples, the kings swearing that
they would not make their rule more arbitrary, while the peoples
swore that they would never overthrow the monarchy so long as

---

[1] Diogenes Laertius, *De Vitis Philosophorum*, x. 150. Cf. Stobaeus, *Florile-
gium*, 43. 139: οἱ νόμοι χάριν τῶν σόφων κεῖνται, οὐχ ἵνα μὴ ἀδικῶσιν, ἀλλ' ἵνα μὴ
ἀδικῶνται. In fairness to Epicurus, however, we must remember, as Newman
pointed out (Introd. to Ar. *Pol.* i. 28, note), that Epicurus' teaching was not
purely destructive, like that of the sophists. 'He had a philosophical discipline
to set in the place of the State, which they had not. They struck down the
traditional guide of human life without having anything to substitute for it.'

[2] E. Barker, *Gk. Pol. Theory, Plato*, p. 70.

[3] *De Rerum Natura*, v. 1154:
nec facilest placidam ac pacatam degere vitam
qui violat factis communia foedera pacis.

These lines follow an account of the origin of government and laws, whereby
anarchy was checked and crime restrained by punishment.

the kings observed their oaths.[1] Another example of a similar bargain between a ruler and his subjects occurs in Xenophon's *Cyropaedeia*. Cambyses is here described as addressing the Persians, and suggesting the conditions upon which Cyrus shall be their king: he and his future subjects are to offer joint sacrifices to the gods, and, calling them to witness, to make a contract (συνθέσθαι), Cyrus undertaking to use all his might to defend the country in case of a foreign attack, or an attempt to overthrow its laws, while the people undertake to come to his assistance in case of a rebellion against his rule.[2]

As Sir Ernest Barker suggests, this may be Xenophon's way of expressing in a kind of parable his somewhat imaginary ideal of Cyrus as a limited monarch,[3] but in any case this and the previous passage from the *Laws* are interesting as anticipations of the theory which in later years was to play such an important part in schemes for making monarchy a limited and constitutional instead of an absolute and arbitrary form of government. The distinction between the good monarch, who ruled for the benefit of his subjects, and the tyrant, who ruled for his own selfish ends, was a commonplace in both Plato and Aristotle, and seems to have led naturally, then as since, to contractual phraseology. Perhaps a link lay in the conception, strongly recommended by both philosophers, of the constitutional king who was not sovereign, but governed in accordance with a fundamental law. However that may be, the governmental contract is of no more than casual and sporadic occurrence in Greek political thought, and merely anticipates the similar contract of later epochs. That seems to have developed anew from fresh sources, and there seems no reason to suppose that there was any historical connexion between it and these early occurrences of the same mode of thought. The social contract of the sophists, however, is more important, even if here too we can hardly claim it as the direct ancestor of the social contract of later times; for it was closely associated with the outset of a perennially recurrent attitude to political questions, which, while it underwent many developments in the course of its history, led in due time into the heart of modern political theory.

Before leaving the Greeks we must not forget what is perhaps the best-known example of contractarian thought to be found in

[1] Plato, *Laws*, 684 A.
[2] Xenophon, *Cyropaedeia*, VIII. v. 25–27.
[3] *Cambridge Ancient History*, vi. 516.

their literature, where Socrates, in Plato's *Crito*, is explaining to his friends, after his trial and condemnation to death, why he is unwilling to avail himself of their offer to help him to escape from prison. Here the laws of the city are personified, and are represented as addressing Socrates; they say that they have never hindered a man who does not like the city from departing with his goods and making his dwelling elsewhere, but if he chooses to remain, he has really entered into a covenant with the laws to obey their commands (φαμὲν τοῦτον ὡμολογηκέναι ἔργῳ ἡμῖν ἃ ἂν ἡμεῖς κελεύωμεν ποιήσειν ταῦτα); if he disobeys, he commits a threefold wrong, for in addition to his covenant, the laws have been his parents and his nurses, and as such his duty is to obey them. But Socrates never departed to Sparta or Crete, which he was fond of praising for their good government; instead, he remained at Athens, and begot children there; if he were now to try to escape from prison, he would be acting shamefully, like a runaway slave, breaking his covenant and contract, according to which he had agreed to be a citizen (. . . ἅπερ ἂν δοῦλος φαυλότατος πράξειεν, ἀποδιδράσκειν ἐπιχειρῶν παρὰ τὰς ξυνθήκας τε καὶ τὰς ὁμολογίας, καθ᾽ ἃς ἡμῖν ξυνέθου πολιτεύεσθαι).[1]

This whole argument is interesting in several ways. With its reference to the possibility of departure, it anticipates Locke, who thus sought to include later generations within the scope of a social compact to which only the first founders of the state had been individually parties; its ὡμολογηκέναι ἔργῳ, again, is like the 'implicit' or 'tacit' compact which Locke and others conceived as binding on these later inhabitants of the state. But in Locke these were merely subterfuges to avoid some of the difficulties of his individualist premisses; here in the *Crito* they do not imply, nor are they efforts to defend, a contractarian theory of the origin of the state. The inference to be drawn is a very different one; in fact, as Hume wittily put it, Socrates 'builds a Tory consequence of passive obedience on a Whig foundation of the original contract'.[2] Strictly speaking, Socrates' contract is not an 'original' one; but at any rate the emphasis is on the duty to obey the laws, not on the right to resist, for besides the covenant or promise to obey, he pictures the relationship between the laws and the citizen as that

---

[1] Plato, *Crito*, 51 D–52 A, 52 C–53 A; cf. 50 C: τί οὖν, ἂν εἴπωσιν οἱ νόμοι, Ὦ Σώκρατες, ἢ καὶ ταῦτα ὡμολόγητο ἡμῖν τε καὶ σοί, ἢ ἐμμένειν ταῖς δίκαις αἷς ἂν ἡ πόλις δικάζῃ;

[2] D. Hume, *Essays, Moral, Political, and Literary*, Part i, Essay xii, 'Of the Original Contract', *ad fin.*

between parents and child. Plato is really the convinced enemy of the whole contractarian standpoint,

teaching rigorously the inevitable nexus which binds man to man in a State, and—as a corollary—the dominant claims of the State upon its members. What Plato means [Sir Ernest Barker continues] is that every man who regards himself as a member of a State has thereby really and implicitly, though not verbally and explicitly, subscribed to the obligations of membership. He has claimed rights, and has had them recognized: he has acknowledged duties, and is bound to fulfil them. This is implied in membership of the State: it is implied in the membership of any group.[1]

In the Roman world there was little political philosophy worthy the name, and what speculation we find in Cicero, for instance, was largely an amalgam of ideas from various sources, partly Stoic, partly Platonic or Aristotelian, modified by the practical experience of an active Roman lawyer. We can find passages in his works that show some affinity with the idea that government is based on consent, even if not definitely on contract;[2] in fact, he has one sentence which explicitly repeats the theory of a contract (or at least of a 'kind of contract') between the people and their rulers, consequent upon fear and dissension within the ranks of the state.[3] This theory, however, was not Cicero's own, but is put by him into some one else's mouth; Cicero himself seems to have held that while the state involves a common will and consent, it is an organic development from the natural association of the family, and can rightly command the loyalty of its members.[4] As against the theory that man is by nature unsociable, and is only driven into society by fear of the dangers of solitary life, he held that justice, which is the foundation of law and of organized society, is not the product of a convention, but is itself rooted in the nature of things.[5]

[1] E. Barker, *Gk. Pol. Theory, Plato*, p. 123. If Plato really meant this, he was expressing a view which, though not explicitly contractarian, is nevertheless inherently contractual: perhaps this was the view of Socrates himself.

[2] Cf., e.g., Cicero, *De Rep.* III. xxxi. 43: 'Ergo illam rem populi, id est rem publicam, quis diceret tum, cum crudelitate unius oppressi essent universi? neque esset unum vinculum iuris nec consensus ac societas coetus, quod est populus.'

[3] *De Rep.* III. xiii. 23: 'Sed cum alius alium timet, et homo hominem, et ordo ordinem, tum, quia sibi nemo confidit, quasi pactio fit inter populum et potentes, ex quo exsistit id quod Scipio laudabat, coniunctum civitatis genus.'

[4] Cf. *De Officiis*, I. xvii. 53.

[5] Cf. *De Legibus*, I. xiv–xvi; *De Finibus*, II. xviii. 59. What is essentially this

Although the Roman Empire generally stood for order and
obedience, echoes of a theoretical individualism can be heard all
through its history. In Seneca the Stoic idea of the law of nature
and the brotherhood of man actually appears in the form of a
definite golden age in the past, from which man had lapsed into
violence, and so necessitated the artificial creation of the state.[1]
It is clear, again, from the writings of Lactantius that in the fourth
century the idea of a law of nature and the contractarian origin of
society was still current.[2] Lactantius' view, derived ultimately from
Aristotle, but thrown into a Christian form, was that God gave
wisdom to man, and especially *hunc pietatis affectum*, that man
should love, cherish, and protect his neighbour, for God wished
man to be *animal sociale*. But, he proceeds, opinions vary about the
origins of political life. Some describe primitive man as living a
savage life and a prey to the attacks of animals, and attribute the
foundation of cities to a desire for protection against these perils.
Others reject this theory as *delira*, and hold that not the attacks of
wild beasts but *ipsam humanitatem* was the *causam coeundi*. Even
if we imagine this theory to be true, he continues, surely the moral
is that if men have come together because they need protection,
man's duty is to succour his neighbour when he needs assistance.
It would be the height of wickedness to break the compact entered
into at the outset of society (*foedus illud inter homines a principio sui
ortus initum, aut violare, aut non conservare*); at least, if any man
were thus to dissociate himself from the body politic, it would
mean that he was choosing to live no longer as a man, but as a wild
beast.[3] But this is really impossible, so that we must study to
preserve the bonds of human society, seeing that no man can live
without his fellows, and the real explanation of society lies in
human nature itself (*humanitatis ipsius causa facta est hominum
congregatio*).

Lactantius thus, like Socrates in the *Crito*, draws a conservative

point of view, while it admits the element of consent, is put into the mouth of
Scipio Africanus in *De Rep*. I. xxv. 39: 'Est igitur, inquit Africanus, res publica
res populi, populus autem non omnis hominum coetus quoquo modo con-
gregatus, sed coetus multitudinis iuris consensu et utilitatis communione
sociatus.' Cf. R. W. and A. J. Carlyle, *History of Medieval Political Theory in the
West*, i. 5, 13–14.

[1] Seneca, *Epistulae Morales*, XIV. ii (90), §§ 3, 5, 36, 38, 40. Cf. A. J. Carlyle in
The Social and Political Ideas of some Great Medieval Thinkers (ed. F. J. C.
Hearnshaw, 1923), p. 43.

[2] F. Lactantius, *Divinae Institutiones*, vi. 10.

[3] i.e. he would revert to the state of nature.

moral from the hypothesis of a contract, and while contractarian thought and phraseology were evidently still in being under the Roman Empire, the whole political atmosphere was one of absolutism and submission. Christianity, too, could find maxims in the Scriptures which enjoined the same lesson. But the Roman system itself contained elements the implications of which, though submerged at the time, led away from this attitude towards one of revolt. The Roman citizen, while he had to obey the law, was essentially the possessor of rights, and it was a maxim of Roman Law that, by the *lex regia*, the authority of the emperor himself was derived from the people. Though under the sway of the military Caesars this might seem a rather empty and theoretical survival from the republican past, it was to be fruitful of unforeseen consequences in future. So also was the inclusion within the body of Roman Law of the conception of the law of nature, descending from the Stoics and their ultimately individualist philosophy, and yet regarded as superior to the ordinary civil law. Here could be found such sentences as 'All men are by nature equal', and though proclaimed at first as a purely legal maxim, such a doctrine was potentially revolutionary, even if centuries elapsed before it was put into effect.

III

THE EARLY MIDDLE AGES AND THE
CONTRACT OF GOVERNMENT

THE Dark Ages, after the fall of the Roman Empire in the West, though they did not produce definite political treatises, were by no means lacking in political ideas, which formed the background for the more elaborate and developed theories that were to follow. These ideas were derived from two main sources. One was Roman Law, as embodied in Justinian's *Corpus*, and itself coloured by its own inheritance from Stoic philosophy; the other was the teaching of the Christian Church. From both these sources two opposite theories of government could be derived, and the seeds of much subsequent controversy lay in the alternative interpretations that could be put upon them. Roman Law, developed and codified under an absolute imperial authority, lent itself, on the one hand, to the support of an absolutist rule: the emperor's pleasure, ran one of its most famous texts, has the force of law—'quod principi placuit legis habet vigorem'. But it was equally a principle of Roman Law that the emperor's authority was ultimately derived from a grant by the sovereign people, and this is embodied in the words, less often remembered than the famous text itself, though they immediately follow it: 'utpote cum lege regia, quae de imperio eius lata est, populus ei et in eum omne suum imperium et potestatem conferat.'[1] Here was a doctrine which, though not one of contract, could be regarded as one of popular consent, and on which a theory of contract could easily be grafted. At the same time, however, the commentators were equally able to interpret the *lex regia* in an absolutist sense by maintaining that by it the people had made a total and irrevocable alienation of all their powers—a doctrine which has an obvious affinity with the theory of Hobbes.[2]

From Christianity, in so far as it bore on politics, a choice of similar alternative theories could be derived. On the one hand were the texts that upheld the divine authority of the secular power: 'The powers that be are ordained of God', and 'Render unto Caesar the things that are Caesar's'. But on the other hand

[1] *Digest*, i. 4, 1.   [2] See below, p. 32, note 1.

there was a strong and persistent theory, which had behind it all the weight of St. Augustine's authority, that the secular power had its origin in sin. This theory, which found support in the doctrine of the Fall of Man, was partly influenced by such Stoic ideas of a golden age as have already been noticed in Seneca; combined with the equally corresponding Christian and Stoic ideas of the brotherhood and equality of all men (ideas incorporated, in the law of nature, in the body of Roman Law itself), it would suggest that the political was not the 'natural' condition of man, but that the state was artificially imposed upon him. It would be a mistake to suppose that the theory of the sinful origin of the state was in any way a theory of popular government, for in the hands of the Church (whether or not St. Augustine intended his City of God to be interpreted as the Papacy)[1] it became a lever to exalt the majesty of ecclesiastical authority;[2] but at any rate it tended to diminish and limit the powers of secular monarchs. Here again, then, the way lay open for the theory of contract to make its entrance; for this notion of the sinful origin of secular government was essentially the ancestor, via the ideas of Hooker, Locke, and the Benthamites, of the liberal theory of the state, popularized in England by Herbert Spencer and the nineteenth-century radicals, which reduced the functions of government to the mere protection of life and property, and with which the social contract was always more or less closely associated.[3] At the same time it should be observed, while the secular power was supposed to have originated in sin, this did not imply that it was itself sinful. It could be interpreted as the divine remedy or punishment for sin, and so, as with the *lex regia*, defenders of the monarch's authority could parry possible attacks, and still maintain that obedience was due to it, as having the sanction of the will of God.[4] This, in fact, was the usual medieval theory.

So far, then, we have no explicit mention of contract as the basis of government, but we have a way of thinking with which a contractual theory would readily cohere—on the one hand, the impli-

---

[1] On this point see J. N. Figgis, *The Political Aspects of St. Augustine's 'City of God'* (1921).

[2] This became especially evident at the time of the Investiture Contest in the eleventh century.

[3] Cf. Carlyle, *Hist. Med. Pol. Theory in the West*, iii. 5.

[4] This appears, e.g., in the doctrine of the 'two swords' (in allusion to St. Luke xxii. 38), generally associated with Pope Gelasius—the dual and parallel authorities of Pope and Emperor, both appointed by God to rule the world.

cation of the *lex regia* that secular authority arose from a specific act on the part of the people, and on the other hand the Augustinian and Stoic notion that the secular power was created artificially after the Fall, and stood in contrast to the natural (or Divine) state of affairs. In St. Augustine, moreover, we can find not only this idea of the artificiality of the state, but also an essentially individualist standpoint—another regular concomitant of the contract theory. 'Quid est autem civitas', he asks, 'nisi multitudo hominum in quoddam vinculum redactum concordiae?'[1] In defining the state, again, he practically copies Cicero, but with the important difference that he omits Cicero's reference to law and justice, and so severs the connexion with the tradition of Plato and Aristotle, and their belief in the state as itself the highest and most 'natural' embodiment of human excellence.[2]

The actual word *pactum* occurs in St. Augustine's *Confessions*, where he says: 'generale quippe pactum est societatis humanae obedire regibus suis'; and a few lines above he refers to the breach by sin of the 'pactum inter se civitatis aut gentis, consuetudine vel lege firmatum'.[3] *Pactum* here appears to contain some of the meaning of the social as well as the governmental contract, but this use of the word should not be interpreted as implying the existence as yet of a regular contractual theory of the state. Nevertheless, the occurrence of such a word in so influential a writer as St. Augustine was not forgotten, and became, as we shall see, of the greatest importance when a regular contract theory began to be developed.[4]

Over the foundations of Roman Law and Christian teaching just described, the Teutonic kingdoms of early medieval Europe deposited a principle of government, and especially of the relationship between the king and his subjects, which profoundly affected the whole of medieval political theory. Briefly, this principle was that the king was no arbitrary or absolute ruler, but that the allegiance

---

[1] *Epist.* cxxxviii. 2. 10. Cf. *Epist.* clv. 3. 9: 'cum aliud civitas non sit, quam concors hominum multitudo.'

[2] It was perhaps inevitable that a gulf should open between Aristotle, whose vision was confined to this world, and a Christian writer, for whom perfection lay only in Heaven.   [3] *Confessions*, iii. 8.

[4] Whether or no St. Augustine had in mind some unknown, possibly Stoic, writer who had used contractarian phraseology, or whether perhaps he was echoing Cicero (*De Rep.* III. xiii, quoted above, p. 19), and whether Cicero in turn was echoing Plato (*Laws*, 684 A above, p. 16), must remain conjectural. Professor Mario d'Addio regards St. Augustine as the chief source of the contractual idea throughout the Middle Ages. See his *L'Idea del Contratto Sociale dai Sofisti alla Riforma* (Milan, 1954), pp. 188, 189.

owed to him by his subjects was dependent on his recognizing their rights, and that in his legislative capacity he could only make laws after getting the advice and consent of his wise men, and in some sense of his whole people. Dr. Fritz Kern brings evidence to show that in the Visigothic kingdom in Spain this principle found expression in the notion of a definite *pactum* between ruler and subjects, the earliest example of this being in the Acts of the Fourth Council of Toledo, held in the year 633.[1] Even earlier than this, the fifth-century Laws of the Burgundians were stated to have been drawn up by the common will of all, and published in order to bind posterity by an everlasting *pactio* (*ut definitio, quae ex tractatu nostro et communi omnium voluntate conscripta est, etiam per posteros custodita perpetuae pactionis teneat firmitatem*).[2]

Among the Franks there appears to have been only one occasion when this reciprocity of rights and duties between king and people was actually referred to as constituting a compact (*pactum*); this was in the *Capitula ad Francos et Aquitanos missa de Carisiaco* of 856.[3] This occasion was specially marked by the inclusion of penal sanctions (resembling those in the final clause of Magna Carta) in case the arrangement should be broken, but it is clear from the various capitularies of the ninth century that the Frankish kings were normally regarded as ruling conditionally rather than absolutely, and that their legislative functions were in some degree shared by their subjects. This doctrine, in fact, received a formal and definite statement in 864, in the *Edictum Pistense*, where we read that 'lex consensu populi fit et constitutione regis'.[4] Vigorous kings in the Middle Ages were often successful in imposing their will on their subjects, but the modern, post-Renaissance conception of absolute monarchy, and of laws as the mere expression of the monarch's will, was foreign to early medieval thought. Not only was positive law regarded as inferior and bound to conform to the dictates of the law of nature (or of God), but to begin with, at any rate, there was hardly a conception of positive law at all, in the sense of the command of the sovereign, just as there was no con-

---

[1] F. Kern, *Gottesgnadentum und Widerstandsrecht* (Leipzig, 1914), pp. 367, 368. Professor S. B. Chrimes has published an English version of this work with the title *Kingship and Law in the Middle Ages* (Oxford, 1939). For the Fourth Council of Toledo see Mansi, *Concilia*, x. 638 (c. 75): 'Sacrilegium quippe est, si violetur a gentibus regum suorum promissa fides; quia non solum in eos fit pacti transgressio, sed et in Deum quidem, in cuius nomine pollicetur ipsa promissio.'

[2] Monumenta Germaniae Historica, *Leges Nat. Germ.* II. i, § 14, p. 34.

[3] M.G.H. *Leg.* i. 445.   [4] M.G.H. *Leg.* i. 490.

ception of sovereign power itself, which is the modern correlative of positive law. Law, in the earliest times barely distinguishable from custom, was in medieval thought prior to rather than the creature of government; the whole people, in some sense, was its repository, and though the king's function was to declare it, it was not in his power to manufacture it arbitrarily.[1]

This medieval Germanic theory of kingship appears most clearly in the ceremonies that attended the accession of a new king. Though kinship and descent gave a candidate to the throne a strong claim to succeed, hereditary succession by primogeniture, later the established medium of divine right, was unknown in the early Middle Ages, and a king's subjects had a definite share in his appointment. The least that was required was the people's assent to a king's accession;[2] often the people, or at any rate their leaders, the nobles, had the right of electing the new king, and could impose conditions which he must observe. The king on his part had to swear to give justice and good government to all, a pledge which in the formal shape of the coronation oath has survived down to our own time. When the new king did not belong to the direct line of succession, all the more insistence was laid, at his election, on his observance of these conditions. Thus, when Boso became king of Arles in 879, we find what amounts to a formal statement of the terms on which he was elected, and similarly with Guido, who was elected to the kingdom of Italy in 889. Another statement of the same principle of mutual obligation, amounting to a contract, though not actually so called, occurs in the *Capitula Pistensia* of 862.[3] Nor was it only on election that such formal promises were demanded and given. Just as English kings some centuries later were repeatedly pressed to confirm their charters, so the Carolingians, when they were in difficulties during their reigns, and wished to regain popular confidence, had to issue solemn assurances that they would maintain law and justice, provided their subjects in return would render them true help and obedience.[4]

---

[1] The classical English expression of this doctrine of law is in Bracton's famous sentence that the king, while not below any man, must be 'sub Deo et sub lege, quia lex facit regem' (*De Leg. et Consuet. Ang.* i. 8. 5). But cf. p. 33, note 1, below.

[2] Cf. the instances cited by Carlyle in *Hist. Med. Pol. Theory in the West*, i. 240 ff.

[3] M.G.H. *Leg.* i, 547–9, 554–6, 478–83.

[4] Cf. the document published at Mersen by Lothair, Lewis, and Charles in 851, repeated at Coblentz in 860, and again by Charles the Bald in 869: ibid. 407–9, 468–73, 509–12. Prof. Kern cites evidence of there also having been

The contractual principle, in terms of which these ninth-century Frankish kings occupied their thrones, was not, it will be observed, a social contract, explaining the formation of society; that was something more theoretical, which only appeared with the growth of philosophy. Nor was it an 'original' contract that took place once and for all in the past; it was, rather, a perfectly practical statement of actually existing conditions. Nor, we may remark, was it open to the historical objection that it treated as prior to law what is really posterior, for the Middle Ages, as we have seen, did not accept the modern conception of law, implied in this criticism, as created by the government; on the contrary, the law of the kingdom continued always, and kings were elected, and the conditions of their rule laid down in accordance with that continuing law. The medieval contract, therefore, is completely immune against the sting of this particular criticism.

If we ask whence the Franks and other Germanic peoples derived the idea of expressing the conditions governing their monarchy by the formula of a *pactum*, the answer may be, partly from their inheritance of Roman and other classical traditions, no doubt familiar in some degree, if not at first hand, to the lawyers by whom the elections were managed; but another source, it can hardly be doubted, was the Old Testament. The history of the Jews is full of covenants of various kinds, and their whole career as the chosen people rested on such a basis. It is recorded, for instance, how God made a covenant with Noah and his posterity, that the flood should not destroy all flesh, neither should there any more be a flood to destroy the earth;[1] so again with Abraham and his posterity, whereby God promised to be their God, and to give them the land of Canaan for an everlasting possession.[2] These divinely initiated covenants are followed by covenants in which the people or their leaders take the initiative, as when under Joshua the people promised to serve God, and Joshua 'made a covenant with the people that day, and set them a statute and an ordinance in Shechem'.[3]

Undertakings of this kind, while to some extent bilateral, are primarily solemn promises by one party to act in a certain manner towards the other party; this is clearly the meaning where Josiah gathered the people and inaugurated a covenant to observe the

---

an *Urvertrag* in the late ninth century in the kingdom of Hungary (op. cit., p. 370).   [1] Gen. vi. 18; ix. 9–17.
[2] Gen. xvii.   [3] Joshua xxiv. 24–25.

law of God, 'and all the people stood to the covenant'.[1] But there are also instances in the Old Testament of regular bilateral pacts between king and people, embodying the mutual rights of ruler and subjects, and foreshadowing the future political constitution of the land. The best example of this is when 'all the elders of Israel came to the king to Hebron; and king David made a covenant with them in Hebron before the Lord: and they anointed David king over Israel'.[2] A similar covenant, preceded by a renewed covenant with God, was made when the priest Jehoiada arranged the killing of Athaliah and the setting up of Joash on the throne of Judah: 'Jehoiada made a covenant between the Lord and the king and the people that they should be the Lord's people: between the king also and the people.'[3] Here, then, we have clear examples in Scripture of the rights and duties of kings and their subjects founded in a covenant or compact, and there could be no better authority for medieval peoples, whose theory of government already corresponded with the principle of contract, and whose ceremonies of unction and coronation were similarly derived from the East, to adopt the contract itself in defining the status of their kings.[4]

A contractual principle, then, was implicit in the political system of Carolingian times, and explicit references to an actual contract occur sporadically from now onwards. It must be admitted that such references are relatively infrequent,[5] but we must remember that theoretical treatises on politics, which are the natural home of the social contract, were yet to be written, and the lawyers and statesmen were more concerned with practical affairs. The contest for supremacy between Papacy and Empire in the eleventh and twelfth centuries, centring round the question of investiture, and

---

[1] 2 Kings xxiii. 1–3. This is the kind of *pactum*, or solemn undertaking, that was meant by St. Augustine in the passage quoted above, p. 24. Cf. 2 Chron. xxiii. 3.   [2] 2 Sam. v. 3; 1 Chron. xi. 3.

[3] 2 Kings xi. 17; 2 Chron. xxiii. 16, but omitting the political covenant.

[4] The application of these biblical covenants can be seen, e.g., in Rufinus, *De Bono Pacis*, ii. 9 (A.D. 1056: in Migne, *Patrologia Latina*, vol. cl, p. 1617), who remarks with reference to the classical and Augustinian tradition: 'Unde cum rex instituitur, pactio quaedam tacita inter eum et populum initur, ut et rex humane regat populum, et populus regem statutis tributis et inlationibus meminerit venerari.' He then mentions the covenant arranged by Jehoiada.

[5] Prof. Kern remarks (op. cit., p. 368) that it is a mistake to suppose that the formula of contract was at all common between the seventh and the eleventh centuries, and that it often had more of a theological than a *volksrechtlich* significance; but at any rate the idea was evidently alive at that period, and ready to be developed into a regular political theory in due time.

its concomitant revolts in Germany, stimulated the output of political literature, and here, sure enough, the contract made its appearance again. The mutual relations of kings and people were not, of course, the main issue in this controversy, but the right of the secular government to intervene in ecclesiastical affairs. But the protagonists of the Church sought to resist the imperial claims by advancing counter claims on behalf of the Papacy to intervene in secular affairs, and to depose an emperor who misgoverned, and here was the point where the contract made its entry.

In this connexion the name of Manegold of Lautenbach has been quoted by a number of modern historians, and he is usually regarded as the first writer to have hit upon the terminology of contract in dealing with politics.[1] Thus, according to Mr. Carlyle, Manegold presented the world with 'the crystallisation of a movement of political thought and principle into a great phrase'. He gave 'the first definite expression to the conception which came in later times to be known as the theory of the "social contract" ', and there is 'no other writer of the eleventh or twelfth century who expresses the principle in exactly the same phrases'.[2] But apart from the earlier occurrences of the phrase mentioned above, Dr. Georg Koch has shown that Manegold was by no means alone in his day in using the language of contract, and that the phrase occurs in several other writers connected with the Investiture Contest.[3] If Manegold was unique, then, it was not because he invented a phrase.

Before dealing with these, however, let us read what Manegold himself wrote, for often though he has been quoted before, we certainly cannot omit him here. The position and powers of a king, he tells us, excel all other earthly powers, so that base or wicked men are not fitted to exercise them; rather, a man who as king is to govern and have the care of all should outshine his fellows in all virtue and wisdom, and study to rule in strictest equity. The people does not exalt him above itself (*neque enim populus ideo eum*

---

[1] O. Gierke (tr. F. W. Maitland), *Political Theories of the Middle Age*, p. 146; id., *Johannes Althusius und die Entwicklung der naturrechtlichen Staatstheorien*, p. 77; D. G. Ritchie, *Darwin and Hegel*, p. 203; R. L. Poole, *Illustrations of the History of Medieval Thought and Learning* (2nd edn.), pp. 203 ff.; J. N. Figgis, *From Gerson to Grotius*, p. 6.

[2] Carlyle, *Hist. Med. Pol. Theory in the West*, iii. 168, 169.

[3] G. Koch, *Manegold von Lautenbach und die Lehre von der Volkssouveränität unter Heinrich IV* (*Historische Schriften*, ed. E. Ebering, no. xxxiv, Berlin, 1902). The occurrence of the phrase in the ninth-century *Capitula de Carisiaco* was noticed by Carlyle himself in a previous volume, op. cit. i. 248.

super se exaltat) in order to give him scope to play the tyrant, but in order that he may be a guard against the tyranny and injustice of others. So if he who is chosen (*eligitur*) to repress the wicked and protect the just begins to cherish wickedness in his own heart, to oppress the righteous, and to impose on his subjects the cruellest tyranny, from which it was his duty to shield them, is it not clear that he deserves to be deposed from the position that was granted to him (*merito illum a concessa dignitate cadere*), and that the people is free from all subjection to him, since he was the first to break the compact, in accordance with which he was set up (*cum pactum, pro quo constitutus est, constet illum prius irrupisse*)? Manegold then, with an apology for taking an illustration *de rebus vilioribus*, proceeds to his well-known simile of the swineherd: if some one hired a man to feed his pigs, and later discovered that the man instead of feeding them was slaughtering, mutilating, and destroying them, would he not dismiss him in disgrace, and refuse to pay him his wages as well?[1] Nor is this all that Manegold has to say in condemnation of tyranny, for he returns to the subject in a later chapter. If a king violates the compact under which he is elected (*si quando pactum, quo eligitur, infringit*), and disturbs and confounds what it was his business to set in order, the people is justly and reasonably absolved from its allegiance, since he was the first to break that faith which bound them together (*quippe cum fidem prior ipse deseruerit, que alterutrum altero fidelitate colligavit*). The people never binds itself by an oath to obey a ruler who is possessed by fury, and is under no obligation to follow such a man wherever his madness drives him.[2]

Manegold was here going considerably farther than his party can have liked. For although Hildebrand restated vigorously the Augustinian view that secular monarchy is rooted in sin, and that the Pope had the power of deposing unrighteous kings,[3] Manegold contended that the subjects of kings who became tyrants were already absolved from their allegiance, and that the Pope merely gave effect to what was already implied in the monarch's breach of faith.[4] As is clear from his language in several places, Manegold took the historical matter of fact that monarchy in his time was

[1] Manegold of Lautenbach, *Ad Gebehardum Liber* (written 1083–5), c. xxx (in M.G.H. *Libelli de Lite*, i. 365). The chapter is headed: 'Quod Rex non sit nomen nature, sed vocabulum officii.'

[2] c. xlvii, ibid., pp. 391–2.   [3] Cf. Gierke (tr. Maitland), pp. 12, 109.

[4] Cf. Carlyle, *Hist. Med. Pol. Theory in the West*, p. 166; Poole, *Illustrations*, p. 204.

elective and conditional, and erected on that basis a definite theory of popular sovereignty. In this he was indeed an innovator, and was doing much more than merely repeating what was currently accepted by his contemporaries.

If we now turn to some of the other writers of the period of the Investiture Contest, we shall see how Manegold was exceptional, and how the language of contract had no necessary connexion at that time with the doctrine of popular sovereignty. Paul von Bernried, for instance, who wrote a life of Gregory VII,[1] makes no reference to the people, for although he says that 'free men' (*liberi homines*) made Henry king over them on condition that (*Henricum eo pacto sibi praeposuerunt in regem, ut ... &c.*) he would ensure that his electors got justice and good government, it is clear from his later remarks that he was thinking in terms of the princes who actually exercised the electoral rights. Even they can only refuse to acknowledge him as king after the Apostolic See has pronounced judgement upon him, for to the Pope belongs the power to depose and excommunicate a king, and to absolve all Christians from their allegiance. Henry, he proceeds, did not cease to violate and contemn the pact (*quod pactum ille postea praevaricare et contemnere non cesserit*), oppressing some with tyrannical cruelty, and compelling all whom he could to go astray from the Christian religion; accordingly, as he has refused to keep the pact which he promised them as the condition of his election (*cum pactum adimplere contemserit, quod eis pro electione sua promiserit*), the princes can rightly refuse to have him as king.

A similar standpoint, though it is used to urge the opposite conclusion, is taken up by the author of the anti-papal *Liber de Unitate Ecclesiae Conservanda*, who complains that Hildebrand has claimed the power to absolve the 'princes of the realm' (*principes regni*) from their oath, by which they had sworn to the king that they would keep their faith and compact[2] (*sacramentum, quo fidem vel pactum promiserant regi suo*). Manegold, therefore, was not unique in referring to the mutual ties between ruler and subjects as constituting a *pactum*, but for another reason he may justly be regarded as of unique importance among the political writers of his age. A contractual element was implicit in early medieval mon-

[1] Paulus Bernriedensis, *Vita Gregorii VII*, in Watterich, *Vitae Pontificum* (Leipzig, 1862), i. 474 ff.
[2] M.G.H. *Libelli de Lite*, ii. 205. Cf. his phraseology on p. 207, where he refers to 'testes sive iudices pactae fidei in nomine Domini'.

archy, and at times, as we have seen, became explicit; the popular origin of sovereignty also was by no means an unheard-of doctrine. It was implied in the Roman *lex regia*;[1] and in a work like the *Policraticus* of John of Salisbury (1120–80), though there is no mention of contract, the distinction between the king who rules according to law, and the tyrant who rules arbitrarily,[2] is elaborately developed, and the argument even culminates in a defence of tyrannicide. But Manegold was the first writer to combine the notion of contract with a doctrine of popular rights, and in so doing he anticipated the essential characteristic of the contractarian position in years to come.[3]

Many years, however, were yet to elapse before a regular political theory of contract can be said to be established.[4] Meanwhile another factor was developing, whose influence, added to that of the factors already described—the elective status of monarchy, and the character of law in the early Middle Ages—helped to prepare the ground for the contract theory. This factor was feudalism. While it contained the element of personal loyalty and devotion,

[1] See Carlyle, *Hist. Med. Pol. Theory in the West*, ii. 57 ff., for the work of the medieval civilians of the twelfth and thirteenth centuries who commented on the Roman Law. The doctrine that the people were the only ultimate source of political power was generally accepted, but there was a division of opinion among medieval authorities on the question whether the people had totally alienated their power, or whether they retained some of it, or at least could resume the use of it. The civilians of the fourteenth and fifteenth centuries frequently discussed the relationship between ruler and subjects in terms of contract: cf. Carlyle, op. cit., vol. vi (1936), pp. 15, 16, 19, 20, 152–6, 300, 323. See also Gierke (tr. Maitland), pp. 39, 43, 147, 150, and the quotations in F. Kern, *Gottesgnadentum und Widerstandsrecht*, p. 252, note 461.

Carlyle also mentions an opinion that custom could prevail against law, especially if it were such that it could be confirmed by a compact: 'alii autem dicunt, consuetudinem juri contrariam demum servari debere, quae pacto expresso potest confirmari: nihil enim aliud est consuetudo quam tacitum pactum' (*Dissentiones Dominorum*, Codicis Chisiani Collectio, 46; quoted op. cit. ii. 61).

[2] This distinction, indeed, was a commonplace from the time of Plato and Aristotle onwards.

[3] On the whole connexion of the right of resistance with the *Herrschaftsvertrag* and the doctrine of popular sovereignty see Kern, op. cit., pp. 251–66, esp. p. 255. On its first appearance in medieval German political thought the doctrine of popular sovereignty, he points out, was as much a stranger as the doctrine of absolutism (p. 254).

[4] Dr. Koch (op. cit., pp. 54 ff.) subjects Manegold's theory to a ponderous analysis on the lines of the distinctions drawn by later contractarian lawyers, but this is unnecessarily elaborate, for it is absurd to expect Manegold to have been aware of difficulties that really arose in later theory, when the contract was no longer a statement of actual conditions, as it was in the Middle Ages, but was thrust back into an imaginary past.

symbolized in the act of homage, feudalism as a form of government was essentially contractual. The vassal swore fealty to his lord, and was bound to discharge certain obligations, but he was only so bound provided the lord also discharged his obligations to the vassal. The feudal system, in fact, was the natural outcome of the whole theory of law and government which, as we have seen, was normal and general in the early Middle Ages. The whole 'legal atmosphere of feudalism', as Dr. Figgis puts it, was congenial to the contract theory.

The two elements [he writes], the assimilation of public to private rights, and the mutual nature of the tie between governed and governor, existed in the feudal system far more obviously than in any other; and these two elements were necessary to the contract theory. It could not have arisen except in an age when public rights were conceived inductively, inferred that is from particular rights of ruling lords, and in an age dominated by the idea of private law; for the contract theory assumes the existence of private rights and private legal obligations as anterior to all public rights, and indeed to the existence of the State.[1]

This view of the importance of feudalism in relation to the theory of contract is not merely an inference from the general similarity of the assumptions common to both. The final clause of a document like Magna Carta, to take a well-known illustration, clearly implies a theory of monarchy involving the recognition of bilateral rights and obligations, which is contractual in effect if not actually so-called. Examples can be found to show that feudalism was present in the minds of medieval thinkers themselves as a corroboration of their use of the terminology of contract. Thus, to return to the writers at the time of the Investiture Contest, Paul von Bernried clinches his argument against Henry IV[2] by the reflection that the knight is bound by his oath of fealty to submit to his lord only on the condition that the lord will not fail to perform his duty to the knight (*miles domino suo fidelitatis iuramento subiicitur eo pacto, ut et ille sibi non deneget, quod dominus militi debet*), and if he does fail, the knight is free to leave him for another

---

[1] J. N. Figgis, *From Gerson to Grotius*, p. 10; cf. pp. 130 ff. It is perhaps going too far to derive all public law and rights from private ones, for medieval thought contained an equally strong tradition that the king's position and powers were authorized by God, and the study of Roman Law helped the development of the idea of the state and of legislative action as capable of correcting and overriding custom by law. The notion of absolute monarchy, which by the end of the Middle Ages confronted that of popular sovereignty, was equally a development out of an earlier tradition. [2] Above, p. 31.

lord.[1] Similarly Guido, Bishop of Ferrara, who wrote on behalf of Gregory VII, quotes his enemies as saying that if it were once admitted that the Pope could depose kings, the consequences would be incalculable. The oath of fealty, which is referred to as a *foedus*, is on the same footing, they urge, as all other oaths, such as that binding man and wife, or the giving of a pledge (*pignus*) as security; if this principle were lost sight of, knights would cease to respect the oath that bound them to their lords, children would rise against their parents, subjects against their kings, and right and wrong would be confounded.[2]

In all these ways, then, the political ideas current in the Middle Ages combined to suggest that contract was the basis of government—the election and coronation ceremonies of medieval kings and emperors, the conception, embodied in feudalism, of law as anterior to the state, the examples of covenants in the Bible, the interpretation of Roman Law which attributed the source of political authority to the people—and from time to time the result was the actual use of the term contract (*pactum*, *foedus*) itself. At the same time it should be clear that this was not yet the *theory* of contract—obviously not of the social contract, and hardly even of the governmental contract as it came to be understood in the age of the Renaissance and after.[1] It was at the same time less unhistorical, and less theoretical than that was. That was the counterpart of, and the attempt to reply to, the theory of absolute sovereignty, which was appropriate to the political conditions of the sixteenth

---

[1] Paulus Bernriedensis, loc. cit.

[2] Wido, Episcopus Ferrarensis, *De Scismate Hildebrandi* (M.G.H. *Lib. de Lite*, i. 539). Cf. Hugo, Monachus Floriacensis, *Tractatus de Regia Potestate et Sacerdotali Dignitate*, in opposition to Gregory VII (ibid. i. 479), who alludes to the wickedness of breaking one's oath to one's lord, 'cui iuramento divini nominis fuerat *federatus*'. For other instances where the relationship between subjects and king is treated as one of *fides*, or *fidelitas*, and is thus equated with the feudal tie between vassals and lord, see Kern, op. cit., p. 259, note 477. The contractual conception of allegiance may also be illustrated in the fourteenth century from Dauphiné and Castile: cf. Carlyle, op. cit., vi. 69, 70.

[3] F. Kern suggests that even in the tenth and eleventh centuries the *staatsrechtliche Band zwischen Herrscher und Untertanen* can hardly be regarded as genuinely contractual, and that the contractual standpoint was something foreign to German political thought, which regarded the relation of subject to ruler as resting on a basis of *Recht* rather than *Vertrag* (op. cit., pp. 157–8, 177). It is true that German political thought did not regard rights and duties as being simply created by contract, as the Greek sophists did, but as resting in a fundamental *Recht*, ultimately the Will of God; but in political affairs, nevertheless, this issued in a *Vertrag*, which regulated the relationship between ruler and subjects.

and seventeenth centuries, just as the medieval idea of contract was appropriate to medieval conditions. After the Renaissance politics were dominated by two sharply contrasted theories of government—the theory of popular rights, enshrined in the contract theory, and the theory of the divine right of kings. In the Middle Ages, which could regard government as caused by sin, yet divinely ordained to meet the consequences of sin, and monarchy as an office, the product of election, yet marked through the ceremonies of unction and coronation with a stamp of the divine, the social contract and the divine right of kings were not incompatible.[1] It was only when both had changed their meaning with the change in the meaning of law and government itself that they became irreconcilably opposed.

[1] Cf. E. Barker, 'Medieval Political Thought', in *The Social and Political Ideas of some Great Medieval Thinkers* (ed. Hearnshaw), p. 22.

IV

THE LATER MIDDLE AGES AND THE
SOCIAL CONTRACT

WE have seen that the principle of the contract of government was implicit in the political structure of medieval Europe, but that it was not as yet interpreted as an act that was supposed to have taken place in the distant past, before any states existed. This conception appeared later, with the development of more speculative interests. As long as the medieval, essentially juristic, conception of government as the offspring rather than the parent of law remained true to life, and as long as the contract remained in its medieval form, it could not be called unhistorical, or abstract, or self-contradictory.

Gierke has shown how such 'properly medieval' conceptions of government gave way at length before the advance of what he called 'antique-modern' ideas,[1] until by the time of the Renaissance the whole medieval fabric was shattered, and in its place there arose the independent, territorial state, ruled by the sovereign, territorial monarch, whose will was law. The contract theory was no longer appropriate to this type of government, so that when writers who sought to combat the monarch's claim to absolutism built out of the surviving traditions of the older, medieval conception of the state a regular doctrine of contract, it could not help being imaginary and doctrinaire.

The normal medieval political theory, then, was that government is monarchical, but that the monarch's rule is subject to law, and that his person is exalted only by reason of his office. An absolute monarchy was theoretically conceivable, but, in the light of the traditional contrast between monarchy and tyranny, it was almost universally condemned as an undesirable form of government, and it was widely held that men were not obliged to obey tyrannical rule. St. Bonaventura, for example, in the thirteenth century, after a discussion of the question of political liberty, raises the question

---

[1] O. Gierke (tr. Maitland), *Pol. Theories of the Middle Age*, passim. By 'antique-modern' ideas he means 'ideas which proceeding from Classical Antiquity are becoming modern in their transit through the middle Ages . . .' (p. xliv; cf. p. 4).

how far Christians must submit to tyrants, and replies that they are obliged to obey their earthly lords, but only in such things as are not contrary to God, and then only in such things as are ordained reasonably in accordance with right custom.[1]

St. Thomas Aquinas himself, while stopping short of the approval of tyrannicide, and holding that if it is necessary to check the cruelty of tyrants, action should be taken by public authority and not *privata praesumptione aliquorum*, clearly identifies himself with the idea that royal power had a popular origin (*si ad ius multitudinis alicuius pertineat sibi providere de rege*), and that the people had a right, in case a king abused his power, either to restrict or to abolish the king's power altogether. If the people depose a tyrant, he continues, they cannot be held to have broken faith, even if they had previously submitted themselves to him in perpetuity (*nec putanda est talis multitudo infideliter agere tyrannum destituens, etiamsi eidem in perpetuo se ante subiecerat*); because it is he who has broken faith, in not ruling the people according to his duty as king, so that it is only what he deserves if his subjects do not keep their compact with him[2] (*quod ei pactum a subditis non reservetur*). Many of the elements in this passage are clearly recognizable. The idea that a king is established in office by the people, and that the people make a definite submission to him, is evidently derived from the medieval principle of election,[3] combined with the Roman Law doctrine of the *lex regia*; while in the end we have the idea of fealty or *fides*, and the actual word *pactum* once more, in much the same sense as that in which they were used by Manegold and his contemporaries in the Investiture Contest.

The development of Scholasticism and the recovery of the ethical and political works of Aristotle, in the thirteenth century, were accompanied and followed by the development of a more purely speculative and theoretical attitude to political questions

---

[1] S. Bonaventura, *Commentaria in IV Libros Sententiarum Mag. Petri Lombardi*, II. xliv. 3. I. Cf. the views of Augustinus Triumphus of Ancona, *Summa de Ecclesiastica Potestate* (Rome, 1479; written in the first quarter of the fourteenth century), qu. xxvi, where it is asserted that the Pope has the power to depose tyrants on the ground that 'videtur quod tyranni resistentes pape sunt heretici'.

[2] S. Thomas Aquinas, *De Regimine Principum*, I. vi.

[3] St. Thomas, in fact, specially commends an elective monarchy because of the opportunities it affords for placing restraints on the royal power. His general position, however, is really conservative: by public authority he apparently means some other power to whom the king is subject; if there be no such power to appeal to, there is no practical remedy for misgovernment, and the people can only be patient and trust to God. Cf. Poole, *Illustrations*, p. 212.

than had yet been common in the Middle Ages. The fundamental problem of political philosophy—the ultimate justification, or explanation of the state—began to demand a solution, as distinct from the rights or powers of this or that monarch in this or that particular situation. With this question that of the origin of the state was closely connected. Aristotle's political philosophy contained a complete answer to this problem, but the Christian Middle Ages had also inherited the strong, Augustinian tradition that the cause of secular authority was sin, and that government was something artificial; moreover, when the ultimate explanation of things was being sought, they could not wholly accept a philosophy whose outlook was confined to earthly affairs. We are not concerned with the whole systems which St. Thomas Aquinas and the other schoolmen constructed in the attempt to reconcile the Augustinian and the Aristotelian philosophies, but the fundamental conflict between these two points of view on politics is important in the history of the social contract theory.

On the one hand was the Aristotelian doctrine that the state had developed from the family, and that man was naturally political; on the other lay the whole medieval tradition, reaching back to the Romans and the Stoics, with its doctrines of the fall of man, its contrast between natural law and civil or positive law, and its theory that government was set up by the people on a contractual basis.[1] A common solution of this difficulty was to accept the Aristotelian doctrine that man was intended by nature to be political, adapting this to Christian teaching by substituting for nature the will of God, but to regard nature or the will of God as merely a *causa remota* or *causa impulsiva*, which required the co-operation of human will and action for it to be translated into effect.[2] This necessary human action was identified with the contract of subjection, by which the people set up a government to rule over them; and this contract, which had been embodied in the everyday operation of medieval political life, began now, as the origins of the state were investigated, to be thrust back into the past, to form the threshold of organized political society, with a non-political 'state of nature' in the background.

[1] According to Gierke, it was an axiom of philosophical *Staatslehre* from the end of the thirteenth century onwards that the *Rechtsgrund* of all *Herrschaft* lay in the voluntary and contractual submission (*in freiwilliger und vertragsmäßiger Unterwerfung*) of the governed community (*Althusius*, pp. 78, 79).

[2] Cf. Gierke (tr. Maitland), pp. 89, 187. This in itself is not so un-Aristotelian as might at first appear: cf. above, p. 13.

An interesting example of this combination of Aristotelian and medieval ideas is to be seen in the *Tractatus de Potestate Regia et Papali*, written about 1303 by John of Paris.[1] In the opening chapter we find it stated that men must live together, and in sufficient numbers to provide for the needs of life. But every community needs a man to rule over it and direct it for the common good, for if each individual were to look after his own affairs, the community would be scattered and dissipated. But it is clear, the writer proceeds, that this rule is not derived only from the law of nature, namely, that man is by nature a civil or political animal, for before the days of Belus and Ninus, who were the first kings, men did not live naturally, nor like men, but like beasts, without any rule. How, then, did men emerge from this bestial condition, and come to live under government? The author avoids the absurdity, current later, of supposing that these primitive men could make a political agreement together; *huiusmodi homines*, he says, could not be brought out of their bestial life to the common life for which they were naturally fitted *per verba communia*.[2] What happened was that men more able to use their reason, pitying them, endeavoured to persuade them to live together and submit to the rule of one man, and so bound them under fixed laws to live in common.

This somewhat fanciful account of the origin of the state does not, it is true, employ the formula of a contract, but it implies that men entered the state of their own consent; for it was by persuasion, and not by force or conquest, that they were induced to accept the authority of a ruler. If we turn to the contemporary Engelbert of Volkersdorf, however, we shall find a similar mixture of Aristotle and medieval tradition, but with a definite contract of subjection at the origin of the state.[3] Kingdoms and principalities, he tells us, arose *secundum hunc ordinem et modum naturae*: impelled by nature and reason, and under the experience of their natural wants, men chose one of their own number (*unum aliquem ex se*), of powerful reason and intelligence, and set him up (*praeficiebant*) to rule and preserve the rest, and they bound themselves

---

[1] Printed in Schard, *De Jurisdictione, Autoritate et Praeeminentia Imperiali* (Basel, 1566), pp. 142–224; Goldast, *Monarchia Romani Imperii* (Frankfort, 1614), ii. 108–47.

[2] It should be observed, too, that though his *vita bestialis* corresponds to what later writers called the state of nature, John of Paris, under the influence of Aristotle, does not call it natural, but reserves that epithet for political life.

[3] Engelbertus, Abbas Admontensis, *De Ortu et Fine Romani Imperii Liber* (Basel, 1553; written 1307–10), c. ii.

to obey him by a pact and bond of subjection (*sub pacto et vinculo subiectionis*). It was not *per ambitionem potestatis*, he continues, but *per electionem virtutis et probitatis*, that men were promoted to be kings.

It is clear from a study of fourteenth- and fifteenth-century political treatises that in spite of the admixture of Aristotelianism, the medieval, contractarian tradition was too strong to be overcome by it. That man is naturally political was a commonly repeated dogma, but it tended to be thrust into the background, while emphasis was laid on the voluntary origin of the state in a definite act of subjection. The inference drawn from this was not necessarily or usually a justification of popular rights against the existing ruler, for the act of subjection, like the *lex regia*, could be interpreted as a total surrender by the people of all their power; but it was generally held that the law of God, or of Nature, set a limit to the authority of the most absolute king. William of Ockham, for instance, held that human society was bound to observe the obligations it had undertaken, which included an obligation to obey its rulers, whether kings, or still more the emperor. But even the emperor's *plenitudo potestatis* was not unlimited, in that he must not break the law of God and of Nature; moreover, he had no more power than what the people had who gave it him, and he must use it for the common good.[1] As yet, in fact, the contract theory had no necessary connexion with democracy, and by far the most radical political treatise of the whole Middle Ages, the *Defensor Pacis* of Marsiglio of Padua,[2] is at the same time the most Aristotelian in its treatment of the origin of the state. Marsiglio held that laws should be made by the people, that is the whole body of the citizens, *aut eius valentior pars*,[3] and observes that a citizen would be more willing to obey a law which he thought he had imposed upon himself;[4] but there is no mention of contract in the book.[5] Though not a contractarian, however, Marsiglio occupies

---

[1] William of Ockham, *Dialogus* (in Goldast, ii. 398–957), bk. III, tr. ii, bk. 2, cc. 26, 27 (Goldast, pp. 923 ff.). In c. 28 it is worth noting that William of Ockham repeats St. Augustine's sentence that the *generale pactum societatis humanae* is to obey their kings, but he qualifies it by limiting it (as in St. Bonaventura, above, p. 37) to those things 'quae spectant ad bonum commune' or 'quae ad utilitatem communem proficiunt'.

[2] Written 1324–6; edited by C. W. Previté-Orton, Cambridge, 1928.

[3] Bk. I, c. xii, §§ 3, 5.   [4] Ibid., § 6.

[5] These pleas for popular representation, however, are another example of how widespread was the general medieval view of the relation between ruler and subjects, which, as we have seen, lay behind the contract theory. Marsiglio's

an important place in the evolution of the doctrine of popular sovereignty, which, both in the Middle Ages and afterwards, was commonly, though not universally, associated with the contract theory in one or other of its forms.

Less radical, and more in the general line of medieval tradition, was the theory advanced by Nicholas of Cusa in his *De Concordantia Catholica*.[1] God, according to Nicholas, is the primary source of all earthly power, but a definite law-making government can only arise from the voluntary act of men who agree together and submit themselves to its authority (*ex concordantia subiectionali eorum qui per eam ligantur*).[2] The use of violence is wrong. Here again, then, early in the fifteenth century, we find expressions which, though they do not include the mention of an actual contract of government, clearly involve the theory of deliberate popular consent as the origin of legislative authority, and approach very closely to an explicit *pactum* itself. In this respect, therefore, Nicholas of Cusa clearly belongs to the same political tradition as John of Paris and Engelbert of Volkersdorf a century or so earlier.

A contract of government, then, or if not an actual contract, a voluntary act of popular submission, which, regarded in the light of the distinction between monarchy and tyranny, and of the monarch's duty to observe the law of God and secure the common good of his subjects, was really a conditional submission, and so practically amounted to a contract, was well established by the fourteenth and fifteenth centuries as an explanation, not only of the status of existing kings, but also of the origins of government in general. With this theory of the origins of government there is already associated the notion, itself inherited from biblical and classical sources, of a primitive condition, in effect a 'state of nature', before governments arose. This might be a golden age,

reference to the 'whole body of the citizens' (*civium universitas*) recalls the language of the thirteenth-century English *Song of Lewes*, written in support of Simon de Montfort's representative experiments, with its advice that *quid universitas sentiat, sciatur*, and the tag which Edward I subsequently quoted, 'ut quod omnes tangit ab omnibus approbetur'; but Marsiglio's meaning went much farther than this in the direction of positive democratic control of legislation.

[1] Written 1431–3; printed in Schard, pp. 465–676. On his opinions see Gierke (tr. Maitland), pp. 47–48, 153.

[2] Bk. II, c. 12. Cf. bk. III, c. 4, where we are told that governments cannot be 'recte et sancte constitutae' except 'per viam . . . voluntarie subiectionis et consensus in praesidentiam'. Cf. also the contractual principles expressed later in the fifteenth century by Wessel of Groningen, quoted in Carlyle, *Hist. Med. Pol. Theory in the West*, vi (1936), 180.

in which all obeyed the law of nature; more often it was represented as a quasi-bestial form of life, in which men were solitary.
In any case all men were free and equal in it, and there was no
private property, nor established laws and government to protect
it. In seeking to explain the beginnings of organized society men
first discussed the origin of *dominium*, a conception including both
government and property; then, when the question of the establishment of government began to be distinguished from that of the
establishment of private property, the answer to the first question
began to be found, as we have seen, in a contract of submission.
But this led on to a further question; if men in the state of nature
were merely isolated individuals, how did they become a corporate
people with a common will, and a common power to negotiate
such a transaction with their future ruler, and to compel every
member to accept it?

John of Paris, as we have seen, avoided this question by assuming that the state was actually founded by some wise men who
persuaded the rest to accept the rule of a king; but generally the
result of holding that government could only arise as the effect of
a free act of will, combined with the essentially individualist conception of the freedom of every man in the state of nature, was to
create the idea that a corporate people itself, able to establish a
government, could only come into existence through the free act
of all the individuals composing it. There began to arise, in fact,
the conception of a social contract proper, explaining the origin of
society itself, and antecedent to the contract of submission, by
which that society established a government over itself. For a time,
however, political ideas were still fluid, and the answer to the
question how society came to be formed, as Gierke says, was
doubtful and hesitating.[1]

Aegidius Romanus Colonna,[2] who wrote about the end of the
thirteenth century, is a good example of an author who advances
alternative solutions of the problem without making it clear
whether they were complementary or contradictory. After describing the state, in the manner of Aristotle, as natural, and man as
animal civile, he tells us that there are two modes by which the
origin of the state and of government may be explained,[3] both of
them natural, but the one more natural than the other. One of

[1] Cf. Gierke, *Johannes Althusius*, pp. 93–95; *Pol. Theories of the Middle Age*
(tr. Maitland), pp. 88–89.   [2] *De Regimine Principum* (1473), bk. III, part i, c. 6.
[3] Cf. Hooker's explanation (below, p. 72) of the twofold foundation of the state.

these modes is the increase of families, leading the household to become a village, the village a city, and the city a kingdom. The other mode is agreement between those who establish the city or the kingdom (*concordia constituentium civitatem vel regnum*); for of old men lived singly (*dispersi*), but there came a time when in order the better to secure the necessaries of life, they made an agreement to form a unity, and founded a city for themselves (*aliquando concordabant in unum, constituentes sibi civitatem aliquam*).[1] A kingdom was made when a number of cities and encampments, fearing the power of their enemies, made a compact and agreement together to live under the rule of one king (*simul confoederarentur et concordarent, ut sub uno rege existerent*). Both of these modes is natural, but the first is more natural than the second. We can add yet a third mode, he concludes, which is simply that of violence, when some man rose up as a tyrant over the scattered individuals, and in order to coerce them the more easily, forced them to come together and form a *civitas*.

Now of these modes the first two are not necessarily incompatible, for Aristotle himself conceived of the amalgamation of households into villages, and villages into cities, as the result of voluntary action.[2] For Aegidius, however, they appear to be alternatives, and this mixture of Aristotle and the social contract may well strike us as characteristic of the whole political thought of the post-Scholastic age. But as the Middle Ages drew to a close, the time was at hand when such divergent accounts of the origin of the state as these could no longer lie side by side in the same treatise, with no very decided preference for one rather than another, but were to form the weapons with which the partisans of hostile factions contended against each other on behalf of rival political ideals. Meanwhile Aegidius' second 'mode', which is clearly that of an explicit social contract,[3] was becoming the accepted theory by which a whole school of political thought explained the genesis of political communities.

This involved two stages in the creation of the state—the for-

---

[1] *Civitas* here probably means 'city' and not 'state', because a few lines lower down *multae civitates et castra* unite to form a *regnum*. It might indeed be a city-state, but there is no mention of a government at this stage, whereas the *regnum* is under a *rex*, so that the *civitas* may be in the same condition as the *societas* in Aeneas Sylvius' work (next page), after the social but before the governmental contract. [2] Cf. above, p. 13.

[3] Aegidius' account of the origin of the *regnum*, however, does not include any definite contract of submission with the king, but a *confoederatio* of *civitates*, and in this respect it to some extent anticipates the theory of Althusius.

mation of the community, and then the erection of a government—
and these can be clearly seen in a work written in the middle of the
fifteenth century by Aeneas Sylvius Piccolomini, who subsequently
became Pope Pius II.[1] In the first chapter he describes how men,
after our first parents were driven out from the delights of Para-
dise, wandered like beasts in the fields and woods. But God had
implanted in them the faculty of reason, and they perceived that
society was necessary for the attainment of a good life (*ad bene
vivendum*). Accordingly these men who hitherto had lived apart
from one another like beasts in the woods, whether guided by
nature, or by the will of God, who rules all nature, all came together (*insimul convenere*) and founded societies, built houses and
towns, and invented the arts. For a time they lived thus in great
content; but in the second chapter we read that presently men
began to break their faith, disturbing the peace and injuring their
fellow citizens, stealing other people's property, and so *violare
societatem* and *fas omne abrumpere*. At length the people could no
longer endure being oppressed in this way by the strong and
violent; therefore they decided to resort to some one man of outstanding virtue, who should protect the weak from injury, and by
establishing justice secure that all alike got equal judgement.
This happened not among one people only, but generally, and so
arose the rulers who were later called kings.

Here, it is true, we have no explicit mention of a *pactum* in either
of these two proceedings, and, as Atger has pointed out, *convenere*
means 'ils se rassemblèrent', not 'ils ont convenu';[2] nevertheless,
as is borne out by the subsequent reference to breaking faith,
a social contract is clearly implied, just as the second stage, the
institution of government, is a voluntary act on the part of the
society, and the monarch is established, as in the regular medieval
tradition, for specific purposes, and, implicitly, on specific conditions. In effect, therefore, Aeneas Sylvius' account is an anticipation of the regular theory of two contracts, social and governmental,
which was common among the *naturrechtlich* jurists in Germany
in the seventeenth century.

Gierke suggested that it was inevitable that medieval theorists,
in spite of the richness of their experience of all sorts of groups
and organized communities, should have found in contract the

[1] *De Ortu et Authoritate Imperii Romani*, printed in Schard, pp. 314–28.
[2] F. Atger, *Essai sur l'histoire des doctrines du contrat social* (Nîmes, 1906),
p. 68.

explanation of the state. According to Gierke, the most appropriate clue to medieval experience would have been his own doctrine of the real personality of groups, and had they been able to apply this to their non-political communities, they might well have applied it also to the state, and so have avoided all the difficulties and contradictions that an individualist theory involves. But unfortunately, though the Middle Ages had their *Körperschaftsbegriff*, they had no adequate *Korporationstheorie*.[1] Their lawyers wrote in Latin, and inherited the technical phraseology of Roman Law, and with it a conception of corporate life which was fundamentally at variance with their own experience. Roman jurisprudence, in the first place, made a sharp distinction between *ius publicum* and *ius privatum*, and thought in terms of an absolute state over against a number of individual citizens; the Roman Empire was jealous of associations, and *collegia illicita* were suppressed. But in genuinely medieval thought there was no such severance between private and public right, and in the age of feudalism the state was but an aggregation of estates.

In seeking to name and describe their various corporate bodies, medieval theorists, in adopting Latin phraseology, necessarily inherited the distinction between the *universitas* and the *societas*. The *universitas* was the Roman corporation, but according to Roman Law, which conceived of no real legal personality other than that of the individual, the *universitas* was a *persona ficta*;[2] it could act in certain ways (own property, sue and be sued, &c.) as though it were a person, but its personality was artificial, and depended for its existence on a grant or concession from the state. The *societas* was a mere partnership of individuals, in the sphere of private law; it had no corporate character, not even a fictitious one, but was only a collective name for the individuals who composed it. To the Roman lawyer a *societas* involved a merely contractual relationship, and was in the same legal category as *emptio* and *venditio*, or *conductio* and *locatio*.

Now when medieval theorists applied these conceptions to their own experience, it was possible to treat a corporation below the state as a *universitas*, though the garment fitted badly. But a *universitas* owed its existence to a concession of fictitious person-

[1] Cf. Maitland's Introduction to Gierke, *Pol. Theories of the Middle Age*, p. xxviii.
[2] This famous phrase was first used in the thirteenth century by Sinibald Fieschi, later Pope Innocent IV, and does not occur in Roman Law itself, but it exactly epitomized the Roman doctrine of corporations: cf. Maitland, Introd. to Gierke, op. cit., p. xix.

ality by the state, so that strictly speaking the state itself could not be a *universitas*, for there was nothing above it whence it could have derived its corporate status. It followed, therefore, that the state must be only a *societas*. This may seem a very paradoxical conclusion, but medieval theorists found confirmation for it in various ways.[1] For one thing, there were a number of passages in Cicero where the state was described as a *societas*, or was said to be *sociatus*.[2] There is indeed no reason to suppose that Cicero was using these words in their technical legal meaning of a contract of partnership, for he often used them in a general sense of any common association, and even of the whole human race.[3] But then in St. Augustine, who had repeated Cicero's definition of the state, the words *societas* and *pactum* are actually found in conjunction,[4] and a whole succession of medieval writers afterwards either adopted or adapted this definition.[5] At any rate, by the end of the Middle Ages it was an accepted belief that the state originated in a contract of society, and since it is by contract that individuals enter into partnership together, this doctrine seemed to cohere well with the notion that in the 'state of nature' that preceded society the world was populated by entirely independent individuals.

[1] Actually, like *societas* (cf. note 3), the word *universitas* had a general as well as a technical legal meaning, and was sometimes used in the Middle Ages and later of the whole body of the people. Cf. above, p. 40, note 5.

[2] e.g. *De Rep.* I. xxv. 39; III. xxxi. 43, quoted above in Chap. II, p. 19, notes 2 and 5. Cf. also *De Rep.* I. xxxii. 49: 'cum lex sit civilis societatis vinculum, ius autem legis aequale, quo iure societas civium teneri potest . . . Quid enim civitas nisi iuris societas?' Ibid. IV. iii. 3: 'civium beate et honeste vivendi societatem.' Ibid. VI. xiii. 13 (*Somn. Scip.*): 'concilia coetusque hominum iure sociati, quae civitates appellantur.' Cf. *De Officiis*, I. xvii. 53, where the state is included as one of a list of various *societates*.

[3] Cf. *Lael. de Amicitia*, V. 20: 'Ex infinita societate generis humani, quam conciliavit natura.' *De Legibus*, I. x. 28: 'si hominum inter ipsos societatem coniunctionemque perspexeris.' Ibid. I. xi. 32: 'cum omne genus hominum sociatum inter se esse intellegatur.' *De Finibus*, IV. ii. 4: 'natosque esse ad congregationem hominum et ad societatem communitatemque generis humani.'

[4] Cf. above, p. 24. It is true that strictly speaking a *pactum* in Roman Law fell short of a *contractus*, but it was next door to it. Cf. Maine, *Ancient Law* (ed. Pollock, 1906), pp. 335, 336.

[5] e.g. St. Thomas Aquinas, *Summa Theol.* II. i, qu. cv. art. 2; II. ii, qu. xlii, art. 2 (both Cicero via St. Augustine); Vincent of Beauvais (thirteenth cent.), *Speculum Doctrinale*, vii, c. 6 (Cicero via St. Isidore of Seville); ibid. c. 7 (Cicero via St. Augustine); Dominicus de Sancto Geminiano (early fifteenth cent.), *Lectura super libro sexto Decretalium* (Lyons, 1520), p. 290, 2nd side, col. 2, no. 6, where he cites a number of definitions of the state, including Cicero's, via St. Isidore. Gerson, *Tractatus de modis uniendi ac reformandi Ecclesiam in Concilio Universali* (in *Works*, ed. du Pin, Antwerp, 1706, vol. ii, p. 171; cf. p. 163), applies Cicero's definition to the Church.

It would be a mistake, however, to suppose that the theory thus elaborated was individualistic or libertarian in its operation. In spite of its contractualism, medieval thinkers and their successors evolved a theory of corporations, and of the state itself, from which it is clear that they were well aware of, and could find expression for, the difference between a community and a mere aggregate of individuals. St. Thomas Aquinas based an organic view of the state on a combination of Aristotle's principle that man is naturally a political animal with a doctrine of natural law, which formed a rational basis for government and political allegiance. So also, as we shall see, writers like Suarez and Hooker,[1] whose theories were built on Scholasticism, reached conclusions which were far from 'atomistic'. The same can be said of Althusius; and the idea of 'moral personality', developed by Pufendorf and his successors[2] in the German school of natural law, led finally to Rousseau's theory of the general will. Gierke's theory of the real personality of groups, which is open to serious objections, both theoretical and practical, is by no means the only alternative to an extreme individualism.

The development of the social contract can be seen very clearly in the work of the Italian Marius Salamonius, who wrote early in the sixteenth century.[3] A discussion between *Philosophus* and *Jurisperitus* on the difference between a *princeps* and a *tyrannus* leads to the admission that the *princeps* is bound by the *lex regia*, which is a *lex populi*, and that the power of the people which creates the *principatus* is greater than that of the *principatus* itself.[4] From this the discussion passes on to the question of custom and law, custom being defined as *tacita quaedam civium conventio*, and law as *expressa civium conventio*; a further inquiry about the meaning of a *conventio* elicits the reply that it is a voluntary agreement, and the conclusion is reached that the law is a kind of compact between the citizens (*lex ergo inter cives ipsos pactio quaedam est*).

The nature of the state is next discussed, and the definition of Cicero and St. Augustine is quoted; the ensuing dialogue is so illuminating that it deserves to be translated in full:

PHILOSOPHER. If the state (*civitas*) is nothing but a kind of civil

---

[1] Cf. below, pp. 70, 74.　　　　　　　　[2] Cf. below, p. 122.

[3] *De Principatu libri septem.* This was first published at Rome in 1544, but appears to have been written between 1512 and 1514. It was dedicated to Pope Leo X (1513–22). On the work of Salamonius see Mario d'Addio, *L'Idea del Contratto Sociale dai Sofisti alla Riforma* (Milan, 1954).

[4] *De Principatu* (ed. d'Addio, Milan, 1955), pp. 12–19.

partnership (*civilis quaedam societas*), is any partnership ever formed without contracts (*contrahiturne societas ulla sine pactionibus*)?

LAWYER. No, there must be contracts, either tacit or express.

PHIL. May not these contracts be rightly called the laws of the partnership?

LAWY. Doubtless, but what has this to do with the people, which cannot be pledged to itself?

PHIL. Nor is a partnership pledged to itself, but the partners are pledged to one another (*nec societas sibimet obligatur, sed ipsi inter se socii*). Tell me, does a partnership exist before it is formed?

LAWY. No.

PHIL. Can it be formed before the partners agree upon the conditions?

LAWY. Certainly not.[1]

Here we have the whole story—the association of Cicero's and St. Augustine's definition of the state with the contractual bond of the *societas*, and the individualist principle that in the *societas* it is only the several *socii* who can put themselves under an obligation. Salamonius is thus a cardinal figure in the history of the social contract—comparable with Manegold of Lautenbach in the history of the contract of government.[2] A number of previous authors, as we have seen, were feeling their way towards the theory, but in Salamonius for the first time we find it stated with the utmost clarity and precision. Details of the content of the pact were yet to be filled in, and a number of years were to elapse before it was enunciated again so clearly, but in essence the doctrine was now fully fledged, and ready to enter the modern world.

[1] *De Principatu*, pp. 27–29.

[2] J. W. Allen, in his *History of Political Thought in the Sixteenth Century* (1928), appears to me to have seriously underrated the interest of Salamonius, whom he wrongly described as a Spaniard. After declaring (p. 333) that there is nothing in his views of the nature of law that could not have come direct from the earlier work of Fortescue, *De Laudibus Legum Angliae*, he writes (p. 335) that Salamonius may be said to have formulated a contract theory, but that, unlike that in the *Vindiciae contra Tyrannos* (which he also disparages, pp. 317, 319), God is not a party to the contract, 'and this, perhaps, is the most remarkable thing about it'. But, as far as the contract theory is concerned, this is surely to miss the whole point.

V

THE *MONARCHOMACHI* AND THE
CONTRACT OF GOVERNMENT

ALTHOUGH the contract theory was widespread in the Middle Ages, its modern history really begins in the sixteenth century, when it acquired a wider publicity, and made a fresh start as a commonplace of practical political controversy. Its earlier history was now to be repeated anew, for just as in the early Middle Ages the theory of a contract of government had preceded that of the social contract proper, so now we shall find that at first controversialists were mainly concerned with the governmental contract, and the more theoretical social contract did not appear until a later stage. The ultimate cause of this renewal of political controversy was the Reformation. It has sometimes been suggested that individualism in politics derived encouragement from the essentially individualist attitude of Protestant theology. This may have happened later, especially among the Puritan communities of seventeenth-century New England, and to some extent among the sectaries of England too, but it was not the initial cause of the recrudescence of contractarian thought in the sixteenth century. Nor, although there was much praise of liberty and denunciation of tyranny, were sixteenth-century writers at all disposed to advocate either individual freedom of conscience, or anything approaching political liberty for the masses. Intolerance and persecution were held to be right and desirable by Catholics and Protestants alike, for both were convinced that they alone possessed the truth. But this conviction, while it inspired each side with the belief that it was their duty to exterminate error, made it intolerable that they should themselves be suppressed by rulers whom they conceived to be blind to the truth. In the circumstances of religious minorities, then, rather than in any liberal or tolerant principles, lay the genesis of sixteenth-century contractarianism.

This can be seen, for example, in the attitude of the Presbyterians to the reign and deposition of Mary Queen of Scots; but the religious struggles in France in the second half of the sixteenth century gave rise to the most prolific crop of writings of this school, and also showed clearly how completely opportunist they all were, whether Protestant or Catholic. Under the later Valois kings, and especially after the Massacre of St. Bartholomew, the Huguenots in France were in rebellion against the government that persecuted them, and their pamphlets attacked the monarchy. But when their leader Henry of Navarre became heir to the throne, their hopes became centred in the Salic Law, while the Catholics took up the weapons the Huguenots had discarded, and proclaimed the incapacity of a heretic king to rule. From whatever standpoint they wrote, however, and opportunist as they were, the authors of these opinions made a distinct contribution to the history of political thought. They did not as a rule question the form of the state, but took monarchy for granted; yet in striving for religious freedom —freedom for their own religious groups, although not freedom or toleration for individuals—they had to advance arguments against absolutism. Some of these they found in political traditions inherited from the Middle Ages, but they gave to them a new vitality and a new meaning; they provoked replies in favour of the divinity of royal power, and so gave rise to an active and practical political controversy. And partisan though these controversial writers were, their discussions of the limits of monarchy led on to the whole question of the basis of sovereignty, and so into the heart of general political theory.

In the Middle Ages, as we have seen, the relationship of government to governed was such that it could be expressed in the language of contract without any of the implications of popular sovereignty, or individual rights, which later became associated with the regular contract of government. So also, to describe the state as united by a social contract might only be a logical deduction from the description of it as a *societas*, and did not necessarily imply that states had actually been fabricated by individuals living hitherto separate lives in a 'state of nature', though it might undoubtedly foster such a belief. Medieval thinkers, however, who accepted the doctrines of Aristotle, would say that even if states and governments were established by deliberate action, this was in response to a natural impulse, and in accordance with reason; they would not look on it as simply a matter of utility or convenience. Medieval kings were not autocrats, but were expected to govern according to law, and in their coronation-oaths (which might be interpreted in contractual terms) they promised to do so. Tyrants might be resisted, or even killed, but a contract of government did not imply that there was normally a tension, or conflict of interests, between the ruler with his powers, and the subjects with their rights. Kings were certainly exalted above their subjects, but this was by reason of their office, and as representatives of the whole community which accepted them. They were not inherently superior beings, whose blood was different from that of ordinary mortals. Even if they might be said to rule by divine right, this meant that monarchical government was part of God's order, and corresponded with God's own unity, not that the eldest line of some dynasty inherited a God-given dominion.

By the end of the Middle Ages, however, the concept of unity was wearing thin. The unity of the Empire, never much more than theoretical, was replaced by a plurality of sovereign national states, and now the rise of Protestantism threatened the unity of the Church as well. Protestantism threatened to disrupt also the internal unity of the national state. When religious minorities refused to accept the religious uniformity prescribed by the government, they claimed rights which, they alleged, overrode those of any merely earthly ruler. The contract of government was an obviously useful weapon in these conflicts, but its implications now began to diverge from what they had been in the Middle Ages. The final upshot was the emergence of the theory of the natural rights of individuals, and, in answer to this, monarchy was transformed by claims to personal absolutism. These opposing theories each reacted on the other, and drove their respective champions to wider researches and speculations in their efforts to controvert their opponents. Medieval thinkers had gone on from the contract of government to the social contract proper, and a similar process was now repeated. A contract theory of the basis and origin of government carried in its train a similar theory of the origin of society itself, until eventually the natural rights of individuals found their appropriate setting in a supposedly pre-social state of nature.

The best known of the political writings of the Huguenots is the *Vindiciae contra Tyrannos*, but its importance consists more in the clarity and decisiveness with which its views are stated, and the popularity it enjoyed, than in the originality of its contents; for practically all it has to say can be found in a group of smaller pamphlets published during the previous ten years or so. A few of these are the work of known authors, others are anonymous; but they have much in common, and it has been suggested that they may even have been the work of 'a kind of syndicate for the production of political pamphlets'.[1] All are agreed that political authority is divinely ordained, and that the duty of obedience is a duty owed to God. But all are equally certain that to God belongs the only absolute authority; earthly rulers are bound as much as all other men to respect the will of God, which includes the worship of God in the right way. If a king persecutes the true religion, the people's duty to God overrides their duty to the king, and a right to resist the king comes into play. Opinions differed as to the extent of this right of resistance, but monarchy, it was maintained, was always limited, never absolute.

These views appear clearly at the outset of the earliest of the Huguenot pamphlets, the anonymously published *De Jure Magistratuum in Subditos*, which in fact was almost certainly the work of the Calvinist theologian Theodore de Beza.[2] But the author goes farther than this; if man's prime duty is to God rather than to the magistrate, whence comes the magistrate's authority? It was divinely instituted, but as a means, not as an end in itself. People were not created for the sake of the magistrates, but vice versa, just as a tutor is appointed for his pupil, and not the pupil for the tutor, and a shepherd for his flock, not the flock for the shepherd. This is clear from the nature of things, but may also be proved by historical examples. Rulers, therefore, have a duty to their people, as well as a right to expect obedience from them, and the relationship between rulers and subjects is one of reciprocal obligation.

So far we have nothing more than an adaptation to current needs of what had for centuries been a commonplace of political theory; but it was generally held that this reciprocity of rights and duties between ruler and subjects had at least been overtly recognized by the ruler, who explicitly pledged himself to respect his side of these mutual obligations.[3] Beza goes a step farther, for he refers

---

[1] E. Armstrong, 'The Political Theory of the Huguenots', in *E.H.R.* iv. 34. On the Huguenot writings generally see J. W. Allen, *History of Political Thought in the Sixteenth Century*, pp. 306 ff., and G. Weill, *Les Théories sur le pouvoir royal en France pendant les guerres de religion* (Paris, 1891).

[2] This is said to have been first published in 1550; a French version, *Du Droit des Magistrats sur leurs Sujets*, appeared in 1574, and the Latin text was afterwards more than once reprinted. See *Mémoires de l'Estat de France sous Charles IX* (1576), ii. 735 ff.

[3] This is the argument, e.g., of the *Discours par dialogue sur l'Édit de la révocation de la paix* (1568), quoted in P. F.-M. Méaly, *Les Publicistes de la Réforme sous François II et Charles IX* (Dijon, 1903), p. 114; 'Fausser la foi à ses sujets avec lesquels les rois se lient par obligation naturelle et réciproque, c'est défaillir de roi pour décliner en tyrannie.' Practically the same occurs in

to the relationship between ruler and subject as a *mutuo consensu ac publice contracta obligatio*, and shortly afterwards as an *obligatio solemni et publico consensu contracta*.[1] Here is an unmistakable example of the governmental contract, but Beza's work only indirectly bears on the actual origins of government, for while he prefaces his remarks on the position of magistrates by the heading *De magistratuum origine*, he does not say much more in effect than that peoples existed before they had rulers, and chose their rulers for themselves.[2] It is clear, from the quotations he makes in support of his views, that what really weighed with Beza in the construction of his argument was not any *a priori* consideration of the origins of power, but the historical examples of covenants in the Old Testament. The same is true of the other sixteenth-century Huguenot writers, as it also was to some extent of the lawyers and others in the early Middle Ages who made use of contractarian phraseology. It seems doubtful, however, whether the Huguenots were directly influenced by their medieval predecessors. The truth probably is that similar conditions gave rise to similar thoughts and utterances. The language of contract lay ready to hand, and they furbished it up afresh for their own purposes. At any rate, while they evidently inherited much that was traditional, it is hard to trace in them a specific debt to any previous writers, and their quotation of authorities is much more from biblical or classical history than from medieval political theory.

A similar argument to Beza's in favour of limited monarchy forms the theme of another Huguenot pamphlet published about this time, the *Dialogue de l'authorité des Princes et de la liberté des peuples*, in which 'Archon et Politie parlent'.[3] This, however, does not go beyond the common assumption that royal power was created for the sake of the people, and that wherever it exists it is established on the basis of a contract between king and people. Other writers approached their objective, the necessity of limiting the powers of monarchy, from a somewhat different angle. François

---

Beza's pamphlet (qu. vi): the man who is 'ex rege tyrannus factus' 'apertissime eas conditiones transgreditur, sub quibus Rex designatus fuerat, quarumque observationem ipse iuraverat'.

[1] Qu. vi.   [2] Qu. v.

[3] In *Mémoires de l'Estat de France sous Charles IX*, iii. 87–159. Cf. esp. p. 114: '*Arch*. Il faut donc . . . nécessairement conclure, qu'une mutuelle correspondance doit estre entre le Roy et le peuple, tout regardant à Dieu et à l'équité'; and the reply: '*Pol*. Cela est vray. . . . Mais il y a loy entre les deux parties qui ordonne pactions et convenances réciproques, qui ne se peuvent ny par le prince, ny par les sujets, sans justice violer.'

Hotoman, the author of one of the most famous of the Huguenot pamphlets, the *Franco-Gallia*, published at Geneva in 1573, rests his conclusions not so much on a consideration of the functions of the monarch in relation to the will of God and the needs of the people, as on a systematic and learned inquiry into the historical development of French political institutions from the Romans and the Gauls until his own time. But through it all there runs the same conception of the proper subordination of the interests of the king to those of his people: absolute monarchy is described as 'Turkish' and fit only for brutes, not for rational beings, and although Hotoman does not argue expressly in terms of the contract theory, he quotes with approval the famous coronation oath of the kings of Aragon, and other historical instances of restrictions on royal power.[1]

Such, then, were the current political ideas which formed the background of the famous *Vindiciae contra Tyrannos*, which appeared in 1579.[2] The arguments of its predecessors are here elaborated at some length, and the contractarian basis, hitherto touched on comparatively lightly, occupies a prominent and central position. The book propounds in turn four questions, of which the first is answered in the negative, and each of the others, subject to certain qualifications, in the affirmative. The first question is whether subjects must obey princes if they command what is contrary to the law of God; the second, whether it is lawful to resist a prince who infringes the law of God; the third, whether it is lawful to resist a prince guilty of political oppression; the fourth, whether neighbouring princes or states should come to the assistance of the subjects of other princes who are afflicted for the sake of true religion, or oppressed by manifest tyranny.

The points raised in the first two questions, it will be seen, are in effect the same as those discussed by Beza's pamphlet; Beza, too,

---

[1] *Franco-Gallia* (1573), pp. 80, 81, 85. On p. 83 he alludes to the ephors whom the Spartans appointed 'qui regibus freni instar essent'. He probably borrowed them from Calvin, who mentioned them at the end of his *Institutes of the Christian Religion*.

[2] It was published anonymously, ostensibly at Edinburgh, but really at Basle, over the pseudonym of Stephanus Junius Brutus. Various persons were suggested as the real author, but most scholars came to the conclusion that he was either Languet or Duplessis-Mornay, or perhaps both jointly. Walker's seventeenth-century English translation of the *Vindiciae* was republished in 1924 with an introduction by H. J. Laski. See also E. Barker, 'A Huguenot Theory of Politics', in *Church, State, and Study* (1931), and his articles on the *Vindiciae* in *Cambridge Historical Journal* (1930).

had advanced similarly from religious oppression to political tyranny in general, which is the point raised in the third question of the *Vindiciae*.[1] The fourth question was evidently suggested by contemporary circumstances, with an eye to Queen Elizabeth and the Protestant princes in Germany. In formulating his answers to these questions the author makes use of two covenants or contracts—the words *foedus* and *pactum* appear to be used indiscriminately. The first is between God on the one hand and the king and the people jointly on the other, and is illustrated by the various covenants entered into with God on several occasions in Old Testament history. They are made to apply to his own time by the argument that 'although the form both of the Jewish church and the Jewish kingdom be changed, for that which was before enclosed within the narrow bounds of Judaea is now dilated throughout the whole world; notwithstanding the same things may be said of Christian kings, the Gospel having succeeded the Law, and Christian princes being in place of those of Jewry'. The same covenants, therefore, still hold good, with the same conditions and the same punishments for breach of them.[2]

The first covenant, with God, is clearly not a contract in the ordinary sense of either a social or a governmental contract, but it is made the basis for the legal argument that as king and people have a joint obligation to God (as *correi promittendi*), the people are bound to perform their share even if the king may neglect or violate his. A covenant of this type plays a relatively unimportant part in the general history of the contract theory, but it is of interest because it leads on in the *Vindiciae* to the second contract, and shows clearly what was pointed out above, and is evident again when the writer expounds his second contract, that for inspiration the Huguenots went back behind medieval political theory to the biblical source from which medieval contractarianism itself had largely been derived.

In the second contract of the *Vindiciae* the current Huguenot conception of the reciprocity of rights and duties between king and people is equated with the covenant between Joash and the people that followed their covenant with God, and it so appears as a regular contract of government, from which is deduced the

---

[1] The method of proceeding by a series of questions may also have been taken from Beza, who arranged his pamphlet in a similar manner, though the actual questions do not exactly correspond.

[2] *Vindiciae* (trans., ed. Laski), p. 75.

right of resistance to a tyrannical prince. J. W. Allen considered that though the author of the *Vindiciae* stated his theory of government in contractarian terms, he was not really thinking in terms of a proper contract theory, for a contract implies 'a conscious and deliberate act of will'; he suggested that the author 'was thinking simply of a moral obligation. His *pactum* does not, like a contract, depend on a man's volition. It is something that exists necessarily and universally', from the nature of things and the will of God. He pointed out also that though the author speaks of two covenants, he seems to be uncertain of their number, and sometimes implies that there were three;[1] the explanation, according to Allen, is that the reality of the covenants does not matter, and is not essential to the argument. The political covenant, again, may be expressed in words, but it may equally well be tacit,[2] and Allen concluded that these covenants, about which the author was so vague, are unimportant, and that he was merely stating, in a form corresponding to his scriptural analogues, what all the Huguenots had proclaimed, the obligation of the prince to serve God, and his liability to be resisted and even deposed if he refused to do so.[3] The author of the *Vindiciae*, which he called 'a pretentious book',[4] was simply 'gathering up the content of the earlier pamphlets and presenting it in a logical order and with a great parade of precision. He had really little to add to what had been said already.'[5]

It is true that passages can be found in the *Vindiciae* where the Huguenot political doctrine is stated without any reference to an actual covenant; we read, for instance, that 'there is ever and in all places a mutual and reciprocal obligation between the people and the prince: the one promises to be a good and wise prince, the other to obey faithfully, provided he govern justly'.[6] It is also true that if this obligation arises from the nature of things and the will of God, the promises signify mutual acceptance of the obligation of king and people, and do not, as in a thoroughgoing contract theory, themselves create and constitute the obligation; but the

[1] *Vindiciae* (trans., ed. Laski), p. 89, where there is a 'double covenant' between God and the king, or between God and the king and people, and between God and the people, besides the covenant between king and people only.

[2] Cf. ibid., p. 212: 'In the receiving and inauguration of a prince, there are covenants and contracts passed between him and the people, which are tacit and expressed, natural or civil.'

[3] J. W. Allen, *History of Political Thought in the Sixteenth Century*, pp. 317, 319.

[4] Ibid., p. 313.   [5] Ibid., p. 319.

[6] *Vindiciae* (trans., ed. Laski), p. 199.

Vindiciae gives such prominence to the covenants, and mentions them so frequently,[1] that one cannot help feeling that it is going too far to deny to them any real significance. At any rate, judging by the frequency with which it was quoted, there can be no doubt of the importance of the *Vindiciae* as a source of inspiration to later contractarian writers. Armstrong's verdict, in the article already quoted,[2] was nearer the truth: 'the function of the *Vindiciae* is to sum up and put into philosophical shape the results of these smaller pamphlets. The theory of contract which is constantly taken for granted in the latter is deliberately made the groundwork on which the *Vindiciae* rests.'[3] A few pages later, in fact, Allen admits that 'there is, if you will, in the *Vindiciae*, a "contract" between people and ruler: there is no suggestion of a social contract'.[4]

Social contract proper there is certainly none in the *Vindiciae*; nor is there anything really radical or revolutionary in its politics. Although kings may be resisted if they govern oppressively, the common people has no power to act; it is dismissed as 'that beast of many heads' which would 'run in a mutinous disorder', and measures of resistance may only be undertaken by the magistrates, or the duly constituted assembly of the Estates.[5] Allen justly points out that what is most original in the *Vindiciae* is 'its suggestion of a federal system based on recognition of the rights of natural communities'.[6] This conception was later developed by Althusius, but, as Allen says, it was not followed up by the author of the *Vindiciae*. It may well have a reference to the actual programme of the Huguenot communities in those regions of southern France which were mainly under their control during the Wars of Religion.

The last of the political works of the Huguenots of this school was the *Politices Christianae Libri Septem* of the Calvinist minister Lambert Daneau (Danaeus), published at Geneva in 1596. This is of interest because, much more than any of its predecessors, it attempts to construct a regular political theory. The origin of the state is traced, in Aristotelian fashion, by development from the family,[7] so that there is no social contract in Danaeus, but the

---

[1] e.g. besides the passages already cited, pp. 104, 109, 174–5, and others also.
[2] Above, p. 52.   [3] *E.H.R.* iv. 35.
[4] *History of Political Thought in the Sixteenth Century*, p. 329.
[5] *Vindiciae* (trans., ed. Laski), p. 97.
[6] *History of Political Thought in the Sixteenth Century*, p. 331. See *Vindiciae* (trans., ed. Laski), p. 116, where cities and provinces are to superintend the keeping of the pacts by the ruler.   [7] Bk. I, c. iii.

institution of royal power is treated as a deliberate act by the
people, who had hitherto been living in a state of innocence.[1] This
was pre-political, but not what later writers called a 'state of nature',
wherein individuals were free from any control, for it was governed
by what he calls *domesticum imperium*; but this was *toto genere . . .
diversum . . . a Politico seu Civili imperio*. The latter arose when
kingdoms and states were formed by the union of different families
or clans into a single society (*quum regna et respublicae ex diversis
gentibus conflentur in unam iuris societatem consensu coeuntibus*).[2]
This involved a definite contract of government. The people chose
their kings and princes, and set them up to rule with an authority
definitely limited by fixed conditions (*regum ac principum (quos
sibi eligebant et elegerunt) constrictam et limitatam arctis legibus, a se
mutuo consensu probatis auctoritatem esse semper voluerunt*).[3] Kings
who have ruled too harshly, that is, in violation of the compacts
(*durius, id est praeter pacta conventa*), have often been assassinated;
for when the agreements (*conventiones*) and laws of the kingdom,
which the kings swore to observe, have been broken, their subjects
have felt that they too were released from their promises; and all
men have ever held that vengeance should be wrought, as though
on public enemies of liberty, on princes who thus violate their
sacred compacts and agreements.

From a later book we gather that the contract of government
need not necessarily be an act by which a dynasty was set up once
and for all, to continue as long as the terms of the contract were
not broken (*cum nemine quicquam de perpetua dignitatis successione,
aut de magistratus auctoritate cuipiam uni familiae continuanda
pactus est*). A people which created its rulers could retain the
power of changing the constitution, and in that case no injury
would be done to any man.[4] Danaeus' theory in this respect is
more advanced than that of his predecessors, and it will be observed that he seems, if not actually to encourage, at least to con-
done tyrannicide. His contract of government is no longer merely a
means of expressing the reciprocity of rights and duties between
ruler and ruled, but has an actuality such as is usually associated
with a social contract at the outset of society, and the whole
apparatus of theoretical individualism. It might, indeed, be argued
that there is in Danaeus at least the embryo of a social contract

---

[1] 'Ab hoc statu vis omnis et ἀταξία aberat: ordo vero, et modestia, modera-
tioque animi vigebat summa' (I. iv, p. 31).
[2] p. 41.   [3] p. 42.   [4] III. vi. 214.

proper, for the state is formed *consensu*, and the word *societas*, which is used to describe it, had individualist and contractual associations.[1] But I doubt if these points should be pressed, for the elements combining to form the state are not individuals, but *gentes*; and in other ways Danaeus' theory, though to some extent in this anticipating the ideas of Althusius, is incompletely developed. One may ask, for example, whence the *populus* derived the wide powers it exercises in the contract of government, unless it is supposed to possess them all along; but in the family stage men were already under an *imperium domesticum*, presumably developed from parental authority; in which case whose *consensus* was it that led to the union of families to form a state? On such points as these Danaeus is vague, but his statement of the governmental contract is clear and precise.

If we now turn to the publications of the Catholic *Monarchomachi*,[2] we shall find that on the whole their views were decidedly more advanced than those of the Huguenots. The earliest of them, it is true, Jean Boucher, a clerical teacher and champion of the Catholic League, whose book *De Justa Henrici III Abdicatione* appeared in Paris in 1589, does not make much advance on the *Vindiciae*: by the people he does not mean the multitude, that 'beast of many heads',[3] but rather the assembly of nobles and senators, men of virtue and wisdom. Of actual contracts there is less in Boucher than in the *Vindiciae*; he alludes to the *foedus* made with God on several occasions in the Old Testament, which included king as well as people, and argues that in this covenant the people's part is greater than the king's, so that the people is bound to compel the king to observe the compact with God (*populus ad cogendum regem ut pactum Dei servet est obligatus*).[4] But there is no specific political compact between king and people, whose relations are merely said to be ones of *obligatio mutua*, while the king is described as *regni populique tutor publicus*, and it is pointed out that a tutor who abuses his office is removed.[5] In the account of the origin of the state, however, there is much that is contractual by implication. All men are stated to be free by nature,[6] and it is shown that there may be a people without a king, for

---

[1] Cf. above, pp. 45 ff.

[2] This word, familiarized for English readers by the essay in Figgis's *From Gerson to Grotius*, is derived from the Scotsman W. Barclay, who in 1600 published his *De Regno et regali Potestate, adversus Buchananum, Brutum, Boucherium et reliquos Monarchomachos*.

[3] Bk. i, c. 9.   [4] i, c. 18.   [5] c. 19.   [6] c. 12.

instance under the rule of priests or an aristocracy; but there cannot be a king without a people.[1] Yet nature impelled men to monarchy, since one God rules the universe, and so the people agreed (*multi in id consenserunt*) that the power which had been immediately in their hands (*penes eos immediate*) should, for the public convenience, be transferred to one man.[2] The appointment of kings by the people is supported by examples from the Old Testament,[3] and though it is admitted that some thinkers hold that when the monarch was established, the people deprived themselves of the whole of their authority,[4] Boucher maintains that *potestas* and *maiestas* (i.e. sovereignty, the ultimate supreme authority) is retained by the people. No one, he declares, is ever born king, and no Christian kingdom is subject to rigid rules of hereditary succession, but the people retains the right of constituting and altering them.[5]

Boucher's theory is incomplete, or inconsistent, at several points. It is not clear, for instance, how he would reconcile his general statement of the freedom of all men, and their agreement to transfer their power to the monarch, with his limitation of the *populus* to the nobles and senators, to whom alone, presumably, belong the rights over the king that are ascribed to the people. But we have in this agreement of free men to establish a monarchy, retaining certain rights against him, what amounts to a contract of subjection, which also has some of the features of a social contract; and imperfectly developed though it is, this is really more significant in Boucher than his repetition of the Old Testament covenants that the Huguenot writers had used. These practically disappear henceforth from political theory, but the contractual origins of the state play an increasingly important part in the later *Monarchomachi*, until they become a regular feature of antimonarchical thought.

Sixteenth-century writers, however, had not yet reached the position where it was asserted that the pre-political life was 'natural' for man, and that the creation of the state was something wholly artificial. The next book of this school, for example, the *Liber de iusta Reipublicae Christianae in reges impios et haereticos authoritate*, by Rossaeus,[6] states plainly that man was destined by nature *ad*

---

[1] *De Abdicatione*, c. 11.   [2] c. 12.   [3] c. 14.
[4] c. 18.   [5] cc. 17, 18.
[6] Paris, 1590. Some have identified the author with Guillaume Rose, Bishop of Senlis, another partisan of the League and opponent of Henry IV, but it seems more likely that he was the English exile William Reynolds.

civilem societatem; only so could the arts and manufactures flourish, while the power of speech that man alone possesses marks him out for a social existence.[1] No social contract, therefore, was needed to make men combine; but the institution of political authority was a deliberate act. At first, we gather—for how long is not stated—men lived together in natural but non-political communities; but they were subject to the risks of crime, and so the same common reason which previously induced them to combine now led them to create magistrates to rule over them (*ut singulae societates magistratus sibi quosdam crearent*).[2] Different societies established different kinds of government, but monarchy arose just like other governments, and those who created kings could equally well have created *consules* or *duces*. Some peoples have subordinated their kings too much to popular fury, as the Scots did with their queen, while others put their kings too high above the people, and falsely declare that kings can never be punished or deposed by the people.[3] The truth is that there are limits to the power of Christian kings, and if kings become tyrants, or espouse the Protestant heresy, which is worse than the paganism of old, their subjects can rise against them.[4] The justification for this, according to Rossaeus, is in the nature and purpose of monarchy, and the conditions on which it was established, and though there is no mention of any specific pact, his whole treatment of this subject is manifestly on the lines of a contract of government.

We come now to the book which achieved a widespread infamy for its justification of tyrannicide, the *De Rege et Regis Institutione* of the Spanish Jesuit Juan Mariana.[5] This is noteworthy for us, not so much for its radical views on tyranny, as for its account of the origin of society. To begin with a picture of man's life in what is virtually a 'state of nature' has now become a regular practice of political theorists; in Mariana it is more elaborate, and also markedly more individualistic than before. At first, he tells us, men wandered alone (*solivagi pererrabant*) like beasts, without fixed homes, with no law and under no government.[6] Apart from *latrocinia* and other dangers, what especially made society necessary was the weakness and defencelessness of man's offspring, and their need of the protection and resources of their elders. And so men bound themselves together with others by a compact of

---

[1] c. i, § 1.
[2] Ibid., § 2.
[3] Ibid., §§ 3–5.
[4] cc. ii, ix.
[5] Toledo, 1599.
[6] Bk. 1, c. i.

society (*mutuo se cum aliis societatis foedere constringere*), looking
to some one man of outstanding justice and honesty. Hence first
arose cities, and the sovereignty of kings.[1] The result, while kings
acted righteously, and performed their duty of protecting the
people, was a great improvement on the solitary life. Though
Mariana lays it down that kings must exercise the power they have
received from their subjects *singulari modestia*,[2] they were expected
at first, apparently, to rule equitably by their own discretion; laws
were introduced later, when men became suspicious of the king,
in order to secure equal treatment for all.[3] No king is *solutus legibus*,
and if he becomes a tyrant he deserves no mercy; but there is no
mention of any definitely contractual relationship between king
and people. At the outset, however, we now have what is practically
a social contract between individuals, as is implied in the conjunction of the words *foedus* and *societas*, whether or not we should
read an avowedly contractual meaning into the use of the word
societas by previous writers such as Boucher, Rossaeus, and
Danaeus. It will be remembered that Rossaeus prefaced the state
by a contract of subjection which had some of the features of a
social contract. In Mariana we have a social contract, but one
which has some of the features of a contract of subjection; for
when individuals combined, they chose out someone of whose up-
rightness and wisdom they all approved, and conferred authority
upon him.[4] Mariana does not discuss the question, which exercised
later contractarians, how subsequent generations could be held to
be bound by the rules of a society originally formed by the consent
of free individuals; he seems to be content, having once launched
his state by a social contract, to treat its later development on non-
contractarian lines. However that may be, it is clear that by the end
of the sixteenth century the writings of the *Monarchomachi*,
Protestant and Catholic, had done much to popularize the conception of a contract of government, and also some of the individualist ideas of the origin of the state which naturally found
expression in a social contract, even if they had not yet worked out
the distinctions which later writers drew between these two kinds
of contract, or all the implications of a contractarian theory of the
state.

Much the same theory of the state was current about this time
in Presbyterian circles in Scotland. A well-known illustration of

---

[1] *De Rege et Regis Institutione*, Bk. I, c. i.   [2] cc. v, ix.
[3] c. ii.   [4] Ibid.

this is in the dialogue *De Jure Regni apud Scotos*,[1] written to justify the deposition of Mary Queen of Scots, by George Buchanan, the historian, and tutor of James VI. Primitive men are here shown as living a solitary, lawless life, very much like that later described by Mariana.[2] But this condition is not called a state of nature: their own desires, as well as *commoditas aliqua utilitasque communis*, led them to come together, and a life in common is said to be more in accordance with nature (*naturae magis consentaneum*) than this wandering and solitary existence. Something more than mere *utilitas* was the cause of their union; rather it was *quaedam naturae vis*, so that we may regard God himself as the author of human society.[3]

We can hardly say, therefore, that there is a definite social contract in Buchanan; but in making society originate in the deliberate action of individuals who had hitherto lived solitary lives, he adopts a position which is well on the way towards it. Furthermore, the formation of society immediately involves the establishment and maintenance of a government, and this Buchanan treats as definitely contractual. The people choose out an individual of outstanding merit, and make him king, but on condition that he shall obey the *leges civiles*.[4] His function is to protect his subjects, and a man who seizes power by force or fraud, instead of receiving it at the hands of the people, is a tyrant. Kings born after the first inauguration of the monarchy owe their position to the laws and votes of the people just as much as those who were elected at the beginning: in fact, the law does not derive its force from the king, but the king gets his from the law.[5] It is observance of the law which distinguishes a king from a tyrant, for the law directs and moderates the king's desires and actions.[6]

Buchanan here seems to be thinking in terms of a kind of fundamental law, but he proceeds to treat it as the embodiment of a definite contract of government between king and people, breach

---

[1] Edinburgh, 1579.

[2] p. 8.
                                                                    [3] pp. 8–9.

[4] Buchanan seems to regard the people as already forming a *political* society before the king was elected, for he writes (p. 15): 'In rege autem creando hoc opinor veteres fuisse secutos, ut si quis inter *cives* (my italics) esset singulari praestantia, reliquosque omnes aequitate et prudentia antecellere videretur . . . regnum ad eum ultro deferebant.'

[5] p. 85. We have here an anticipation of the dispute about the relative positions of *lex* and *rex* which agitated the parliamentary lawyers when James I became king of England.

[6] p. 86.

of which on the king's part involves the loss of his rights.[1] An exact application of his theory may be seen in the account in his *History of Scotland* of Morton's speech to the Parliament at Stirling in 1578.

The Scottish nation [we read], originally a free people, created themselves kings upon this condition:—That the government, being intrusted to them by the suffrages of the people, if the state of the country required it, could be taken from them by the same suffrages; of which law, many vestiges remain even in our own day; . . . besides, the ceremonies used at the inauguration of our kings, have an express reference to this law; from all which, it is evident that government is nothing more than a mutual compact between the people and their kings.[2]

This passage is followed by some historical examples, including the remark, *Pro me si mereor in me*, which was said to have been used by the Emperor Trajan when he delivered the sword of justice to the prefect of the city.[3] This 'grim version of the theory of contract', as Ritchie calls it,[4] was stamped, with a drawn dagger, on the reverse of the coins minted at the coronation of James VI.[5]

A similar application of the theory of the contract of government to reality may be seen in the Act of Abjuration, or declaration of independence, issued by the deputies of the United Provinces on 26 July 1581. The preamble states:

All mankind know that a prince is appointed by God to cherish his subjects, even as a shepherd to guard his sheep. When, therefore, the prince does not fulfil his duty as protector; when he oppresses his subjects, destroys their ancient liberties, and treats them as slaves, he is to be considered not a prince, but a tyrant. As such, the estates of the land may lawfully and reasonably depose him and elect another in his room.

---

[1] *De Jure Regni*, p. 96. The dialogue runs as follows:
BUCHANAN: Mutua igitur regi cum civibus est pactio.
MAITLAND: Ita videtur.
B.: Qui prior a conventis recedit, contraque quam pactus est, facit, nonne is pacta et conventa solvit?
M.: Solvit.
B.: Soluto igitur vinculo, quod regem cum populo continebat, quicquid iuris ex pactione ad eum, qui pacta solvit, pertinebat, id, reor, amittitur.
M.: Amittitur.
[2] G. Buchanan, *History of Scotland* (trans. J. Aikman, Glasgow, 1827), bk. xx, § 37.
[3] Ibid., § 38.   [4] D. G. Ritchie, *Darwin and Hegel*, p. 204.
[5] Ritchie points out that in Milton's *Tenure of Kings and Magistrates* (in *Prose Works*, ed. Bohn, 1848, vol. ii, pp. 26–27), where this whole passage from Buchanan's *History* is quoted, the motto is made even grimmer by the omission of the words *pro me*.

Similar views appear in the instructions given by the states to their envoys who were charged to justify the Abjuration before the Imperial Diet held at Augsburg twelve months later.

The delegates of the States [as Motley says] [were instructed] to place the King's tenure upon contract—not an implied one, but a contract as literal as the lease of a farm. The house of Austria, they were to maintain, had come into the possession of the seventeen Netherlands upon certain express conditions and with the understanding that its possession was to cease with the first condition broken. It was a question of law and fact, not of royal or popular right. They were to take the ground, not only that the contract had been violated, but that the foundation of perpetual justice upon which it rested, had likewise been undermined. . . . 'The contracts which the King has broken are no pedantic fantasies', said the estates, 'but laws planted by nature in the universal heart of mankind, and expressly acquiesced in by prince and people.'[1]

As might be expected in a man brought up in this atmosphere, and with Buchanan for his tutor, the idea of the compact between king and people was familiar to James VI, but, as we should also expect, he argues strongly against it. In his *Trew Law of Free Monarchies* (1598), after dealing with a number of reasons by which men sought to limit the powers of kings, he comes to 'the last obiection', which 'is grounded upon the mutual paction and adstipulation (as they call it) betwixt the King and his people, at the time of his coronation: For there, say they, there is a mutuall paction, and contract bound up, and sworne betwixt the king and the people', of which the consequences were that if the king broke his side of the bargain, the people were freed from theirs. James VI flatly denies that any such contract was made then, 'especially containing such a clause irritant as they alledge', though he admits that at his coronation the king freely promises to his people 'to discharge honorably and trewly the office given him by God over them'. Even if there were a contract, he continues, 'no man that hath but the smallest entrance into the civill law' will doubt that one of the parties to a contract is not freed from it because he thinks the other party has broken it, 'except that first a lawful trial and cognition be had of the ordinary Judge of the breakers thereof: or else every man may be both party and Judge in his own cause'.

[1] J. L. Motley, *The Rise of the Dutch Republic*, part VI, c. iv. Cf. also the use of contractual phraseology in the *Apologie* of William of Orange, quoted in Carlyle, *Hist. Med. Pol. Theory in the West*, vi (1936), pp. 384–5.

This consideration, which is undoubtedly a sound criticism of the practical operation of the contract theory, leads him to conclude that between king and people God is the only judge. It certainly does not lie with the 'headlesse multitude, when they please to weary of subjection, to cast off the yoke of government that God hath laid on them, and to judge and punish him whom by they should be judged and punished'.[1]

---

[1] In *Works*, ed. C. H. McIlwain (Harvard Pol. Classics, Cambridge, Mass., 1918), p. 68. King James alluded to the compact again in his speech to Parliament on 21 March 1610 (ibid., p. 309), and there, it may be noted, he seems to have been more prepared to admit the validity of the idea, though once more it is God only who can punish a king.

VI

THE DEVELOPMENT OF THE
SOCIAL CONTRACT

WHILE active politicians and controversialists were thus popularizing contractual theories of government, a succession of more academic thinkers, mainly of clerical or legal training, were engaged in developing and transmitting to posterity the traditional *corpus* of political theory which they inherited from the Middle Ages. In the later seventeenth and eighteenth centuries these studies were carried on mainly in German and Dutch universities by the writers commonly known as the school of Natural Law (*Naturrecht*), but in the sixteenth and early seventeenth centuries political science owed much to the revived Scholasticism of a remarkable group of Spanish theologians. We saw at the end of the fourth chapter how, before the middle of the sixteenth century, Marius Salamonius had already published a theory of the state containing all the essential elements of the social contract. The Spanish writers hardly went as far as Salamonius in the construction of an explicitly contractarian theory, yet the same ultimate presuppositions may be found in them. A good example of this is in the work of the Dominican Franciscus Victoria, who died in 1546, and of whose *Relectiones Theologicae* several editions were published at various cities in the second half of the century.

The state and civil power, he held, are just and legitimate, and have divine authority. Social life is natural and necessary for man, because of his weakness and defencelessness, and on account of his power of speech, which is the index of a faculty of reason,[1] while life in society involves the necessity of government. But before men came together they were all equal,[2] and there was no reason why any one of them should exercise authority over the rest, so that the community must have governed itself.[3] It was incon-

---

[1] Victoria, *Relectiones*, iii, §§ 1, 4, 5. Some of these views, ultimately derived and, in fact, quoted by Victoria from Aristotle, reappeared, as we have seen, in Rossaeus and Mariana.

[2] This is in effect a 'state of nature', though it is not so called, for Victoria regards civil society as 'natural': yet he speaks of men being equal by virtue of the 'law of nature'.　　　　　　　　　　[3] *Relectiones*, iii, § 7.

venient in practice, however, for government to be in the hands
of the multitude, and so it was necessary to choose some person
or persons to whom the exercise of government should be transferred.[1] This arrangement is not described in so many words as
a contract of submission, and is analogous rather to the Roman
and medieval *lex regia*, from which, no doubt, it was derived; but
it is combined in Victoria with the assumptions that frequently
led to a contract theory. Even monarchy, which he regards as the
usual form of government, is held to derive its power from the
people; and that power, although men are said to be naturally
political and to have come together into society naturally, is
stated to arise, not from the nature of society itself, but from
the previously existing 'natural' rights of individuals. Here again,
though there is no explicit social contract, society is a product
of the association of previously isolated and equal individuals,
and it was only a short step from this to a definitely contractarian
position.

There is an evident inconsistency, though Victoria's theory does
not raise it in an acute form, between this theoretical individualism
and the Aristotelian tradition that man is naturally political.
Thoroughgoing contractarians avoided this difficulty by abandoning the organic view of society altogether, and explaining the state
on completely individualist lines, but some Spanish theologians
made an interesting attempt to effect a reconciliation. Thus the
Jesuit Luis Molina[2] follows Victoria's account of the origin of
the state, but reads into it a new interpretation. He tells us in effect
that society is natural, and the first *societas* was that of man and
woman, leading to the family, and the *potestas* of husband over
wife, and parents over children, and master over servants. But
man is impelled by nature to a yet larger society, in which there
can be division of labour and the production of necessaries; and
being naturally prone to sin, so that a government is necessary,
men must unite not in villages only, but in a complete and perfect
state.[3] Monarchy, therefore, was instituted; but Molina points
out that the authority of the state cannot have had its origin simply
in the powers of individuals, for if so how could the state have the
power of life and death over its citizens, which no individual

---

[1] *Relectiones*, iii, § 8.

[2] *De Justitia et Jure* (Mainz, 1614). Molina died in 1601, and his first volume,
with which we are concerned, received its *approbatio* in 1592.

[3] Molina, *De J. et J.*, Tract. ii, Disp. xxii, § 8.

rightly possesses? Some later writers would have concluded that the state does not rightly possess this power at all, but the solution Molina offers is that the power of the state is divine; yet men came together of their own free will to form the state, and although they did not create the power of the state themselves, this voluntary union of them is a necessary condition without which it could not materialize.[1]

Sir Ernest Barker illustrates this theory of the theologians by the analogy of marriage. 'The agreement of husband and wife', he writes, 'is necessary to the existence of marriage. But it does not explain, or create, the institution of marriage. The institution is an inherent part of the divine scheme; and the agreement of the parties is simply an agreement to fit themselves into that scheme, which exists *per se* apart from their agreement.'[2] One might add that this analogy throws light on the defects, and the half-truth, of the social contract theory. Marriage has some of the features of a private contract between individuals, but it is something more than a mere contract that can be dissolved by the will of the parties; so also the state, while it contains elements of consent by the citizens, which are analogous to contract, is something more than a mere product of contractual agreements. Further, just as historical criticism would altogether reject the contractarian account of political authority, and explain it rather in terms of tradition and prescription, following acquiescence in the successful exercise of power, so also, whatever views we hold about the place of marriage in modern society, its history is something quite different. At the same time, this does not prevent those who wish to do so from arguing that the divine scheme (whether in politics or matrimony) is fulfilled by an historical process.

A theory of the state somewhat similar to Molina's was advanced by the great Jesuit philosopher Francisco Suarez. He begins his account of the origin of government by the statement that it naturally belongs to no single man, but to the aggregate of men (*hominum collectio*);[3] and he proceeds to say, more individualistically

---

[1] Ibid., § 9. 'Longe diversa', he continues, is the 'potestas, quae ex natura rei consurgit in Republica, a collectione particularium potestatum singulorum.'

[2] Note in Gierke, *Nat. Law* (tr. Barker), ii. 241–2. This comparison of political obligation with the marriage-tie had already been made (God himself being described as 'the principal author of the contract') in Beza's treatise *Du Droit des Magistrats sur leurs Sujets* in *Mémoires de l'Estat de France sous Charles IX* (1576), ii. 775.

[3] F. Suarez, *Tractatus de Legibus ac Deo Legislatore* (1611; Antwerp, 1614), III, c. ii, § 3. Cf. c. iv, § 2: 'Haec potestas ex natura rei est immediate in com-

than Molina, that the whole community, which is formed by a union of individuals, derives its authority from the free consent of individuals (*a singulis hominibus per proprium eorum consensum derivari hanc potestatem in totam communitatem ex eis coactam*): it was thus that both the community and its power originally came into existence.[1] Suarez appears to be identifying himself with the contractarian standpoint; but he makes an important distinction. The *hominum multitudo* can be regarded in two ways, first as a mere *aggregatum quoddam*, but secondly in that men unite together by common consent into a single political body in one bond of society (*quatenus speciali voluntate seu communi consensu in unum corpus politicum congregantur uno societatis vinculo*), and in order to assist one another to one political end; in this way they form a single mystical body, which can be called a moral unity (*quo modo efficiunt unum corpus mysticum, quod moraliter dici potest per se unum*).[2]

Gierke dismissed this theory as 'a mere *jeu d'esprit*', and complained that Suarez, like the whole individualist school, could not really transcend the conception of the state as only an aggregate, and never achieved any real sense of its corporate character.[3] But here, as with Molina's theory, Gierke hardly did justice to Suarez.

The consenting parties [Sir Ernest Barker pointed out] who are necessary to the existence of a political society (just as they are necessary to the institution of marriage) may be, as such, only an aggregate. But the *institution* which emerges from their act of agreement as a number of individuals is a part of the divine scheme. The distinction is fundamental; and if we accept it the State is really a *corpus*.[4]

It remains true, nevertheless, that Suarez makes more definite use of contractarian terminology than Molina had done, not only in the implied social contract at the origin of the state, but also in dealing with the relationship between the people and the king. Molina had agreed with Victoria that the people could not conveniently retain political authority in their own hands, but must set up a government, whether a monarchy, an aristocracy, or a demo-

munitate, ergo ut iuste incipiat esse in aliqua persona tanquam in supremo principe, necesse est, ut ex consensu communitatis illa tribuatur.'

[1] *De Legibus*, III. iii, § 1: 'Nam idem est principium talis potestatis et ipsius communitatis, in qua residet: sed ipsa communitas coalescit medio consensu et voluntate singulorum; ergo ab eisdem etiam voluntatibus manat potestas.' Cf. c. iv, § 2.

[2] c. ii, § 4. Cf. the theory of Pufendorf, below, p. 122, and note 5.

[3] Gierke, *Nat. Law* (tr. Barker), i. 46.

[4] Ibid. ii. 243, note.

cracy;[1] and that they could confer limited powers on the government, so that if it exceeded those limits, it could be resisted as tyrannical: but this arrangement is not described as an actual contract between government and people.[2] In Suarez, on the other hand, there is a definite contract of government. Royal power, he declares in one place, varies in degree (*maior vel minor existit*), according to the terms of the pact or agreement made between the king and his kingdom (*iuxta pactum, vel conventionem factam inter regnum et regem*);[3] this pact, he points out, is binding on the people as well as on the king, and they cannot refuse him obedience (unless he degenerates into a tyrant, in which case they may wage a just war against him), just as a private individual who had sold himself into slavery would be bound to keep his contract by serving his lord.[4] In a later chapter, indeed,[5] he writes of *veluti conventio quaedam inter communitatem et principem*, saying that the power exercised by the king is not to exceed the *modum donationis vel conventionis*; and he may perhaps be conscious of the unreality of this *veluti conventio*, for he alludes to the possibility of its not being available in writing, and in that case, he remarks, the limits of royal power must be decided by custom. Suarez, however, is steeped in the contractarian attitude to politics; it appears again, for instance, with some justification, in an interesting passage where he anticipates the later evolution of international law. Here he comments on the desirability of justice, peace, and mutual assistance between states, and remarks that they should agree, *quasi communi foedere et consensione*, to observe certain common laws. These, he continues, are what are called the laws of nations, and arise more from tradition than from formal promulgation.[6]

This may be the best point at which to discuss the political theory of Richard Hooker, in whose famous work, *The Laws of Ecclesiastical Polity*,[7] with its judicious combination of views de-

---

[1] The latter is not a government of the whole body of the people by itself, but arises 'cum potestas plurimorum, qui regimini deputantur, a tota Republica . . . instituatur et concedatur' (Molina, II, Disp. xxiii, § 12).

[2] Ibid., §§ 6–11.

[3] Suarez, III. iv, § 5.   [4] Ibid., § 6.

[5] c. ix, § 4. We may compare with this the theory of the Spanish jurist D. Covarruvias (ob. 1577), *Practicae Questiones*, in *Opera* (various editions), vol. i, c. 1: man is naturally a 'civile animal', but 'civilis societatis et reipublicae rector ab alio quam ab ipsamet republica constitui non potest iuste et absque tyrannide. . . . Reges vero et principes ab origine mundi populorum suffragiis creabantur'.

[4] Suarez, III. ii, § 6.   [7] The first five books were published in 1594.

rived from various sources, classical, medieval, and contemporary, the state of political thought at the end of the sixteenth century is significantly revealed. Hooker's work is interesting also, apart from the inspiration that Locke in particular drew from it, in that he was one of the first Englishmen to use contractarian phraseology, and the vehicle by whom much continental political theory reached this country.

He states at the outset that 'we are not by ourselves sufficient to furnish ourselves with a competent store of things needful for such a life as our nature doth desire, a life fit for the dignity of man'. Society, therefore, is natural; yet societies do not occur spontaneously in nature, but must be formed by men deliberately 'seeking communion and fellowship with others', and 'uniting themselves . . . in politic Societies'. Life in society involves government and laws, and these, too, are the product of agreement. The origin of the state, therefore, is twofold, both natural and artificial: 'Two foundations there are which bear up public societies; the one, a natural inclination, whereby all men desire sociable life and fellowship; the other, an order expressly or secretly agreed upon touching the manner of their union in living together.'[1]

'Men always knew', he continues, 'that strifes and troubles would be endless, except they gave their common consent all to be ordered by some whom they should agree upon'; and the reason why this consent was necessary was that without it 'there was no reason that one man should take upon him to be lord or judge over another'.[2] Political life, then, in Hooker's view (as in Victoria's), is in accordance with nature, yet it needs a deliberate act of union by individuals, and an agreement on the terms of their union, which amounts in principle to a social contract, to bring the state into existence. The establishment of government is also the result of deliberate agreement and action by individuals, and at first sight this does not appear to be distinguished from the act of union itself; for the social contract is said to produce 'that which we call the Law of a Commonweal, the very soul of a politic body'.[3] On reading farther, however, we find that Hooker considered the possibility of a social existence without the establishment of actual government. But (as in Locke's state of nature) disputes would arise under these conditions, in the absence of any one to compose

---

[1] Hooker, *Eccles. Pol.* I. x, § I. Cf. the theory of Aegidius Colonna, above, p. 42.

[2] Ibid., § 4; cf. Victoria, above, p. 67.   [3] Ibid., § I.

them, and so a second agreement was necessary for the erection of a government.

To take away all such mutual grievances, ignorances, and wrongs [as he puts it] there was no way but only by growing unto composition and agreement amongst themselves, by ordaining some kind of government public, and by yielding themselves subject thereunto; that unto whom they granted authority to rule and govern, by them the peace, tranquility and happy state of the rest might be procured.[1]

So that in a word [he continues], all public regiment of what kind soever seemeth evidently to have risen from deliberate advice, consultation and composition between men, judging it convenient and behoveful; there being no impossibility in nature considered by itself, but that men might have lived without any public regiment. Howbeit, the corruption of our nature being presupposed, we may not deny but that the Law of Nature doth now require of necessity some kind of regiment,[2] so that to bring things unto the first course they were in, and utterly to take away all kind of public government in the world, were apparently to overturn the whole world.[3]

In a later part of his book, it should be observed, Hooker drops the assumption that the contractual origins and limitations of government are universal. 'In power of dominion', we read, 'all kings have not an equal latitude. Kings by conquest make their own charter: so that how large their power, either civil or spiritual, is, we cannot with any certainty define, further than only to set them in general the law of God and nature for bounds.' There may, in fact, be kings by divine right—'by God's special appointment'—and these will have 'that largeness of power which he doth assign or permit with approbation'. Only some, not all kings, 'were first instituted by agreement and composition made with them over whom they reign'; their powers, indeed, are limited by 'the articles of compact between them', but the historical actuality of this compact now appears to be somewhat dubious. The terms of the compact made 'at the first beginning . . . for the most part are either clean worn out of knowledge, or else known unto very few', so that the determining factor will be, in effect, no definite compact at all, but the actual constitution of the country—'whatsoever hath been after in free and voluntary manner condescended unto, whether by express consent, whereof positive laws are witnesses, or else by silent allowance famously notified through

[1] Ibid., § 4.
[2] The Augustinian tradition again.
[3] Ibid., ad fin.

custom reaching beyond the memory of man'. Hooker's thought is here more in accord with the medieval conception of the contractual basis of all constitutional authority, and it contributed in course of time to the common Whig assumption that the constitution of England embodied an 'original contract'.[1]

Professor d'Entrèves has warned us, however, against reading into Hooker the individualism in support of which Locke and others quoted him in the late seventeenth century.[2] While some of his sentences, especially if they are taken out of their context, appear to be susceptible of an individualist interpretation, Hooker's outlook was essentially medieval and scholastic. He speaks of 'composition and agreement', but not of men making it but 'growing unto' it, and when he considers the question of the obligation of later generations to observe the laws which had been agreed upon by their fathers, but to which they personally had never given their consent, it is clear that his attitude was far from individualist. This problem, when perceived, was always a stumbling-block to a contractarian theory of the state. Hooker simply refers to the immortality of corporations.

To be commanded we do consent [he writes] when that society whereof we are part hath at any time before consented. . . . Wherefore as any man's deed past is good as long as himself continueth; so the act of a public society of men done five hundred years sithence standeth as theirs who presently are of the same societies, because corporations are immortal; we were then alive in our predecessors, and they in their successors do live still.[3]

He does not tackle the problem Molina and Suarez were at pains to solve—how the mere association of individuals at the beginning could create a genuine corporate body with an eternal power to coerce persons who did not freely join it, but had simply been born into it. He combines the notion of the perpetuity of the corporation with the concept of agency or representation, which makes it unnecessary for all laws to receive the approval of every individual; yet this still further weakens the principle of consent. Representation was an obviously convenient device which already had a long parliamentary history behind it, but at bottom it rested

[1] *Eccles. Pol.* VIII. ii, § 11.

[2] A. P. d'Entrèves, *Medieval Contributions to Political Thought* (Oxford, 1939), p. 130.

[3] *Eccles. Pol.* I. x. 8. Locke quoted the sentences before and after this passage, but significantly omitted this passage itself.

on a legal fiction. A kindred problem which exercised theoretical contractarians was that of majority-decision: how the will of the majority, which commonly prevails in a corporation as the will of the whole, can bind a dissentient minority in a society supposed to rest on individual consent. Hooker simply ignores this, and it seems clear that he did not envisage consent in terms of individuals.

It is now time to consider the political theory of Johannes Althusius (Althaus),[1] to whom Gierke ascribed a position of epoch-making importance in the history of political thought, and of the social contract in particular. Many writers before him had argued in terms of contractarian ideas, but he first, according to Gierke, created a real theory of the social contract, in that he took the principle of contract, tacit or expressed, as the fundamental juridical basis, not only of the state, but of every kind of human association (*consociatio*). Althusius divides associations into five classes, each in turn wider than the previous one—the family, the fellowship (*Genossenschaft*), the local community (*Gemeinde*), the province, and finally the state. Each is formed by the contractual union of smaller associations, so that in the wider associations the contracting parties are not individuals but associations themselves. The state itself, created by the union of provinces or local communities, is a federal rather than a unitary organization, for the provinces surrender only such part of their rights as is necessary for the purposes of the higher community, and they retain a right to secede from one state and join in combination with another.[2] In this the plea of the *Vindiciae contra Tyrannos* that provinces and cities should superintend the pacts with the ruler and with God, should resist the ruler who broke the contract, and in the last resort renounce their allegiance, was taken up by Althusius and brought into logical unity with a complete political system.

Gierke's interpretation of Althusius has been challenged by Professor Friedrich.[3] Gierke declared that Althusius placed every form of human association in the category *societas*, and made the

---

[1] His *Politica Methodice Digesta*, first published at Herborn in 1603, was re-issued with some modifications at Groningen in 1610, and again at Herborn in 1614. The third edition has been reprinted with an introduction by Professor C. J. Friedrich (Harvard Univ. Press, 1932). Althusius was Professor of Law at Herborn, and later became Syndic of the town of Emden.

[2] See Gierke, *Johannes Althusius*, esp. pp. 21, 48, 99–100, 244; also his *Nat. Law* (tr. Barker), i. 70–76.

[3] In the Introduction to his edition of the *Politica Methodice Digesta*.

contractus societatis the fundamental explanation of all, but Dr. Friedrich flatly contradicts this.

Althusius does not [he writes][1] attribute systematic importance to the word *societas*, probably because of its individualist connotations. . . . How Gierke can say [he adds][2] that Althusius uses the category *societas* constantly, even for the State, I cannot explain. Similarly the expression *contractus societatis* to which he attaches so much importance, is hardly, if ever, found in Althusius' treatise. . . . It is necessary [he continues] to interpret Althusius entirely anew in this respect. Gierke took the position that Althusius treated all public offices in terms of private rights and obligations, that he dissolved the State into a network of contractual obligations. It would be equally possible and perhaps even more convincing to show from the text that Althusius interpreted all private functions in terms of a hierarchy of groups, more or less public in nature. But the truth is that the difference between public and private functions tends to disappear, just as in modern socialism, if all groups, including the State, are looked upon as natural phenomena to be explained sociologically and not legally. For Althusius the distinction between the State and society which he comprehends in the higher concept of a community or natural co-operative group (*consociatio symbiotica*) is inconceivable.[3]

According to Gierke, Althusius ultimately rested all public right on private right, but his system, though erected on this basis, was one in which the various associations stood as 'necessary and organic articulations between the individual and the State';[4] and in this respect Althusius' system resembles medieval political thought, except that the latter started from the unity of the whole, whereas Althusius stands all the time on natural-law individualism.[5] Dr. Friedrich, however, argues that what Althusius is really expounding is the theory of a corporative state.[6] He also considers it unfortunate 'to characterize the relation of the less inclusive groups or symbiotic consociations to the more inclusive consociations as "federalism", as has been customary since Gierke. . . . Federalism is only a particular form of the general type of a symbiotic group' of which 'Althusius never wearies of emphasizing the unitary, collectivistic nature'.[7] 'What Althusius is aiming at would be much better characterized by what the English call local government and what in modern technical parlance is called decentralization.'[8]

---

[1] p. lxxxiv. [2] Ibid., note 6. [3] p. lxxxv.
[4] Gierke, *Johannes Althusius*, p. 244. [5] Gierke, *Nat. Law* (tr. Barker), i. 71.
[6] p. lxxxvi. [7] p. lxxxvii. [8] p. lxxxvii, note 2.

There are a number of points to be considered here, but what concerns us most is the contract which, according to Gierke, Althusius makes the explanation of all associations, but whose importance Dr. Friedrich denies.[1] Dr. Friedrich admits that 'the *Politica* speaks in its second sentence of a pact by which the symbiotics put themselves under obligation to one another' (*consociatio, qua pacto expresso, vel tacito, symbiotici inter se invicem ad communicationem mutuam eorum, quae ad vitae socialis usum et consortium sunt utilia et necessaria, se obligant*). Dr. Friedrich argues, however, that 'a consideration of this sentence in the light of the entire work will show that this pact is not a contract and that its position within the system is a distinctly minor one'. He also attaches considerable importance to the fact that Althusius altered this sentence from the form in which it had appeared in the original edition, when the *consociatio* was formed *pacto, tanquam vinculo arctissimo*. The pact, then, which had been 'a very strong bond', has become something either explicit or tacit; in fact, it is not really a contract; it 'need not be a single act or decision at all. It may be a series of decisions, even in the form of tacit consent'.[2] 'The pact is no more a contract for Althusius than the adoption of a modern constitution is a contract for us.'[3]

I think Dr. Friedrich has gone too far in his attempt to discredit Gierke's interpretation. It may be quite true that Althusius does not use the words *contractus* and *societas*, but what Gierke meant to convey by these words, as must be evident after reading his work, in which *societas* and *contractus* are treated as correlative and complementary technical terms, was the juridical category (that of the free union of individual elements) which Althusius applied to every association. Even making the maximum allowance

---

[1] Dr. Friedrich points out (p. lxxxvii, note 6) that the word *contractus* is used by Althusius only for the governmental contract between the symbiotic group and its executive ministers, and that it is only in this sense that it appears in the index to the book; it is not used for the social contract by which the group is constituted. The governmental contract in Althusius will be discussed below.

[2] p. lxxxviii. He cites Alth. ix, § 7, where cities and provinces unite to form a *regnum*: 'vinculum huius corporis et consociationis est consensus et inter membra Reipublicae fides data et accepta ultro citroque, hoc est, promissio tacita vel expressa de communicandis rebus et operis mutuis, &c.'

[3] This comparison of Dr. Friedrich's is not a very happy one, for actually Althusius refers to a constitution as a pact: see c. xix, § 49: 'Est autem haec fundamentalis lex nihil aliud quam pacta quaedam, sub quibus plures civitates et provinciae coierunt et consenserunt in unam eandemque Rempublicam habendam et defendendam communi opera, consilio et auxilio. A quibus conditionibus et pactis quando communi consensu receditur, Respublica esse desinit.'

for the difference between the first and the later editions of the
Politica, Althusius' second sentence unmistakably says that in
every *consociatio* the constituent members bind themselves together by a pact. In this sentence at the outset of the book, which
is a completely logical structure throughout, Althusius is defining
his terms, and it seems to me that Gierke was undoubtedly right
in his view that Althusius, in defining the *consociatio* in terms of a
pact, meant to imply that every *consociatio*, of every type, was
always contractual. As regards the occurrence of the actual words
in the text, Dr. Friedrich is no doubt right as far as *contractus* is
concerned, but if we try *pactum* instead (a word much more regu-
larly and commonly used by all writers on the social contract), we
shall find it frequently recurring in Althusius.[1] It is worth noting,
too, that Althusius, who freely cites authorities for his statements,
quotes among others the various Old Testament passages that
seem to vindicate a contractual basis of government. Dr. Friedrich's attempt to explain this away does not strike one as very convincing.[2]

As regards the nature of the *consociatio* which results from the
pact, Gierke and Dr. Friedrich are really, perhaps, not so far apart
as at first appears. The real point is that by applying a uniform
juridical principle to all social and political life, Althusius strikes
down the distinction between public and private rights, and
between the sovereign state and subordinate non-political groups,
and makes them all alike species of the one genus, *consociatio*.
Gierke argues that Althusius ultimately reduces all rights to private
contractual rights: Dr. Friedrich, on the other hand, that Althusius
constructs a corporative state in which all rights are public. The
difference, I think, is explained by the fact that one looks primarily
at the formation, or the logical foundation, the other primarily at
the operation or functions of the symbiotic group. For Gierke
does not fail to point out that once the group is constituted it
becomes a genuine corporation, with a ruling power, which is
maior singulis, though *minor universis collegis*.[3] Much of the importance of Althusius, from Gierke's point of view, consisted in
the fact that he avoided a sharp differentiation between the state
and non-political groups, and constructed a system in which

[1] e.g. i, § 6, where the *symbiotici* are *vinculo pacti conjuncti et consociati*, and
ibid., § 28, where he declares 'caussam efficientem consociationis politicae esse
consensum et pactum civium communicantium'. Cf. also ii, §§ 2, 3, 5.

[2] Introduction, p. xlix.

[3] Gierke, *Nat. Law* (tr. Barker), i. 74.

every kind of social organization was explained by a universal principle, and that so he arrived at a much more adequate theory of society and its obligations than any of his contemporaries. To say, with Dr. Friedrich, that Althusius' theory is really that of the corporative state involves the risk of importing twentieth-century political and economic connotations alien to Althusius; but apart from this Dr. Friedrich's contention is only a more modern way of stating Gierke's own interpretation of Althusius' conclusion, and I do not see that he has proved Gierke wrong in his analysis of the foundation on which Althusius' theory was erected.[1]

This is not the place to discuss the whole of Althusius' political theory, but we may notice finally that when the association is formed, it sets up magistrates to execute its decisions, and there is a definite governmental contract between them and the association. Though they differ over the social contract in Althusius, Gierke and Dr. Friedrich are agreed on this point, as indeed they could hardly fail to be, for Althusius' language is plain and unmistakable.[2] Although we may not accept Gierke's theory of the nature of groups, we can hardly deny the importance of Althusius in the history of political thought. Inheriting the ideas both of the *Monarchomachi* and also of the more academic political theorists, he built on them a logical system which he expounded without partisanship or propagandist intentions. The result was a political theory more complete than any hitherto attempted by writers of the social contract school, and though it may strike us as academic, it in fact reflected the author's local experience. Nor must we suppose that it was uninfluential, for Althusius work was repeatedly quoted by controversialists for years to come, and provided them with a rich quarry of arguments.

[1] It should be borne in mind, as Sir Ernest Barker has pointed out (Gierke, *Nat. Law*, Introd., i, pp. lxxxii ff.), that it is a mistake to suppose that Gierke meant his theory of the real personality of corporations to be used to exalt internal groups against the state (as, for instance, in Figgis's *Churches in the Modern State*), for the state as the supreme group is also a real person, and Gierke's theory is equally if not more likely to lead to state absolutism of the totalitarian, Fascist type. Gierke himself, in fact, was deeply influenced by the romantic exaltation of the Germanic *Volk* which later reached such heights in Germany under the Nazi régime.

[2] The chief reference to the governmental contract is in c. xix, §§ 6, 7, where 'populus et magistratus summus inter se mutuo certis legibus et conditionibus de subiectionis et imperii forma ac modo paciscuntur, iuramento ultro citroque fide data et accepta promissave'. This is called a *contractus reciprocus* and is equated with the *contractus mandati* of Roman Law. Cf. also c. xxxviii, § 39, and c. xix, §§ 12, 13.

The name of Hugo Grotius is most famous for his contribution to the development of international law, which lies outside the scope of this book, but he was an important and influential member of the school of natural law, and shared its usual contractarian theory of the state. In some respects, indeed, he followed Althusius' federal conception, but while assuming that all social union is the result of the free combination of individuals who originally lived in isolation,[1] he allows other methods besides contract or *consensus* by which rights over men can be acquired (e.g. delict, which explains the imposition of servitude by way of punishment), and there can be societies of unequals as well as of equals. The state, for example, is a society of unequal persons,[2] and though he admits that the people may choose what kind of government they will have, he denies that they have any right, once their choice is made, to resume their power, just as a woman is free to choose her husband, but once she is married, she is bound to perpetual obedience.[3] Some governments may be set up on the basis of a governmental contract,[4] but the notion of mutual obligation between king and people does not hold universally.[5] Again, if a state is composed of federated parts, this union is the result of a contract,[6] but there is not the same power of free self-determination as Althusius had allowed; if the whole cannot alienate a part without the consent of the part, neither can a part secede from the whole.[7]

A more authoritarian note is sounded in Grotius than in Althusius, yet for Grotius, too, the ultimate political reality is the individual; and though he speaks of society as natural to man,[8] he implies in effect that the state is formed by a social contract. Most writers took it for granted that the original contract of society was unanimous, and it was then difficult to explain, on the basis of individual consent, how a vote of the majority could rightly bind the minority when subsequent decisions were to be made. Grotius

---

[1] *De Jure Belli et Pacis* (Paris, 1625), ii, c. 5, § 17 ff.

[2] I, c. i, § 3.   [3] I, c. iii, § 8.   [4] I, c. iv, § 8.

[5] I, c. iii, § 9. Even Bodin considered the possibility of a king being bound in some circumstances by contract; cf. his *De la République* (Paris, 1576), i, c. 8.

[6] Grotius, II, c. vi, § 4 (Evats's translation, 1682): 'They that first entered into that society did (as may be presumed) contract a firm and immortal league among themselves, for the defence of all those parts which are called integrants. ... Such a society is constituted by mutual consent and agreement: and therefore its power over its parts depends wholly upon the will and intention of them who first instituted that society.'

[7] Ibid., § 5.   [8] e.g. in the preface, p. v.

assumes that one of the terms of the original contract was that decisions should rest with the majority once society was formed, and this, by an extraordinary fiction, he calls a 'right of nature'. All societies, he remarks,

have this in common, that as to those things for which such a society is instituted, the whole, or major part in the name of the whole, do oblige every particular in that society. For it may well be presumed that it was in the mind of those that first entered into that society, that the power to determine all matters therein treated, should rest somewhere. But because it would be apparently unjust, that some few persons should impose upon the rest, where every person hath equal power; therefore by the right of nature (setting aside those orders and by-laws which do prescribe a form or method to the whole society, in the handling and discussing of matters that are brought before them) the major part should have the power of the whole.[1]

By the early seventeenth century contractarian principles had taken a firm hold of nearly all political thought. The Aristotelian tradition that man was naturally political (or social) was commonly accepted, but this by itself was not regarded as a sufficient explanation of the state. Side by side with it there was the strong individualist principle that all men are naturally free and equal, and that they could have only formed a society by their own volition. Accordingly it was commonly held that though men were naturally inclined for life in society, and in fact needed it, they must create society by a deliberate act. Having entered society by what is in effect a social contract, men felt the need of government, and here the principle of contract was resorted to once more. The Huguenots and other *Monarchomachi* had used the contract of govern-

---

[1] II, c. v, § 17; cf. the language of the preface, p. vii: 'For they that lifted themselves into any society, or otherwise subjected themselves to any one man, or to any society of men: These have also expressly promised, or from the very nature of the thing itself, ought so to be understood, as if they had tacitly promised to observe and fulfil whatsoever the major part of that society, or they unto whom their power was transferred, had constituted or ordained for the general good.'

Though a fiction, this assumption that the majority-principle was introduced as part of the original contract was more logical than the mere application to a society, supposedly originating in the contractual union of free individuals, of the rules of procedure in the Roman law of corporations. The same theory reappears in Hobbes, *De Cive*, c. vi, § 2: 'Considerandum deinde est, unumquemque ex multitudine, quo constituendae civitatis principium fiat, debere consentire cum caeteris, ut in iis rebus, quae a quopiam in coetu proponentur, pro voluntate omnium habeatur id, quod voluerit eorum maior pars.' See also the theories of Pufendorf (p. 124), Locke (p. 137), Thomasius (p. 149), Hertius (p. 154), &c.

Cf. Burke's criticism of this view in his *Appeal from the New to the Old Whigs* (1791), quoted below, pp. 194, 195.

ment to justify limitations to the powers of the monarch, and this remained a constant function of this type of contract. Different writers advocated many different methods of keeping monarchs within the bounds set by the contract, ranging from Mariana's threat of tyrannicide to orderly and constitutional action by the Estates of the Realm, as in the *Vindiciae*. Several writers also borrowed the idea of the Spartan ephors, persons appointed by the people to supervise the government of the kings, and adapted this to their own theories,[1] and they form a prominent feature in Althusius' scheme.

But the theory of the contract of government had a much wider currency than that simply of propaganda on behalf of popular rights. Just as medieval writers had differed over the construction of the Roman *lex regia*, so now it was possible to erect a strong monarchical authority on the basis of a contract of submission, and although there was a general agreement that a just king differed from a tyrant, some writers argued from a contractual standpoint that the people had no right to do anything but endure the tyranny of a lawfully constituted ruler. There were thinkers, indeed, who upheld the principle that monarchs got their right to rule from God, and were responsible only to God; but it was at least equally common to hold that the rights of monarchs had been created by the people by way of their deliberate submission.[2]

The governmental contract, in fact, by implying a ruler distinct from the people, was incompatible with a truly democratic theory, such as that of Rousseau, in which the people constituted the state and set up officials whose function was merely to execute the general will. In the seventeenth century men could hardly avoid thinking in terms of the monarchy which everywhere met their eyes, and the result was a conception of the state as being com-

---

[1] e.g. Hotoman, *Francogallia*, p. 83.

[2] The general acceptance of contractarian principles in academic circles, apart from their use for propagandist purposes, might be illustrated from the writings of numerous authors. A good example is that of P. Hoenonius (von Hoen), a German teacher of law at Herborn, who, so far from being a radical, was in the service of several German princes. In his *Disputatio Politica* (Herborn, 1608) we read (i, § 4) of the natural sociability of man; yet society was made, so to speak, not born: men *confluxerunt, operas coniungentes*. The state once formed contains two parts, subjects and ruler, and these are held together by a double pact (*duplici pacto*), with God (as in the Old Testament, with references to the *Vindiciae*, Danaeus, &c.) and with each other (ii, § 1 ff.). Kings do not hold sovereignty or its rights of their own nature, but received them from the whole people, which is *prior et potior Monarchis, quippe quos rectores et curatores Reipublicae is creavit et constituit* (ix, § 6).

posed of two distinct, if not opposed and rival, parts, the monarch and the people. These, as Gierke puts it, came to be regarded as having each a separate 'personality',[1] for this was essential if they were to be the parties to a contract of government. But as long as this theory of the contract of government held the field, the people could never be all-powerful: they might have rights, but so must the monarch too, by the terms of the contract. We may find some anticipations of Rousseau's position,[2] but this dualism meant that the farthest a political system could go in one direction would be a limited monarchy; and in the other direction, while falling short of complete theoretical absolutism, it might leave very little effective action open to the people themselves.[3]

Some writers, indeed, inheriting the traditional classification of constitutions, admitted that government might be in the hands of the few or of the many as well as of one man, but this theoretical democracy was made to conform to the current contractarian form, with its division of the state into the two elements or 'persons' of ruler and people, so that the ruling popular assembly stood over against the people as ruled.[4] And in this case, though the contract of government was supposed to have been made by the people unanimously, the sovereign popular assembly, once set up, could decide by majority-vote, and thus a part of the people might have more authority than all the people taken together.

When the conception of the personality and rights of the people was combined, through the adoption of a social as well as a governmental contract, with the idea of the original rights of individuals, thinkers were confronted with a number of contradictions which they could never satisfactorily resolve.[5] These were the inevitable result of the attempt to build society on a foundation of contract, but as yet they were only partially realized, and it was left for later writers to grapple with them.

[1] Gierke, *Nat. Law* (tr. Barker), i, 44.

[2] e.g. in Buchanan (*De Jure Regni*), especially in such passages as that on p. 86, where the *populus* is said to be *rege praestantior*, and again *cum lex sit rege, populus lege potentior*. Rossaeus (I, c. 1, § 4) even reproached Buchanan with having gone too far in disparagement of the right of rulers. On Milton and Locke see below, Chapters VII, IX. Cf. also Althusius' *contractus mandati*, above, p. 79, note 2.

[3] Cf. the attitude of the *Vindiciae*, or of Boucher, above, pp. 57, 59.

[4] Cf. Victoria and Molina, p. 71, note 1, above.

[5] For some of these theoretical contradictions, and the ways in which different writers sought escape from them, see Gierke, *Nat. Law* (tr. Barker), ii. 237–8.

VII

PURITANISM AND THE CONTRACT

IT was remarked at the beginning of Chapter V that the connexion between the Reformation and the contract theory,
though a close one, was mainly the result, at any rate in Europe
generally, of external political circumstances. Among English-
speaking communities, however, on both sides of the Atlantic,
where more radical views made their appearance, the contract
theory of the state seems to have had a more direct connexion with
the development of individualist theories of ecclesiastical organization. This tendency is particularly noticeable in the foundation of
the Puritan commonwealths in New England in the early seventeenth century. Among these refugees from persecution the theory
was widely current that any number of individuals could constitute themselves by voluntary agreement into a church, which was
essentially a congregation of believers under a covenant with God,
rather than an institution rooted in the Apostolic Succession.

This theory of the church, which was found in England in
Browne and Barrow, and was one of the fundamental principles
of sectarian Christianity,[1] received its clearest definition in America
in the 'Cambridge Platform' adopted in 1648. Here a congregational church is said to be 'by the institution of Christ a part of
the Militant-visible-church, consisting of a company of Saints by
calling, united into one body, by a holy covenant, for the publick
worship of God, and the mutuall edification one of another, in the
Fellowship of the Lord Jesus'. Any of the inhabitants of a New
England township who were 'satisfied of one another's faith and
repentance' could form themselves into a congregational church
by entering into a covenant with one another, a 'visible Covenant,
Agreement or Consent, whereby they give themselves unto the
Lord, to the observing of the ordinances of Christ together in the

---

[1] On the principles of the Brownists cf. D. Neal, *History of the Puritans*
(1822 edn.), i. 303: 'They apprehended . . . that every church ought to be
confined within the limits of a single congregation; and that the government
should be democratical. When a church was to be gathered, such as desired to
be members made a confession of their faith in the presence of each other, and
signed a covenant, obliging themselves to walk together in the order of the
gospel, according to certain rules and agreements therein contained.'

same society, which is usually called the Church Covenant'. This covenant is identified with that made with God by Abraham and the Israelites, by virtue of which they became the chosen people of God.[1]

The Independents and sectaries in England itself, instead of controlling the government, as they did in New England, for the most part found themselves under the threat of persecution; they were disliked almost as much by the Presbyterians as by Anglicans themselves, and had to struggle hard for bare existence. Except for a brief period after the Civil War, when through their prominence in the ranks of Cromwell's army they were able to gain a hearing, and made a characteristic contribution to the political discussions of that time, they were scarcely in a position to develop to the full the political consequences of their religious views. But in America, where they founded new settlements in which the practice of their religion was to be at any rate one of the purposes for which they had crossed the ocean, they had much more scope to put their political theories into effect. They repudiated the constitutional Erastianism of the Anglican Church, and (under the influence ultimately of the doctrines of Calvin, though they disagreed with his Presbyterianism) held that the secular authority should be subordinate to the spiritual—a view which, in spite of their hostility to Rome, resembled in that respect the contentions of medieval Catholicism at the height of its power. They maintained the theocratic view that the state was essentially the secular arm of the church, existing as a means to secure the purposes of the church, and an individualist theory of the state followed naturally from the individualism of their ecclesiastical theory. In order to found a church they made a covenant together; in order to found a state which should protect and maintain their establishment of a congregational church, they entered similarly into a political covenant.

The first to set the example of thus translating the social con-

---

[1] On the 'Cambridge Platform' and early Congregationalism in America see Williston Walker, *The Creeds and Platforms of Congregationalism* (New York, 1893), and his *History of the Congregational Churches in the U.S.* (American Ch. Hist., vol. iii, New York, 1894), pp. 102, 217–18. See also C. E. Merriam, *History of American Political Theories* (New York, 1903), pp. 16–27, and V. L. Parrington, *The Colonial Mind* (New York, 1927), pp. 59–69. Richard Mather, in his *Apologie of the Churches in New England for the Church Covenant* (1639), defends the congregationalist principle on the ground that 'all voluntary relations which are neither natural nor violent are entered into by way of covenant' (quoted in Merriam, op. cit., p. 21).

tract into actual fact were the Pilgrim Fathers themselves, in November 1620,[1] but a number of other instances could be quoted from the New England colonies in the early years of the seventeenth century. At Portsmouth, for instance, on 7 January 1638, the settlers pronounced as follows: 'We whose names are underwritten do here solemnly in the presence of Jehovah incorporate ourselves into a Bodie Politick, and as He shall help, will submit our persons, lives and estates unto our Lord Jesus Christ.'[2] The same principle governed the adoption of the 'Fundamental Orders' of Connecticut on 14 January of the same year: 'We . . . doe . . . assotiate and conioyne ourselues to be as one Publike State or Commonwelth and doe, for ourselues and our Successors and such as shall be adioyned to vs att any time hereafter,[3] enter into Combination and Confederation togather', in order to preserve their liberty and the purity of the Gospel of Jesus Christ, and in civil affairs to be governed by the laws which were thereupon enumerated.[4]

The social contract, thus enshrined in the earliest constitutions of the New England colonies, constantly reappears in the writings of seventeenth-century American theorists on ecclesiastical and political questions, reinforced by references to the Old Testament covenants with which we met in dealing with the political theories of the Huguenots. A clear statement of it may be seen in Thomas Hooker, the Connecticut divine, whose *Survey of the Summe of Church Discipline* appeared in 1648. Here two classes of covenant are mentioned, explicit and implicit, but with a preference for the explicit, and the effect of the covenant is to make every part subject to the whole; but the people may proceed against any officer 'that goes aside', and this they may do 'by the power of judgement which they do possess'.[5]

One of the best-known American exponents of the theory of the popular origin of government at this period was Roger Williams,

---

[1] The words of the covenant are quoted on p. 2, above.

[2] *Rhode Island Records*, i. 52.

[3] New members of a congregation had to make a personal profession of their acceptance of its rules; but, although new immigrants to a colony might be presumed to know the laws in force there, and by their coming might perhaps be plausibly held to have given their tacit consent to them, the individualist principle which demanded the personal consent of all the original settlers can hardly be stretched to cover later generations born within the colony.

[4] *Connecticut Records*, i. 20–21; cf. the similar agreement at Providence in 1636 (*Rhode Island Records*, i. 14).

[5] Quoted in C. E. Merriam, *Hist. Amer. Pol. Theories*, p. 20.

who published *The Bloudy Tenent of Persecution* in 1644.[1] Here he declares that 'the *Soveraigne, originall,* and *foundation* of *civill power* lies in the *people*', and although 'a *civill Government* is an *Ordinance* of *God,* to conserve the *civill peace* of people, so farre as concerns their Bodies and Goods', yet the civil power (i.e. the people) is distinct from the government, and may in fact 'erect and establish what forme of *civill Government* may seeme . . . most meet. . . . It is evident', he proceeds, 'that such *Governments* as are by them erected and established, have no more *power,* nor for no longer time, than the civill power or people consenting and agreeing shall betrust them with.'[2] In this phrase Williams anticipates the concept of trusteeship (often associated with Locke) as the basis of the relationship between government and people, but the idea is not developed at all, and in a later book he expresses similar ideas in language which recalls the Roman Law contract of *mandatum;* but it is doubtful how far he was consciously influenced by, or aware of, political writers who had used this conception.[3] 'Every lawful magistrate,' according to Williams,[4] 'whether succeeding or elected, is not only the Minister of God, but the minister or servant of the people also . . . and that Minister or Magistrate goes beyond his commission, who intermeddles with that which cannot be given him in commission from the people.'

Roger Williams does not refer to any explicit contract, though he approaches it closely in his remark about the people 'consenting and agreeing', and he also refers to Josiah's 'covenant before the Lord', and compares the actions of the kings of England, to their disadvantage, with those of Josiah. For whereas Josiah was 'a precious branch of that Royal Root King David, who was immediately designed by God, . . . Gentile Princes, Rulers and Magistrates', on the other hand, '(whether Monarchicall, Aristocraticall, or Democraticall) . . . (though government in generall be from God, yet) receive their callings, power and authority (both Kings and Parliaments) mediately from the people. . . . What commission from Jesus Christ', he asks, 'had Henry the eight,

---

[1] Reprinted in *Publications of the Narragansett Club* (Providence, R.I.), 1st series, vol. iii.

[2] *Pub. Narragansett Club*, I. iii. 249–50.

[3] Cf. p. 79, note 2, above.

[4] *The Bloody Tenent yet more bloody* (1652), reprinted in *Pub. Narragansett Club*, I. iv. 187. Williams also anticipated Rousseau in the idea that sovereignty (as distinct from executive government) belongs to the people (or rather, to the general will) and cannot be alienated; but so did Althusius, and Locke also.

Edward the 6, or any (Iosiah like) to force' the consciences of Englishmen?[1]

But while the New England Puritans stood up for religious liberty and denounced persecution, they were more anxious to preserve the privileges and independence of their own societies than the liberty of individuals. Nor did they believe in the equality of all men. They drew a sharp distinction between the elect and the unregenerate mass of mankind, and, as their later history shows, their government tended to become a highly intolerant kind of theocratical oligarchy. How this could be justified on a basis of contractarian individualism can be seen in an interesting passage in a speech by John Winthrop, delivered in July 1645. Here he distinguishes between two kinds of liberty, the one 'natural', the other 'civil or federal'. Natural liberty is 'common to man with beasts and other creatures. By this, man, as he stands in relation to man simply, hath liberty to do what he lists; it is a liberty to evil as well as to good. This liberty is incompatible and inconsistent with authority, and cannot endure the least restraint of the most just authority.' The other kind of liberty, however, the 'civil or federal', which 'may also be termed moral', is what is constituted by 'the covenant between God and man, in the moral law, and the politic covenants and constitutions amongst men themselves. This liberty is the proper end and object of authority, and cannot subsist without it': it is a liberty not unlimited, but 'a liberty to that only which is good, just and honest'.

Men, in fact, have surrendered their natural liberty by the social contract, and at the same time, under their covenant with God, they are pledged to live righteously.

This liberty is maintained and exercised in a way of subjection to authority; it is of the same kind of liberty wherewith Christ has made us free. The woman's own choice [he continues] makes such a man her husband: yet being so chosen, he is her lord, and she is subject to him, yet in a way of liberty, not of bondage. . . . Such is the liberty of the Church under the authority of Christ. . . . Even so, brethren, it will be between you and your magistrates.[2]

Winthrop's 'civil or federal' liberty is not the same as the liberty of the post-Kantian idealists, which consists in obedience to one's 'real will' embodied in the state, or its forerunner in Rousseau,

[1] The Bloudy Tenent (Pub. Narragansett Club, I. iii), p. 343.
[2] J. Winthrop, Journal (Hist. of New England), 1630–49 (ed. Hosmer, New York, 1908), ii. 238–9.

whereby men were to be 'forced to be free', but it is curiously like it. The latter was wholly secular, while what Winthrop was expounding was the familiar doctrine of Christian liberty—that the service of Christ is perfect freedom, and that the Gospel has freed men from bondage to the Law. Nevertheless it is interesting, in the middle of the seventeenth century, to find the social contract used in this way to justify the subordination of the individual to the state, rather than to vindicate his rights against it.[1]

The contract theory, however, had an essentially individualist trend, and in course of time, partly under the influence of the constitutional theories of European writers, it was this aspect of it which prevailed, and the intolerant and oppressive tendencies of the early colonial period receded into the background. By the time of the struggle for independence the contract theory of the state, firmly embedded in American political thought from the beginning, became prominent in its traditional role as an argument for political liberty, and, later, in the characteristically American form of a plea for state rights against the federal government, it found frequent employment until well into the nineteenth century.[2]

In England itself the ideas of contract and the popular origin of government were thoroughly familiar. James I had alluded to the contract theory in a speech to Parliament, and the parliamentary lawyers frequently resorted to these notions. Selden, for example, described a king as 'a thing men have made for their own sakes, for quietness' sake', and in his article on 'War' he openly avowed the contract theory. 'To know what obedience is due to the prince, you must look into the contract betwixt him and his people; as if you would know what rent is due from the tenant to the landlord, you must look into the lease. When the contract is broken, and there is no third person to judge, then the decision is by arms. And this is the case between the prince and the subject.' But the question then arises, how is one to decide when the covenant is broken? There is no law to guide one, Selden admits, but one may be guided by custom, and the question has often been decided in this way in English history.[3]

---

[1] Cf. also Kant's remark that as a citizen man has 'abandoned his wild, lawless freedom', but finds 'all his proper freedom . . . in the form of a regulated order of dependence, that is, in a Civil State, regulated by laws of Right' (*Rechtslehre*, § 47, tr. W. Hastie, *Kant's Philosophy of Law*; see below, p. 183).

[2] See below, Chap. XIV.

[3] J. Selden, *Table Talk*, s.v. 'War'. Cf. also his remark (s.v. 'King') that 'a king that claims privileges in his own country, because they have them in another,

As the contest between king and Parliament proceeded, the contract theory in one or other of its forms was constantly advanced and as constantly challenged. In the end the king was faced by open claims for parliamentary (ultimately for popular) sovereignty, but in the earlier stages of the struggle the claims of his opponents were less radical. They sought to keep his prerogative powers within bounds, and there was much talk of the fundamental laws, by which the liberty and property of Englishmen were supposed to be protected from arbitrary power. Fundamental law was a vague term, open to various interpretations, but it seems clear that in seventeenth-century England its primary meaning was that government should be constitutional, not autocratic; it was, in fact a legacy from the common medieval principle that kings should always rule according to law.[1] There were various ways of securing, and expressing, the same end. Some of the king's functions could only be exercised through certain constitutional channels: he could only tax and legislate, for example, in co-operation with Parliament. Thus the English monarchy, it was said, was a mixed monarchy, and in his coronation-oath the king solemnly undertook to respect the legal and constitutional limits to his action.

These notions of limited, constitutional rule found ready expression in terms of a contract of government. This was often thought of as an 'original' contract, an historic event in the past when the foundations of the constitution were supposed to have been laid; but, like its medieval forerunner, it was not necessarily individualist or democratic in its implications. As the king's supporters resisted the parliamentary claims, and made more sweeping counterclaims, the parliamentarians found themselves being led on, step by step, to more radical positions. If their interpretation of history could be challenged, they must needs base their demands on more abstract and general grounds, and appeal, over the head of the historic common law, to reason and natural law; over the head of the king, even of a king claiming his throne by divine right, to the people, and to God. In the last resort, *salus populi* must be *suprema lex*; kings themselves derive their power from the people, and the people have a duty to God to resist a tyrant. English supporters of the parliamentary cause found all these ideas in the

is just as a cook, that claims fees in one Lord's house because they are allowed in another. If the master of the house will yield them, well and good.'

[1] On this subject cf. my *Fundamental Law in English Constitutional History* (Oxford, 1955).

writings of continental publicists, whom they quoted freely, particularly the Huguenot pamphleteers of the previous century, and it is clear that they saw a close parallel between the religious wars in France and the struggle now coming to a head in their own country.

Space forbids more than a cursory glance at a few of the publications that poured out from the presses in a vast flood in the years of the Long Parliament, the Civil War, and the Interregnum. A good example of a moderate parliamentarian view may be seen in the answer composed by Charles Herle to Henry Ferne, one of the king's chaplains, who had denied the theory that the people were the source of royal power and that their representatives in Parliament might resist a king who failed in his trust.[1] Herle refused to be dislodged from his belief in the fundamental laws. Challenged to say exactly what they were, he identified them with 'that original frame of this co-ordinate government of the three Estates in Parliament, consented to and contrived by the people in its first constitution, and since in every several reign confirmed both by mutual oaths between king and people and constant custom time (as we say) out of mind, which with us amounts to a law'.[2] This identification of fundamental law, in the sense of the constitution itself, with an original contract of government, renewed and confirmed in successive coronation-oaths, closely anticipated the position taken up by the Whigs in 1688, and it had in fact become almost a commonplace by the time of the Revolution.

Another writer of some interest, who adopted a somewhat similar position to Herle's, was Philip Hunton.[3] He begins with a discussion of monarchy in general, and agrees with previous contractarians that 'the Root of all sovereignty individuated and existent in this or that Person or Family' is 'the Consent and fundamental Contract of a Nation'. It is this that 'puts them in their Power, which can be no more nor other than is conveyed to them by such Contract of Subjection. . . . Till this come and lift him up', he continues, the king 'is a private Man, not differing in State from the rest of his Brethren'.[4]

---

[1] The idea of trust recurs in the disputes of this period almost as freely as that of the contract itself.   [2] C. Herle, *A Fuller Answer* (1642), p. 8.

[3] His chief work, *A Treatise of Monarchy*, was first published in 1643. It evoked a reply from Sir Robert Filmer, entitled *The Anarchy of a Limited or Mixed Monarchy*, vigorously upholding the necessity for unlimited and undivided sovereignty. Locke, who later wrote to refute Filmer, held views closely resembling some of Hunton's. Cf. C. H. McIlwain, *Constitutionalism and the Changing World* (Cambridge, 1939), pp. 196–230.

[4] Part I, c. ii, § 4.

Once so exalted to monarchy, however, the king acquires a sacred character, and his subjects have only a limited right of resistance. 'Respect must be had to the original Contract, and fundamental Constitution', and it is unreasonable to suggest that if the people have invested one man with sovereign power they still 'have it in themselves, or have a Power of recalling that Supremacy, which by Oath and Contract they themselves trans-ferred to another; unless we make this Oath and Contract less binding than private ones; dissoluble at pleasure, and so all Monarchs Tenants at will from their People'.[1] To this length, we gather, Hunton was not prepared to go, though he admitted that it was difficult to decide who should judge 'the excesses of the Monarch'.[2] At the same time he declared that 'in the first Original all Monarchy, yea any individual frame of Government what-soever, is Elective: That is, is constituted, and draws its Force and Right from the Consent and choice of that Community over which it swayeth'.[3] Like Hobbes, however, he included in this consent the submission of a conquered people, who in order to avoid a continuation of the miseries of war 'submit to a Com-position and Contract of Subjection to the Invader'.[4]

He then applies these general principles to England, and argues that the English monarchy is both limited and mixed. The king was set up by a 'public compact', and if parliament failed to resist a king who exceeded his legal powers 'they should betray the very trust reposed in them by the fundamentals of the kingdom'.[5]

The king, of course, did not lack defenders, particularly among the clergy of the established Church. John Bramhall, for example, Bishop of Derry and later Archbishop of Armagh, who took up the 'Arminian' and anti-contractarian position, urged that the positive laws of a kingdom 'are the just measure and standard of the liberty of the subject'. The liberties and privileges enjoyed by different societies vary, but if some are better off than others, this is 'thanks to a favourable charter, not to any antecedaneous pac-tions'; the source of privilege (as James I himself had urged) is 'custom and the pleasure of the donor, who imposed what condi-

---

[1] § 6.

[2] § 7. If one makes the people the judge it amounts to giving them liberty to break off their allegiance at discretion, and in this way it is difficult in practice to prevent a contract theory merging into one of complete popular sovereignty, where kings are mere delegates of the popular will.   [3] c. iii, § 2.

[4] c. iii, § 5.   [5] *A Treatise of Monarchy*, II. iii, § 4, V, § 3.

tions he liked'. Then, to make his doctrine a little more palatable, he points to history. 'We have a surer charter than that of nature to hold by, Magna Charta, the Englishman's jewel and treasure, the fountain and foundation of our freedom, the walls and bulwarks, yea, the very life and soul, of our security.'[1]

On the other side, however, the Rev. Samuel Rutherford published a reasoned defence of the contract of government. Government, and even the kingly office, he admits, are from God, yet kings are made by the people, and the people have a natural power of self-defence which they cannot alienate, and of which they may resume the exercise. The Royalists argue that kings and subjects are not on an equal footing, and there is no covenant between them; for there is no court which could compel the king to keep his part of the covenant, or inflict any punishment upon him, and he is accountable only to God. But Rutherford, following the Huguenots, points to the covenants in the Old Testament, and maintains that there is indeed a covenant between king and people, and, further, that king and people are pledged to God to preserve the true religion. 'The people, as God's instruments, bestow the benefit of a crown on their king, upon condition that he will rule them according to God's word', and the king is 'made king by the people conditionally': there is a 'mutual coactive power on each side'.

Where, then, it may be asked, is this covenant? There may, indeed, be no 'positive written covenant', though Rutherford refuses to admit this definitely; at any rate, he contends, 'there is a natural, tacit, implicit covenant', which ties the king by the nature of his office. 'And though there were no written covenant, the standing law and practice of many hundred acts of parliament is equivalent to a written covenant.'[2] Writers like these challenged any pretensions to absolutism on the king's part, but went no farther than ascribing to his powers a popular origin, and encouraging Parliament, as representing the people, to take steps to keep the

---

[1] J. Bramhall, *The Serpent Salve* (1643), in *Works* (Oxford, 1844), ii. 366. This quite unhistorical conception of the nature of Magna Carta was common in the seventeenth century.

[2] S. Rutherford, *Lex Rex or The Law and the Prince* (1644), quu. 1–14. Later on (qu. 40) he quotes Aristotle on the difference between the king and the tyrant, and remarks that by feudal custom a vassal was released from allegiance if the lord broke his covenant. An absolute king is contrary to Scripture and to the nature of his office.

A number of writers reverted to the idea that the constitution of a country could be regarded as a contract of government. Cf. below, pp. 102, 193, 210, 211.

king's powers within constitutional limits. It was only another step forward for Parliament to claim full powers for itself, but for some time most members seemed reluctant to take it, although several writers urged them to do so. When war broke out, however, sovereignty was implied in the actions of Parliament, and a definite claim to it naturally followed.

Meanwhile, even more radical views were expressed by the Levellers, who were to become prominent in the ranks of Cromwell's army. The political ideas of their leaders, both inside and outside the army, reflected their membership of the various sectarian churches; they were the instrument, in fact, by which left-wing Puritanism made its chief impact on English political theory. Their best-known spokesman, John Lilburne, who had suffered a barbarous punishment at the hands of the Star Chamber for his attacks on the bishops, was an enthusiastic supporter of the Long Parliament at the beginning of the Civil War, and shared the widely held view that resistance to the king was justified because he had broken his compact with the people. At the end of the war, however, Lilburne found himself at loggerheads with the Commons, and was committed by them to prison. He held the typically sectarian view that a church is a voluntary society formed by agreement or covenant between its members, and resented Parliament's design to impose a Presbyterian uniformity. This helped to convince him that a victorious and sovereign Parliament might be as tyrannical as the king himself, and he not only stood out for liberty of conscience but became the irrepressible champion of the rights and interests of the 'small' man, to whom sectarian Christianity made its chief appeal. The Leveller movement became a campaign, first, for government by a truly representative Parliament, elected at frequent intervals on a wider and more equal franchise, in order to secure for the ordinary Englishman his legal, fundamental rights and liberties. Before long, however, the Levellers realized that to get rid of the king and to substitute for his rule a parliamentary sovereignty was no safeguard for the liberties they valued, and they came to demand that the 'native rights' of Englishmen should be guaranteed by a written constitution, under which Parliament, instead of being sovereign, should itself be obliged to govern according to law.

We cannot examine in detail the numerous pamphlets which Lilburne and his Leveller colleagues issued at frequent intervals in the course of his chequered career. The compact of government, accompanied by ideas such as popular consent, fundamental law, and trusteeship, was a regular weapon in their armoury, but there was nothing specially remarkable or novel about their use of it.[1] In the course of the year 1647, however, when the Long Parliament, jealous of the power of the army that had won its battles for it, was scheming to disband the soldiers unpaid, the army was impelled to bring forward its own designs for national reconstruction. The Levellers' policy took the form of a paper called *The Agreement of the People*, which was drafted by the 'Agitators' of certain regiments and put before the council of officers in October of that year in the hope that it would be adopted as a practical programme. It not only embodied the principle of a written constitution to limit the powers of Parliament, but is an interesting indication that the Levellers had moved on from the contract of government to a form of the social contract. Like the Pilgrim Fathers in the *Mayflower* covenant, or the other New England communities mentioned above, they intended it to be a translation of the contract theory into actual effect, for the paper was to be taken round the country-side for signature by as many as would, so that personal consent to the proposed government might be as wide and as real as possible.

In devising this plan of an 'Agreement of the People' it is possible that the Levellers were influenced to some extent by the example of the Scottish National Covenant of 1638, which had been signed by large numbers of persons, ministers, noblemen, and commons. This in turn was based upon an earlier practice among the Scottish nobility and gentry, who 'in the days when life and property had found no security from the law, ... had been in the habit of entering into "bands" or obligations for mutual protection'. The immediate forerunner of the Covenant of 1638 was a 'band' or covenant entered into in 1581, with encouragement from the king, when there had been a threat of a Catholic conspiracy assisted from Spain. On this occasion all loyal subjects were urged to sign the covenant, pledging themselves to 'renounce the Papal doctrines, to submit to the discipline of the Scottish Church, and to "defend the same according to their location and power" '.[2] As Ritchie re-

---

[1] Examples of the use of the governmental contract by Lilburne, Overton, Walwyn, and other Levellers may be seen in collections such as W. Haller's *Tracts on Liberty* (New York, 1934) and *Leveller Tracts* (New York, 1944), D. M. Wolfe, *Leveller Manifestoes of the Puritan Revolution* (New York, 1944), and A. S. P. Woodhouse, *Puritanism and Liberty* (London, 1938).

[2] S. R. Gardiner, *History of England* (1603–42), viii. 329–30.

marks, ' the absence of a firm government in Scotland had driven men to form compacts among themselves in order to escape the evils of perpetual lawlessness and warfare. It was an easy step from this actual condition to the theory that contract is universally the means by which men pass from the non-social state into that of orderly and peaceful society.'[1]

There can be little doubt, however, that their immediate source of inspiration was the common sectarian notion of a church covenant, which they thus transferred to the political sphere. There is no need here to analyse the contents of the Agreement in detail,[2] either in its first draft, or in any of its later more elaborate forms,[3] but we may note the prevalence of contractarian and individualist ideas in Puritan circles in England at this time by examining some of the speeches in the debates that took place on the subject of the Agreement in the council of the army at Putney. The ideas of natural rights and of the social contract were usually associated together, but the seventeenth-century English Puritans

[1] D. G. Ritchie, *Darwin and Hegel*, p. 213. Although Republicans were grievously disappointed by the turn taken by events when the Commonwealth led to Cromwell's military Protectorate, they continued to advocate a literal social contract to secure national consent for a new settlement of government. Sir Henry Vane, for instance, wrote a pamphlet called *A Healing Question* (1656), in which he advocated 'a generall councill, or convention of faithfull, honest and discerning men, chosen for that purpose by the free consent of the whole body of adherents to this cause in the several parts of the nations . . .

'Which convention is not properly to exercise the legislative power, but only to debate freely, and agree upon the particulars; that, by way of fundamentall constitutions, shall be laid and inviolably observed as the conditions upon which the whole body so represented doth consent to cast itself into a civil and politick incorporation, and under the visible form and administration of government therein declared, and to be by each individuall member of the body subscribed in testimony of his or their particular consent given thereunto.' (*Somers Tracts*, vi. 312.)

[2] Among its more interesting points are a demand for an extended suffrage, more equalized electoral districts, biennial single-chamber parliaments, and the reservation from the power of parliament of certain matters (e.g. religious liberty, no military conscription, equality before the law, and several other points) which are declared to be 'our native rights'. See S. R. Gardiner, *Const. Docts. of the Puritan Revolution*, nos. 74 and 81.

[3] *The Agreement of the People* appeared in a number of different forms in the course of the next two years: for details see my article in *History*, xv (1931), pp. 334–41. It is worth noting that the army leaders (e.g. Cromwell and Ireton), though they ultimately accepted some of the Levellers' ideas in a modified form, refused to allow the paper to be sent round the country for general subscription; instead, it was to be submitted to Parliament. This is an interesting anticipation of the objection sometimes expressed in modern times to the idea of a referendum in England, on the ground that it would undermine the authority of Parliament.

distinguished between them in a way which, as far as I know, was peculiar to themselves. The Levellers, while they proposed to found the constitution on individual consent through a kind of actualized social contract, rested their arguments fundamentally on natural rights, and tended to maintain that a contract might involve unjust restriction of liberty; the officers, on the other hand, or at any rate their most thoughtful spokesman, Ireton, who represented the Independent point of view, more conservative than that of the sectaries, argued against natural rights on the ground that they were subversive of security, and particularly of property, and used the idea of contract as a guarantee of stability and authority.

Thus in the course of the discussion the question arose whether an engagement once entered into was always binding, and Wildman, one of the most prominent of the Levellers, spoke of it as

a principle much spreading, and much to my trouble, . . . that when persons once be engaged, though the engagement appear to be unjust, yet the person must sit down and suffer under it; and that therefore in case a Parliament . . . doth anything unjustly, if we be engaged to submit to the laws that they shall make, if they make an unjust law, though they make an unrighteous law, yet we must swear obedience.[1]

Ireton's reply to these sentiments was to the effect that the only foundation of right between man and man was the general principle that we must keep the covenants we have made. The law of nature he repudiated largely on the ground (in contrast to Locke's argument) that it contradicts the principle of private property. 'But here comes the foundation of all right that I understand to be betwixt men, as to the enjoying of one thing or not enjoying of it; we are under a contract, we are under an agreement' to submit 'to that general authority which is agreed upon amongst us for the preserving of peace and for the supporting of this law.' It is the law which guarantees the enjoyment of property; the reason why my neighbour is prevented from seizing my property under a claim that by natural law he has as much right to it as I have is that 'that man is in covenant with me to live together in peace with one another, and not to meddle with that which another is possessed of, but that each of us should enjoy . . . that which in the course of law is in his possession. . . . This is the general thing:

[1] *Clarke Papers*, vol. i (ed. C. H. Firth, Camden Soc., N.S., vol. xlix, 1891), p. 260. The Putney debates are also printed in A. S. P. Woodhouse, *Puritanism and Liberty*, pp. 1–124.

that we must keep covenant one with another when we have contracted one with another.' Abandon this principle and the result will be chaos.[1]

In the debate on the following day, when the question of universal suffrage was under discussion, another Leveller, Col. Rainborough, reverted to the idea of natural right in another form—the natural equality of all men. 'Really', he said, in an often-quoted passage, 'I think that the poorest he that is in England hath a life to live as the greatest he: and therefore truly, Sir, I think it's clear that every man that is to live under a government ought first by his own consent to put himself under that government: and I do think that the poorest man in England is not at all bound in a strict sense to that government that he hath not had a voice to put himself under.'[2] A little later Wildman makes the same point. 'I conceive that's the undeniable maxim of government: that all government is in the free consent of the people. If so, . . . there is no person that is under a just government . . . unless he by his own free consent be put under that government.'[3]

Ireton's reply once more is that 'if you make this the rule . . . you must fly for refuge to an absolute natural Right, and you must deny all Civil Right',[4] and he urges that the suffrage should belong only to those who have 'a permanent fixed interest' in the country. If one allows a claim to universal suffrage, based only on the law of nature, the foundations of property will vanish.[5] Later on he appears to shift his ground somewhat, or at any rate he shows that his theory of political obligation involves no more than a tacit contract. It is quite right, he contends, that men should have to obey laws that they never consented to.

If any man will receive protection from this people, this man ought to be subject to those laws, and to be bound by those laws so long as he continues among them, though neither he nor his ancestors, nor any betwixt him and Adam, did ever give concurrence to this constitution. . . . A man ought to be subject to a law that did not give his consent, but with this reservation, that if this man do think himself unsatisfied to be subject to this law he may go into another kingdom.

[1] *Clarke Papers*, i. 263. Though he makes the right of property depend on the social contract, and not on the law of nature, he makes an exception of a man's right to dispose of his own person (p. 264). In this respect Locke, who made a natural right to property the consequence of a natural right to one's own person, was at any rate more logical than Ireton, even if his whole argument was unsound.

[2] Ibid., p. 301.   [3] Ibid., p. 318.
[4] Cf. Winthrop's remarks, above, p. 88.   [5] *Clarke Papers*, i. 301.

The laws of the land should be made by those who have a fixed property in the land: those with no permanent interest in the kingdom are on the same footing as aliens.[1] Rainborough disagrees with this rather Whiggish insistence on the importance of private property, and urges that 'the chief end of this government is to preserve persons as well as estates'.[2]

Cromwell himself did not contribute much to this rather abstract discussion of political obligation, and confined himself mainly to practical issues, but it is clear that he too was influenced by the contractual theory of the nature of monarchy. Burnet tells us that when commissioners were sent from Scotland to protest against the execution of Charles I, 'Cromwell entered into a long discourse of the nature of the royal power, according to the principles of Mariana and Buchanan: he thought a breach of trust in a king ought to be punished more than any other crime whatsoever'.[3] In the course of the Putney debates, also, when the king's 'negative vote' was being discussed, he declared: 'I think the king is king by contract.'[4]

After the execution of the king, the contract theory became what may almost be called the official theory of the Commonwealth party. It was expounded by Milton, the Latin Secretary, in his pamphlet *The Tenure of Kings and Magistrates*, written as an express justification of the regicides, and it was adopted by the Rump when on 21 March 1649 they issued a declaration stating their reasons for establishing a Commonwealth.

They suppose it will not be denied, that the first institution of the office of king in this nation was by Agreement of the People, who chose one for that office for the protection and good of them who chose him, and for their better government, according to such laws as they did consent unto. And let those who have observed our stories, recollect how very few have performed the trust of that office with righteousness, and due care of their subjects' good.[5]

Milton's political ideas, like those of most of his contemporaries in England, were largely borrowed from continental writers, but

[1] Ibid., p. 319.

[2] Ibid., p. 320. Shortly before this (p. 312) Mr. Pettus (i.e. Maximilian Petty) took up a kind of mediating position: 'I judge every man is naturally free; and I judge the reason why men when they were in so great numbers chose representatives was that every man could not give his voice: and therefore men agreed to come into some form of government that they who were chosen might preserve property.'

[3] Burnet, *History of my own Time* (ed. Airy, Oxford, 1897), i. 71.

[4] *Clarke Papers*, i. 368.   [5] *Parly. Hist.* iii. 1293.

he was one of the earliest English publicists to expound a thorough-going contract theory, and in certain directions he carried it some distance ahead of most of his contemporaries. *The Tenure of Kings and Magistrates* begins with the lawless 'state of nature': all men were naturally born free, but ever since the transgression of Adam they had wronged and hurt each other, until, perceiving that this would lead to mutual destruction, they made a social contract. 'They agreed by common league to bind each other from mutual injury, and jointly to defend themselves against any that gave disturbance or opposition to such agreement.' Hence came cities, towns and commonwealths. But 'no faith in all was found suffi-ciently binding', and so the need for government arose. Men 'saw it needful to ordain some authority that might restrain by force and punishment what was violated against peace and common right. . . . The power of kings and magistrates is nothing else, but what is only derivative, transferred and committed to them in trust from the people to the common good of them all, in whom the power yet remains fundamentally, and cannot be taken from them, without a violation of their natural birthright.'[1]

The foundation of society, then, is a social contract, but this does not itself involve the creation of a political state, with a government: the state of nature is superseded by a kind of inter-mediate stage in which men agree to co-operate, but are under no compulsion to do so. Only when they broke faith with one another did it become necessary to establish a government, and it is not clear from Milton's account whether this followed immediately after the social contract, because men knew from the start that they would never keep their engagements unless compelled to, or whether they only gained this experience after an interval. At any rate, the government was established, at whatever time this took place, by a delegation of the people's natural sovereignty, and their relationship with the king is not one of contract, but of trusteeship.

This conception was used by Locke, and is often associated with his name, but we have already met with it in English political thought as a substitute for the contract of government.[2] The more

---

[1] J. Milton, *The Tenure of Kings and Magistrates* (1649, republished with additions in 1650), in *Prose Works* (Bohn's edition, ed. J. A. St. John, 1848), ii. 8–11.

[2] Cf. above, p. 99. It also occurs in Roger Williams (above, p. 87). Actually the first reference to it that I have found is in Bishop Ponet's *Short Treatise of Politike Power*, written as long ago as 1556: 'Kings, princes and governors

usual governmental contract theory, however, was also widely held in England, and it is not clear that all writers were quite certain of the difference between a contract and a trust, for they sometimes appear to use the two conceptions indiscriminately. Milton himself is not wholly consistent on this point, for to illustrate his argument he alludes to the Old Testament covenants such as that with Joash, and also quotes Buchanan's account of the deposition of Queen Mary,[1] in which royal power was stated to be 'nothing else but a mutual covenant or stipulation between king and people'.[2] In spite of this, however, it is fairly clear that Milton's general view is that king and people are not parties to a contract of government, for in that case the people could only resume their power if the contract were broken; but Milton goes even beyond Locke's conception of trusteeship, and (like Rousseau) makes the king the mere servant of the people, dismissible at will. Since the king's authority is entirely derived from the people, he says, the people, 'as oft as they shall judge it for the best, may either choose him or reject him, retain him or depose him *though no tyrant*, merely by the liberty and right of free-born men to be governed as seems to them best'.[3]

This doctrine, however, never gained widespread acceptance even in England, where there was more republicanism than anywhere else in Europe, except Holland; and both before and after the Restoration political controversy generally revolved on the more usual ground of the contract of government. This appears, for instance, in *A Holy Commonwealth* (1659), one of the works of the Puritan divine, Richard Baxter, written 'for the healing of the mistakes and resolving the doubts' by which England was then troubled, and for 'directing the desires of sober Christians that long to see the kingdoms of this world become the kingdoms of the Lord and of his Christ'. Baxter's opening does not suggest a contractarian conclusion, for the best form of government, he main-

---

have their authority of the people, as all laws, usages and policies do declare and testify. . . . And is any man so unreasonable to deny, that the whole may do as much as they have permitted one member to do? Or those that have appointed an office upon trust, have not authority upon just occasion (as the abuse of it) to take away that they gave? All laws do agree, that men may revoke their proxies and letters of attorney when it pleaseth them, much more when they see their proctors and attorneys abuse it.' Cf. W. S. Hudson, *John Ponet, Advocate of Limited Monarchy* (Chicago, 1942), p. 107. For a sketch of the history of the trust as a political metaphor see my *John Locke's Political Philosophy* (Oxford, 1950), c. vii.

[1] Cf. p. 64, above.   [2] *Tenure*, p. 26.   [3] Ibid., p. 14 (my italics).

tains, is a theocracy, so far as it can be attained—the reign of
Christ and his saints on earth[1]—since God is the sovereign ruler
of mankind[2] and government is necessary by divine ordinance.[3]
There is no question of a popular commonwealth of believers;
the people as such have no sovereign power,[4] nor is the power of
rulers derived from the people,[5] and of the divers sorts of commonwealths democracy is the worst.[6] But then, he admits, neither do
kings 'naturally' possess any more right to rule than other men,[7]
so that if a king arises who unjustly endeavours to destroy his
people, resistance may be allowable, and this leads him to a
contract theory of government which is not altogether consistent
with his opening remarks on the origins of power.

The terms of the contract of government may vary: the people
may have 'expressly tyed themselves not to resist a king', and if
so 'they are wholly at his will'; but such an arrangement is not to
be presumed unless it be definitely expressed, for the usual object
of covenants is to secure rights, not to abandon them.[8] Whatever
the terms of the contract may be, they limit the king's power, and
he must not overstep those terms; but it does not follow that every
breach of covenant involves a total forfeiture of the crown.[9]
Baxter appears to identify the covenant or contract of government
with the constitution of the state, for he mentions the possibility
that the 'fundamental contracts' may prescribe that government
is to be shared by king and parliament, and that in case of disagreement between them the subjects must adhere to one side or the
other;[10] and in another passage he speaks of such disagreement as
threatening the dissolution of 'the fundamental constitution'. In
these circumstances, he adds, 'when the ship is sinking, it's time
for the passengers to save themselves and their goods as well as
they can. . . . When the government dissolveth itself, they that
possessed it turn us loose to rule ourselves and defend ourselves. . . .
The Law of Nature stands, when men do sinfully dissolve the
Commonwealth.'[11]

Farther on he says that if the power of kings is limited by the
constitution, 'their acceptance of the government is an implicite
Consent and Covenant.' He does not hold that every private
individual may resist the government, but 'the body of the Nation'
may do so. 'To break the Covenants, and reject the terms on which

---

[1] c. 8.   [2] c. 2.   [3] c. 4.   [4] c. 5.
[5] c. 7.   [6] c. 6.   [7] c. 12, p. 430.
[8] Ibid., p. 429.   [9] p. 430.   [10] p. 436.   [11] p. 433.

they did receive their Crowns, is to disoblige the people to whom they covenanted, and cast away their crowns, and turn into a state of enmity.'[1] When a new government is to be set up after a revolutionary disturbance, he continues, it must be done by contract, 'for they can *command* no one to become their governour, and submit to their terms, but they may *offer* it to any that is fit, who is free to accept it, or refuse it.'[2] With his allusion to the law of nature that prevails on the dissolution of the commonwealth, when men are 'turned loose' to rule and defend themselves—a state of nature, in effect—and the foundation of a fresh government on a contractual basis when the people offer the position to a new ruler, Baxter, in spite of his theocratic opening, is clearly expounding the regular contractarian doctrine; but this takes on a new element in a passage in his thirteenth chapter, where he deals with the position of Parliament, particularly with reference to the powers it has claimed during the Civil War.

It is no way necessary to the cause in hand [he writes][3] to prove the antiquity of their Being, or their Power. Whenever they were established in that Power, it was by an Explicite, or Implicite Contract between the Prince and the People, there being no other ground that can bear them, except an immediate Divine Institution, which none pretend to. And the Prince and People have as much power in this Age to make such a Contract, and alter the Constitution, as they had three thousand years ago. . . . When I say that the Parliament representeth the People as free, I take it for undeniable, that the Government is constituted by contract, and that in the contract, the People have not absolutely subjected themselves to the sovereign, without reserving any Rights or Liberties to themselves, but that some Rights are reserved by them, and exempted from the Prince's power. And therefore that the Parliament are their Trustees for the securing of those exempted Rights, and so represent the People as free, not as wholly free, but as being so farre free as that exemption signifies.[4]

---

[1] pp. 443–4.   [2] p. 451.

[3] p. 458. Most contractarians treated a popular assembly (unless it were a purely consultative body under a monarchy) as the ruling body in a democracy, with which the people had contractual relations, just as with the king in a monarchy. But the English Parliament, after the struggle with the king, had ceased to champion the popular cause, and had set up a tyrannical rule on its own account; and many felt that their rights must be safeguarded as much against parliamentary as against royal encroachment. Baxter, therefore, has three parties to deal with, king, parliament, and people. King and people he makes parties to a contract, and he borrows the idea of trusteeship for parliament, which has the duty on the people's behalf of seeing that the terms of the contract are observed.

[4] Baxter's work provoked a reply, *The Rebel's Plea*, by Thomas Tomkins

But though political theorists in England continued for many years—down to the Revolution of 1688 and after—to debate on the familiar assumption that the people had certain rights, which were guaranteed by a contract of government, a new and highly disturbing element had made its appearance in political theory in the intransigent doctrine of Thomas Hobbes, and to this we must now turn.

(1660), which attacks his theory on historical grounds—the lack of evidence that any contract of government was ever entered into. On the contrary, 'in all the Chronicles that ever I met with, the higher I go, the more absolute I finde the king'. What privileges the people enjoy were 'wrested . . . by force and fraud from weak and indigent kings, or given as acts of grace, and acknowledged with thankfulnesse for such' (p. 8). Tomkins's political theory is like Filmer's: 'a nation is families multiplyed, and a king but the common Father.'

VIII

HOBBES, SPINOZA, AND PUFENDORF

HOBBES'S political theory[1] is explained by his general theory of human nature, which closely resembles that put forward by Glaucon in Plato's *Republic*. Men are not naturally sociable, but pugnacious and competitive, and their ideas of right and wrong are determined by their pleasures and desires.

> Whatsoever is the object of any man's Appetite or Desire, that is it which he for his part calleth *Good*: And the object of his Hate and Aversion, *Evill*. . . . For these words of Good, Evill . . . are ever used with relation to the person that useth them: There being nothing simply and absolutely so; nor any common Rule of Good and Evill, to be taken from the nature of the objects themselves.[2]

Men are by nature practically equal in their faculties of body and mind, for none is so weak as not to be able to threaten the safety of the strong. Hence arises mutual distrust, or 'diffidence', so that in the state of nature there can be no co-operation among men, and no civilization. The state of nature is a state of war, a war of everybody against everybody else, giving rise to 'continuall feare, and danger of violent death'. There is no place in the state of nature for the notions of justice or injustice, for 'where there is no common Power, there is no Law: where no Law, no Injustice'.[3]

What, then, of the law of nature, of which earlier political theory had been full? Hobbes rejects the whole of it, and, though he retains the phrase, gives it an entirely different meaning. In the first place, he distinguishes 'Right of Nature' from 'Law of Nature'. The right of nature is simply 'the Liberty each man hath, to use his own power, as he will himselfe, for the preservation of his own Nature; that is of his own Life';[4] in other words, might is right, and a man, as far as nature is concerned, may seize what he can, and keep it if he has the strength and cunning to drive off his natural enemies, the rest of mankind.[5] By a law of nature Hobbes

---

[1] This is set out at length in *Leviathan* (1651), but essentially the same theory had been stated more briefly in the Latin work *De Cive* (1642).

[2] *Leviathan*, c. vi. Cf. c. xiv: '*Good* and *Evill* are names that signifie our Appetites and Aversions.'

[3] *Leviathan*, c. xiii.   [4] c. xiv.

[5] Man in fact, is on a level with the animals, and has as much 'right' to any-

means a 'Precept or generall Rule, found out by Reason, by which a man is forbidden to do that which is destructive of his life, or taketh away the means of preserving the same'; and the first and fundamental law of nature (seeing that 'from this diffidence of one another there is no way for any man to secure himself so reasonable as Anticipation'[1]) is 'That every man ought to endeavour Peace, as farre as he has hope of obtaining it; and when he cannot obtain it, that he may seek and use all helps and advantages of Warre'. Man's course, therefore, is to 'seek Peace and follow it', but also, 'by all means we can, to defend ourselves'. Hobbes mentions a number of other laws of nature, but ultimately they are all the consequences of the first, and can be reduced in effect to the rule, 'Do not to another that which thou wouldest not have done to thyself.'[2]

These so-called laws of nature are stated by Hobbes as obligations, but they have no binding force in the state of nature.[3] He admits, in fact, that 'these dictates of Reason, men use to call by the name of Lawes; but improperly: for they are but Conclusions, or Theoremes concerning what conduceth to the conservation and defence of themselves; whereas Law properly is the word of him that by right hath command over others'. In practice men often disregard them. 'The Lawes of Nature oblige in *foro interno*', as he puts it; 'but in *foro externo*; that is, to the putting them in act, not always.'[4] This is very evidently true of the third law of nature, which lays down 'That men performe their Covenants made',[5] for Hobbes admits that in the state of nature there is no guarantee that they will do so: 'Covenants, without the Sword, are but words,

thing as a tiger has to its prey. Hobbes's right of nature recalls what T. H. Huxley called 'tiger-rights', which, in fact, are no rights at all (cf. E. Barker, *Political Thought from Spencer to To-day*, p. 122). In this peculiar sense, 'every man has a Right to everything, even to one another's body' (c. xiv).

[1] c. xiii.

[2] c. xiv. Hobbes equates this with the law of the Gospel, 'Whatsoever ye require that others should do to you, that do ye to them', but he characteristically inverts it into a negative form.

[3] c. xv.

[4] Ibid. Hobbes says a man *ought* to endeavour peace, &c., but he really has no more business to use this word than Bentham (another psychological hedonist) had, when he said it 'ought to be banished from the Dictionary'. (Cf. H. Rashdall, *The Theory of Good and Evil* (Oxford, 1907), i. 224.) What Hobbes means strictly is that this is how a man would in fact behave if he were prudent, and also confident that other men were prudent too. Similarly when he says a man 'is forbidden' to do what is destructive of his own life, he means that man's instinct compels him to aim at self-preservation: the compulsion is psychological, not moral.   [5] *Leviathan*, c. xv.

and of no strength to secure a man at all.'[1] In nature, according to Hobbes, there is no right or wrong, and there can be no obligation, for the only motives from which men can be relied upon to act are their likes and dislikes; therefore force, which arouses their fears, is the only effective method of controlling them.[2]

Such, then, is the state of nature, but it is an intolerable condition, and men's 'Fear of Death; Desire of such things as are necessary to commodious living; and a Hope by their Industry to obtain them' lead men to agree upon 'convenient Articles of Peace', suggested by reason;[3] namely, 'that a man be willing, when others are so too, . . . to lay down this right to [i.e. power to get if he can] all things: and be contented with so much liberty against other men, as he would allow other men against himselfe.'[4] But the only way to secure that such an agreement will be observed is for all to submit to the authority of a ruler with power to enforce it; and so men are brought to the social contract, by which the state of nature gives place to civil society through the institution of a sovereign government. Though necessary, Hobbes insists that this is a wholly artificial arrangement. 'Men have no pleasure (but on the contrary a great deal of grief) in keeping company, where there is no power able to overawe them all',[5] for they are not naturally gregarious, like bees or ants,[6] and those who say, like Aristotle, that man is a πολιτικὸν ζῷον are wrong.[7]

The terms of the contract are

as if every man should say to every man, 'I Authorise and give up my Right of Governing myselfe, to this Man, or this Assembly of men, on this condition, that thou give up thy Right to him, and Authorise all his Actions in like manner'. [By this means they] conferre all their power and strength upon one Man, or upon one Assembly of men, that may reduce all their Wills, by plurality of voices, unto one Will: which is as much as to say, to appoint one Man, or Assembly of men, to beare their Person: and every one to owne and acknowledge himselfe to be the Author of whatsoever he that so beareth their Person shall Act, or cause to be Acted, in those things that concern the Common Peace and

---

[1] c. xvii. Cf. c. xviii: 'Covenants, being but words and breath, have no force to oblige, contain, constrain, or protect any man, but what it has from the publique Sword.'

[2] Cf. c. xv: 'Before the names of Just and Unjust can have place, there must be some coercive Power to compell men equally to their Covenants, by the terrour of some punishment greater than the benefit they expect by the breach of their Covenant.'

[3] c. xiii.   [4] c. xiv.

[5] c. xiii.   [6] c. xvii.   [7] Cf. De Cive, c. i.

Safetie; and therein to submit their Wills every one to his Will, and their Judgements to his Judgement.[1]

This, then, is the 'generation of that great Leviathan', the state, in which henceforth all men are subjects, except the man on whom all have agreed to confer power, who becomes sovereign over them.[2] Once he is instituted, his subjects are bound to obey him, for by the terms of the contract, says Hobbes, they have surrendered all their liberty of action to him, and whatever he does as sovereign he does by virtue of the powers they have conferred on him. If a subject is killed in resisting his sovereign, 'he is the author of his own punishment, as being, by the Institution, Author of all his Sovereign shall do'.[3] There is no covenant with God in the name of which men may disobey the sovereign, nor is there any covenant between the people and the sovereign; so that whatever the sovereign's actions, 'there can happen no breach of Covenant on the part of the Soveraigne; and consequently none of his Subjects, by any pretence of forfeiture, can be freed from his Subjection'.[4] For the sovereign was no party to Hobbes's contract, but simply the recipient of powers conferred on him by a contract of all with all. A contract, again, implies at least two persons as parties, but the people were not a 'person' capable of acting as a party to a contract with the sovereign before they were united in subjection to him; up to that time they were merely an aggregate of isolated individual persons, and by the terms of the contract the sovereign 'bears the person' of them all. In this way Hobbes destroys the whole foundation on which previous writers had rested the theory of the contract of government as a means of limiting royal power and justifying popular revolt. The only possible contract, according to Hobbes, is one of individuals with one another, and the only enforceable contract is one by which they all surrender their individual liberty to a common sovereign.

German commentators have engaged in a controversy on the question whether Hobbes's contract is to be regarded as a *Vereinigungsvertrag* (a social contract proper) or an *Unterwerfungsvertrag* (a contract of subjection).[5] Gierke suggests that it is a *Vereini-*

---

[1] *Leviathan*, c. xvii.

[2] Hobbes writes that the sovereign may be 'one man or one assembly of men', but it is clear that all the time he is thinking really of absolute monarchy, and he gives reasons (c. xix) for preferring monarchy to alternative forms of government.

[3] c. xviii.   [4] Ibid.

[5] e.g. G. Jellinek, *Allgemeine Staatslehre* (Berlin, 1900), p. 185, note; and see Gierke, *Johannes Althusius* (additional matter in 3rd edn.), p. 378, and

gungsvertrag, because it unites individuals hitherto uncombined; but it also comes under the *Begriff* of an *Unterwerfungsvertrag*, and he concludes with the opinion that it is 'mehr *pactum subjectionis*'. Against this one might argue that as a *pactum subjectionis* was essentially a contract between ruler and subjects, and Hobbes expressly denies that there can be any such contract, we ought rather to classify Hobbes's covenant as a form of *pactum unionis*, though possibly a rather special form. But there is little to be gained by attempting to apply to Hobbes's contract the rigid distinctions drawn by German lawyers in the later seventeenth century. Hobbes was by no means the only writer whose contract would not fit exactly into the standard contractarian scheme, which indeed was elaborated largely in order to refute him.

Gierke particularly censures the suggestion that there are two contracts in Hobbes,[1] and from what we have seen so far of Hobbes's account of the institution of the state it certainly appears that Gierke was right on this point. Yet when Hobbes summarizes his doctrine at the beginning of the chapter on the rights of the sovereign,[2] he introduces a new element which at first sight suggests that, if there were not two contracts, there were at any rate two stages in the completion of the single contract.

A Common-wealth is said to be Instituted [we read] when a Multitude of men do agree and covenant, every one with every one, that to whatsoever Man, or Assembly of Men, shall be given by the major part the Right to Present the Person of them all . . .; every one, as well he that voted for it, as he that voted against it, shall Authorise all the Actions and Judgements of that Man, or Assembly of men, in the same manner as if they were his own. . . .

First of all, then, there is the decision to unite and establish a sovereign, and this must be unanimous, but the actual choice of the particular sovereign follows, and this is decided by a majority. Yet there is no real inconsistency here, for it is evident that this second stage follows immediately after the first, since the union could not subsist without the rule of the sovereign, and the members of the dissentient minority are bound to acquiescence, on the principle that unless they consent with the rest, they may be treated as though they still remained in the state of nature, and 'justly be destroyed by the rest'. By voluntarily entering the

F. Tönnies, *Thomas Hobbes, Leben und Lehre* (3rd edn., Stuttgart, 1925), pp. 302–6 (notes 121 and 122).

[1] Gierke, *Johannes Althusius*, p. 340.   [2] *Leviathan*, c. xviii.

society, a man 'sufficiently declared thereby his will (and therefore tacitely covenanted) to stand to what the major part should or-dayne', and thus by the expedient of a tacit contract Hobbes (like Locke and others) saves the principle of unanimous individual consent, and the choice of the sovereign falls into place as an integral part of the single original contract.[1]

Some critics have attacked Hobbes's theory on the ground that his covenant never actually took place, but as an answer to the contract theory this line of argument misses the real point, even though many contractarians may have believed that the contract was an historical fact. Against Hobbes it is even less effective than usual. On exactly the same footing as 'commonwealths by institu-tion' (i.e. states where the sovereign is established by contract) he places 'commonwealths by acquisition', that is, states 'where the Soveraign power is acquired by Force'. In them men obey the sovereign 'for fear of death', because he 'hath their lives and liberty in his Power',[2] and there is little doubt that Hobbes regarded this as the commonest way by which states had actually come into existence. In spite of his elaborate discussion of the contractual basis of political obligation, it is clear that he did not really rely on the terms of the covenant to explain the necessity of obedience to an absolute sovereign. For if we ask why a man must keep the covenant, and accept all the sovereign's actions, however oppressive, as his own, Hobbes has already admitted that a bare covenant in itself has no obliging force at all, and that it is only fear that can keep men in subjection.[3] Why, then, should we not disobey if we feel confident that we can escape detection, or if there are good prospects of a rebellion being successful? Hobbes's answer is that to do so would be imprudent: 'it is manifest that though the event [i.e. success]

---

[1] In the *De Cive*, it may be noted, these two stages do not appear, and the whole process is unanimous: 'Voluntatum haec submissio omnium illorum unius hominis voluntati vel unius concilii tunc fit, quando unusquisque eorum unicuique caeterorum se pacto obligat ad non resisterídum voluntati illius hominis vel illius consilii, cui se submiserit' (c. v, § 7).

[2] *Leviathan*, c. xx. Hobbes brings these into line with his theory that sove-reignty is acquired by covenant by the assumption that the conqueror can exact obedience from his subjects as the price of sparing their lives; but it will be observed that in this case the contract is one between ruler and subjects, in spite of his denial that there could be such a covenant. A child's obligation to obey his father is placed on similar grounds. Cf. G. Croom Robertson, *Hobbes* (Edinburgh, 1886), p. 147.

[3] He admits that, besides 'fear of the consequences of breaking their word', men may be influenced by 'Glory, or Pride in appearing not to need to break it'. But this is 'a Generosity too rarely found to be presumed on' (c. xiv).

follow, yet because it cannot reasonably be expected, but rather the contrary; and because by gaining it so others are taught to gain the same in like manner, the attempt thereof is against reason.'[1]

Hobbes's basic doctrine, in fact, was his view of human nature as essentially selfish and at the same time timorous. The sovereign's authority is made to consist of the combined powers (or 'rights of nature') of all his subjects, conferred on him by the terms of the contract, but an obligation to abide by that contract is clearly not the real reason why they obey him. Their ruling motive is desire for protection—for the preservation of their lives: this was the reason why they abandoned their liberty in the state of nature and submitted to political authority, and this is ultimately the reason why they continue to obey him—that generally submission is the best way to get security, and rebellion means the risk of punishment. Hobbes admits that the duty to obey ceases when the sovereign issues orders that would endanger his subjects' lives or personal safety.

The obligation a man may sometimes have upon the Command of the Sovereign to execute any dangerous or dishonourable Office, dependeth not on the words of our Submission; but on the Intention; which is to be understood by the end thereof. When therefore our refusall to obey frustrates the End for which the Sovereignty was ordained, then there is no Liberty to refuse: otherwise there is.[2]

Ultimately obedience depends, not on a covenant or promise to obey, but on the continuance of protection:

The Obligation of Subjects to the Soveraign is understood to last as long, and no longer, than the power lasteth by which he is able to protect them. For the right men have by Nature to protect themselves, when none else can protect them, can by no Covenant be relinquished. ... The end of obedience is protection, which, whensoever a man seeth it, either in his own, or in another's sword, Nature applyeth his obedience to it.[3]

This, as Spinoza saw,[4] was a weak point in Hobbes's contract theory. His real doctrine is that man's nature is such that nothing but fear can keep him in order, and that it is generally to his

---

[1] c. xv.

[2] c. xxi. Cf. c. xiv: 'No man can transferre or lay down his Right to save himselfe from Death, Wounds and Imprisonments (the avoyding whereof is the onely End in laying down any Right), and therefore the promise of not resisting force in no Covenant transferreth any right; nor is obliging.'

[3] c. xxi.   [4] Cf. below, p. 115.

interest to obey whatever *de facto* sovereign can make his rule effective; for the alternative to submission is anarchy, which is worse. He purports to justify this necessity of obedience by an elaborate account of sovereignty 'by institution' through a social contract, but the argument really breaks down. It was indeed bound to break down, because by denying the reality of natural law, or rather by simply equating it with the maxims of rational prudence, Hobbes cut away the ground on which a genuine contractual obligation to political obedience might have stood. There was more logic in saying that the conquered subjects of a sovereign 'by acquisition' were contractually obliged to obey him, as the price for their lives being spared.

One reason for his use of the contract theory may have been to give an appearance of legality and respectability to an otherwise unattractive doctrine. Incidentally, by a clever manipulation, he made it an argument for absolutism instead of for the right of resistance, and so turned the tables on his adversaries. There is no reason to suppose that he meant either the state of nature or the institution of sovereignty by contract to be taken as historically true. Though he wrote of the 'causes' and 'generation' of a commonwealth,[1] the contract was really just an hypothesis on which to base a rational explanation of absolute government. His state of nature is not what men once were, but what they potentially are today, except for the repressive authority of government. To support his account of the state of nature he points not to history, but to the fact that, even under government, a man going a journey arms himself, and 'when going to sleep, he locks his doors; when even in his house he locks his chests'; and that the rulers of independent states 'are in continuall jealousies, and in the state and posture of Gladiators'.[2] Though Hobbes employed the terminology of contract, he stood outside the main stream of contractarian thought. In the long run his chief contribution to political theory was his clarification of the principle of sovereignty, and the relation of sovereignty to law.[3] He defined law as the command of a sovereign legislator, and equated right and wrong with legal and illegal,[4] so that natural law was not really law at all. As things have turned out,

---

[1] c. xvii.   [2] c. xiii.

[3] Filmer also insisted on the universal necessity for sovereignty, or 'arbitrary power', but instead of deriving it from a contract he placed it in the hands of a monarch ruling by divine hereditary right. Therefore his views also were unacceptable to the Whigs, whose philosophy prevailed in England from the Revolution onwards.   [4] *Leviathan*, c. xxvi.

the historical process which has located sovereignty in the hands of Parliament (and a Parliament which, through the extension of the franchise, represents the masses instead of only the land-owners) has led to the obsolescence of the devices (fundamental law or original contract) which were valued in the seventeenth century as checks on arbitrary power.[1] The result has been that this element in Hobbes's political theory, though generally repudiated and often misunderstood in his own day, has, as it were, come true in ours. This, of course, is not to say that we need or can accept the premises on which it rested in Hobbes, his cynically one-sided view of human nature, his refusal to admit any obligation but self-interest, and, the ultimate root of all, his whole materialist philosophy.[2] These questions are beyond our concern here, and we must return to the social contract. Another obvious criticism of Hobbes is that men so naturally anti-social as he depicts them could never unite to form a society, and that the social contract, always open to objection on account of its artificiality, is in Hobbes more artificial than ever. There is weight in this criticism, although a partial answer to it is that he did not mean his state of nature or his contract to be taken literally. Hobbes has been both detested and admired, but no one can deny his importance in the history of contractarian doctrine; no subsequent writers could avoid either being influenced by him, or, if they disagreed with him, having to contrive an answer to him.

One of the most eminent of the followers of Hobbes was Spinoza, who constructed a theory of political obligation which in most essentials corresponds closely to Hobbes's. In the state of nature, according to Spinoza, men's actions are determined not *sana ratione sed cupiditate et potentia*, yet what men chiefly desire is a life as far as possible secure and free from fear.[3] Naturally, however, under the influence of passions such as anger, envy, and hatred, men are enemies of one another, and being cleverer and more astute than all other living creatures, they are more capable of injuring one another, and consequently more afraid of one another.[4] There are no natural rights, i.e. no moral obligations,

---

[1] I refer here to Great Britain itself. In the United States the older ideas still prevailed, and the Constitution was expressly designed to exclude the parliamentary sovereignty against which the thirteen colonies had revolted.

[2] He endeavoured to explain sensations, thoughts, and emotions, in fact the whole of consciousness, as varieties of physical motion (*Leviathan*, cc. i–iii).

[3] B. Spinoza, *Tractatus Theologico-Politicus* (1670), c. xvi.

[4] *Tractatus Politicus* (published posthumously in 1677), c. i, § 5, c. ii, § 14.

but only power—in fact, as in Hobbes, might is right.[1] Consequently right and wrong have no meaning except under a government which makes laws to distinguish them; by nature all things are open equally to everybody, and property, and justice and injustice, exist only in the state.[2]

The state of nature is insecure, and without mutual help it is impossible to sustain life or cultivate the mind.[3] Hence men must agree to live under the laws of a society. The attempt to do so, however, would be vain, did not self-interest point to the necessity of such a course. And so men must make a firm compact (*firmissime statuere et pacisci debuerunt*) to restrain their passions when they would lead to the hurt of other people, to do nothing which they would not wish done to themselves, and to defend the rights of others as though they were their own.[4] But it is difficult to enter into a pact when one cannot trust one's neighbour, and so each man must transfer all his power to the society, which alone shall then hold the supreme right of nature, that is, supreme power, over all things, and each man must obey, if not freely, then through fear of punishment.[5]

Spinoza diverges from Hobbes at this point, for instead of men transferring their natural powers to a sovereign ruler, they transfer them to the whole society, and the state so created is a democracy.[6] Experience shows, he says, that the more absolute a king's power, the more misery his subjects have to endure,[7] and the majority of a large community is less likely to make mistakes: consequently democracy is preferable to monarchy.[8] This preference is partly the result of the truer psychology of Spinoza, for he recognizes that men have natural sympathy and pity, and a natural need of one another, as well as hatred and envy; and though he thinks that enmity is usually stronger than friendliness, he does not, like Hobbes, seek to explain away all generous emotions as disguised forms of selfishness.[9] When the sovereign power is established, it is above all law (*nulla lege teneri*) and can command universal

---

[1] 'Unamquamque rem naturalem tantum iuris ex natura habere, quantum potentiae habet ad existendum et operandum. . . . Per ius itaque naturae intellego ipsas naturae leges, seu regulas, secundum quas omnia fiunt, hoc est, ipsam naturae potentiam.' (*Tract. Pol.* c. ii, §§ 3–5; cf. § 18: 'nihil absolute naturae iure prohibetur, nisi quod nemo potest.')

[2] §§ 19, 23.   [3] § 15.   [4] *Tract. Theol.-Pol.* c. xvi.
[5] Ibid.   [6] Ibid.   [7] *Tract. Pol.* c. vi, §§ 4, 5.
[8] *Tract. Theol.-Pol.* c. xvi.
[9] Cf. *Tract. Pol.* c. i, § 5, and c. ii, § 15: if the schoolmen call man an 'animal sociale, nihil habeo quod ipsis contradicam'.

obedience, for such was the pact, tacit or express (*hoc enim tacite vel expresse pacisci debuerunt omnes*), by which men transferred all their powers upon it (*cum omnem suam potentiam se defendendi, hoc est suum ius in eam transtulerunt*).[1] It cannot do wrong, for wrong is defined by law, of which it is itself the author.[2]

In this account of the institution of government, Spinoza is expounding a doctrine essentially similar to Hobbes's; but in a letter written to a correspondent in 1674 he claimed that he differed from Hobbes in that he always kept man's natural right undiminished, and ascribed to the sovereign in any state only as much right over his subjects as he had greater power than they, as is the position in the state of nature.[3] By this Spinoza presumably meant that he did not, as Hobbes did, rest the obligation to obey the sovereign on a supposed law of nature that men must keep their covenants, but frankly equated right with might, and held simply that the government could command obedience because of its superior strength. It is true that Spinoza's account of the law of nature is less ambiguous than Hobbes's, and though the doorway from the state of nature to civil society is a contract of all with all, it is much less prominent and elaborate than in Hobbes's account of the institution of the sovereign. But if obedience depends wholly on self-interest, including the fear of punishment, the question again arises, why should not men disobey, or rebel, if they can escape detection, or are reasonably confident of a successful revolution? Hobbes's reply was that such a risk was never worth taking; Spinoza admits that a contract against self-interest cannot bind,[4] and that if the common interest demands it the contracts by which men handed over their rights to a ruling assembly or individual may have to be broken. But, he asserts, no private man may decide this question, but only the sovereign itself.[5]

In a passage in his *Ethics* he raises the question why a man may

---

[1] *Tract. Theol.-Pol.* c. xvi.

[2] *Tract. Pol.* c. iv, § 4. But (§ 5) there is a sense in which it can be said *peccare*, viz. when it allows any action that might lead to its own downfall. But this is an error of judgement rather than a moral sin.

[3] Spinoza, *Epist.* 50: 'Discrimen inter me et Hobbesium . . . in hoc consistit, quod ego naturale ius semper sartum tectum conservo, quodque supremo magistratui in qualibet urbe non plus in subditos iuris, quam iuxta mensuram potestatis, qua subditum superat, competere statuo, quod in statu naturali semper locum habet.'

[4] *Tract. Theol.-Pol.* c. xvi: 'Nemo contrahit, nec pactis stare tenetur, nisi spe alicuius boni, vel sollicitudine alicuius mali: quod fundamentum si tollitur, pactum ex sese tollitur.'   [5] *Tract. Pol.* c. iv, § 6.

not disobey if he thinks disobedience will be more to his interest than obedience, and feels sure that he will escape the detection and punishment which generally make it more advantageous to obey. If a man by deceit could escape imminent danger of death, he asks, would not reason urge him to be deceitful? Spinoza's answer is that if so, reason would urge similar conduct on all men in similar circumstances, that is, to enter into perfidious social contracts, and so make their common laws of no effect; and this is absurd.[1] On this question, then, his argument is in fact virtually the same as Hobbes's.[2]

This point is interesting because it brings out clearly what is perhaps the most far-reaching difference in outlook and objective between many political theorists of recent times and their predecessors in the seventeenth and eighteenth centuries. That was an age of personal government by kings, and the great political question was one of right. In the eyes of many, kings ruled by divine right, and disobedience was *ipso facto* a sin. Others denied the theory of divine right, but the contract theory which they generally substituted for it was equally a question of right, and one of their motives for adopting it was that it made disobedience justifiable in certain circumstances, on grounds not of mere expediency but of *right*. Nowadays political theory generally moves on a lower—a less theological and a less ethical—plane. Divine right, not only of kings but of peoples too, has been discarded, for democracy and self-determination, open though these are to wide divergences of interpretation, are now so much the accepted basis of government that interest has shifted in democratic states from the question of right to the question of the use that the people shall make of the power it unquestionably possesses. Three factors have contributed to bring about this shift of interest. One was utilitarianism, which brought right itself, once divine, or at any rate natural, down to earth, by making it a question of the greatest happiness of the greatest number; another was the inversion of Hegel's transcendentalism by Karl Marx, who interpreted

---

[1] *Eth.* iv. lxxii, and *schol.* E. F. Carritt suggests (*Morals and Politics* (Oxford, 1935), p. 43) that this 'may be a moral absurdity, but nevertheless it is the only possible conclusion from his premisses already stated. He is only entitled to call it unreasonable when detection is likely.' But if by 'absurd' Spinoza means that widespread perfidy would lead to the disruption of government, and so involve more ultimate disadvantage to myself than if I obeyed, he may well be practically right, and the obligation to obey will still rest on expediency, which is consistent with his principles.

[2] Cf. p. 110 above.

history as a contest for power in terms not of morals but of economics. And at the same time the ideas of the historical school of law tended to displace belief in natural law, with the result that history became its own justification, from which there was no appeal to any higher standard of right or justice. In the seventeenth century, however, the enunciation of a political theory like that of Hobbes and Spinoza, with its explicit repudiation of the validity of any right other than power, so that government (and therefore rebellion also) became a question not of morals but of convenience or expediency, had a profoundly disturbing effect.

Among the hosts of jurists and professors of law in Germany and the Netherlands who published works on political science in the seventeenth and eighteenth centuries, there were a number who simply fell under the influence of Hobbes's clear definitions and systematic argument, and more or less completely adopted his doctrine, shocking though many felt it to be. There is little to be gained by a detailed survey of these secondary figures, for they made no significant addition to the ideas they inherited. One example, Professor J. C. Becmann, of Frankfort-on-the-Oder, may well stand for them all. After remarking that the cause of society is human need, because we are not self-sufficient, but want one another's help, he tells us that besides this wish for our own convenience, we are all afraid of one another. By nature we have an equal right to all things, and our wants are such that we naturally injure one another in trying to get them, for whatever we do, we do from selfish motives. None of us is strong enough to secure his own safety, and so for refuge we fly to society, which is formed by a voluntary contract.[1] This means that we must give up our rights,[2] and no conditional or partial surrender will suffice, for there will be no peace in a state in which individuals are allowed to make reservations on the ground of personal interests or compunctions.[3] Becmann admits that governments were erected for the people's and not the governors' benefit, but it must not be assumed that rulers stand to their subjects like tutors to their pupils. Bad tutors can be removed, but it is not so in the state, for we must recognize that the sovereign has no human superior by whom he can be judged. God alone can punish him.[4]

[1] J. C. Becmann, *Meditationes Politicae* (3rd edn., Frankfort-on-the-Oder, 1679), c. iv, § 3. In § 4 he quotes Hobbes's view that the state of nature is a state of war.   [2] c. v, § 1.   [3] c. xii, § 6.
    [4] Ibid. Hobbes himself had admitted that though the sovereign could not commit injustice or injury 'in the proper signification' (i.e. the legal signification),

But while they had a number of followers, the principal effect of the doctrine of Hobbes and Spinoza on their contemporaries was to antagonize them. In denying the reality of natural law, and recognizing no obligation but that imposed by power, they had made a clean break with medieval and post-Renaissance beliefs, and this constituted a challenge to all who cherished the traditional reality of moral obligation, even if they were content with an absolutist theory of the state. The foundation of the whole idea of natural law had been the conviction that independently of political institutions, or of human passions, there was a real moral difference between right and wrong, which all men had a duty to respect, and by which all human institutions, the state included, must be guided. Some writers had identified this with the Will of God, and while many lawyers, civilians and canonists, had come to treat the actual human systems they expounded, Roman or ecclesiastical, as concrete embodiments of the law of nature, there still remained, at bottom, the idea that there was a real criterion, not merely relative to self-interest, by which actions and institutions should be judged. It was in this atmosphere that the contract theory had developed, and its main function, in the hands of the religious *monarchomachi* and others of their school, had been as a guarantee that this criterion should be respected. Upholders of monarchy by divine right accepted the same basic presuppositions, distinguishing the conscientious king from the tyrant, and acknowledging his moral responsibility, albeit only to God, and not to his subjects.

Hobbes and Spinoza demolished all this, and consequently, in the later seventeenth century and afterwards, the lawyers and political theorists who could not accept their views, and wished to refute them, felt bound to attempt a reconstruction of the theory of natural law and contract in such a way as to avoid the conclusions that Hobbes and Spinoza had drawn. Some of these writers did not do much more than reiterate the traditional contractarian theory, occasionally incorporating such Hobbesian elements as could be made to conform to their general view. Thus Berckringer, a professor of law at Utrecht, constructed a somewhat eclectic account of the origin of the state, by which families united into villages, and villages into states, their union being 'partly natural

---

nevertheless he could commit 'iniquity' (*Leviathan*, c. xviii). It was for God, not man, to deal with this; but the only reason why God must be heeded, according to Hobbes, was that he holds irresistible power (c. xxxi).

and partly voluntary'.[1] It was voluntary because at each stage a *mutua obligatio* was recognized by the express consent of the elements that combined, which consent can be regarded as the efficient cause of the union, and as constituting a quasi-contract.[2] Then there was an unqualified contract by which the people conferred sovereignty on their rulers; this was not an out-and-out alienation of power, but was analogous to hiring rather than selling.[3] This does not carry us very far in the refutation of Hobbes, though it contains some of the ideas (e.g. the distinction between the contract of union and the contract of submission) which were used when a more resolute effort was made.

The most important and influential of the whole school of writers who attempted to construct a complete political theory in answer to Hobbes and Spinoza was Pufendorf.[4] First of all he attacks their conception of the law of nature. It is not to be equated with man's animal desires, nor is the state of nature a state of war. Man's natural condition is peaceful—the condition enjoined by the law of nature, which imposes on him a real and binding obligation. But though man has a duty to observe the law of nature, he is swayed by passions and desires, so that it must be admitted that the peace of the state of nature is precarious and uncertain.[5] Accordingly men are led to enter society. Pufendorf agrees with Hobbes that the dominating human motive is men's desire for their own convenience (*utilitatem*), so that they must have this in view if they are to choose a social life of their own will, and, being free, their entry into society must be voluntary.[6] But he also holds, as against Hobbes, that men are naturally sociable, and that this sociability, or natural inclination to join societies, is the foundation of the law

---

[1] D. Berckringer, *Institutiones Politicae* (Utrecht, 1663), I. i, § 3; ii, § 1.

[2] Ibid. ii, § 6. In calling it a quasi-contract (*quasi ex contractu coëuntium*) Berckringer was presumably conscious of some doubt whether society can rightly be said to originate in a real contract. On the implications of this phrase see below, pp. 225 ff.   [3] c. iv, § 7.

[4] In his *De Jure Naturae et Gentium* (Lund, 1672) and *De Officio Hominis et Civis* (Lund, 1673): both of these were translated into English and other languages, and became standard works on political theory, which left an abiding influence behind them.

[5] *De J. N. et G.* II, c. ii, §§ 3, 5–12: cf. *De Off.* II, c. 1, where he says that the state of nature is a condition of liberty, but must have been uncomfortable and dangerous. Nature itself wishes there to be some *cognatio* between men, enjoining them not to kill but rather to assist one another, but this *cognatio* has little effect among those living in natural liberty. Therefore, though a man need not treat his neighbour as his enemy, he must nevertheless regard him as an uncertain friend.   [6] *De Off.* II, c. v.

of nature, and a necessary condition of a man's willingness to unite with his fellows.[1]

This natural sociability, however, is not by itself a sufficient explanation of the formation of *civil* society. Although outside society man's life is miserable, yet his natural desires and needs could be abundantly satisfied by primitive types of society, and it cannot be inferred from man's sociability that he is naturally impelled to form a *state*. He who becomes a citizen sacrifices his natural liberty, and subjects himself to authority, including the right of life and death, and is forced to do many things he naturally dislikes doing, and to refrain from many things he greatly desires. Also much that is beneficial to society as a whole seems to be opposed to the interests of particular individuals. The genuine and chief reason, therefore, why the patriarchs abandoned their natural liberty and formed states was in order to provide safeguards against the injuries which men may suffer at the hands of their neighbours. There was no other way sufficient to curb the malice of men, for although the law of nature bids men abstain from all injuries, yet reverence for this law is not a sufficient guarantee that men may live safely in natural liberty.[2]

In this account of the origin of society Pufendorf accepts some elements in Hobbes's doctrine, but his view of human nature is essentially sounder and better balanced. Moreover, while Pufendorf seems to have had some doubts about the reality of the state of nature,[3] his account of the origin of the state is not open to the historical objection that he conceived it to be the sudden and artificial product, by contract, of a collection of supposedly disconnected primitive men. Political organization was preceded by a social existence in families, and the parties to the contract were not isolated individuals but the patriarchs. The source of this was not Pufendorf's imagination but the scriptural records of Jewish history, and, as we shall see, Locke took a similar line. Hobbes might have replied that he was not interested in the historicity of the state of nature, and if he pictured it as a condition totally opposed to civil society, this was because he wished to emphasize the tenuousness of the bonds of natural law, and man's indebted-

---

[1] *De J. N. et G.* II. iii. 15.   [2] *De Off.* II, c. v.

[3] Whatever the state of nature may be, Pufendorf will not have it equated with a merely animal existence, for man has a natural duty to worship God (*De Off.* II. i). Men differ also from gregarious creatures like bees or ants in that these lack the 'ratio per quam pacta facere et regimini se submittere possint', and congregate merely for the collection of food so as to survive the winter.

ness to government for all the advantages of society and civilized existence.

In opposition to Hobbes, however, Pufendorf and his school were convinced that the law of nature was a real and binding obligation, and his state of nature therefore was not one of complete detachment between men and men. A real law of nature meant that men had rights and duties in the state of nature, so that the state of nature must itself be a kind of society. Yet it was now a canon of belief that society (any *societas*, whether political or private) could only be formed by a voluntary contract of free individuals, and if one made the state of nature an already social existence (and therefore truer to historical fact), the social contract would be rendered superfluous. From this dilemma Pufendorf and his followers took refuge in the conception of *socialitas*, or natural sociability—a natural tendency to associate together—making the state of nature a life of common intercourse, though formless and insecure.

The ultimate source of this idea was evidently Aristotle's dictum that man is political by nature, as altered and interpreted by the medieval theory that nature is only a *causa remota* or *impulsiva* which led men voluntarily (but artificially) to combine in society. The idea of *socialitas* had already appeared in Hoenonius[1] and again more recently in Grotius;[2] it was a kind of compromise between the completely solitary and separate life of men in the state of nature depicted by writers like Mariana (or Hobbes), and the fully social life of an organized community. It was not a wholly satisfactory solution of the difficulty, for the more social it made the state of nature, the more unnecessary it made a social contract; on the other hand, if the element of sociability were weakened, the more Hobbesian the state of nature became, and the less plausible it was to maintain that the law of nature was a genuine law. But it had the advantage of finding room for the family in the state of nature, and so avoided contradicting the ancient (ultimately Aristotelian) and obviously plausible notion that the family or household was the oldest and most natural of societies. At the same time, whatever the degree of sociability in the state of nature, Pufendorf could not leave men in it permanently, and he had to admit that it was an uncomfortable and precarious existence, from which men's needs impelled them to emerge.

Men therefore form a state, and to do this they must unite their

[1] Cf. p. 82, note 2, above.   [2] Preface, p. iii (Evats's translation).

wills and forces, through compact.[1] Hobbes had denied that there was any contract between people and ruler; the people in his theory were a mere aggregate of individuals before their subjection to sovereignty, and so could not be a party to a contract. Pufendorf was careful, therefore, to arrange that before the ruler appeared on the scene there should be a corporate people to meet him as a capable party to a contract of government. Accordingly he has two clearly distinguished contracts in his system, and the contract of government is preceded by a social contract, through which the future citizens make a covenant, *singuli cum singulis*, promising to live together in a permanent community. For this contract they must be unanimous, and any one who dissents remains outside the future state; he is not bound by the agreement of the rest, although they form a majority, but is left in his natural liberty.[2]

It will be remembered that one of the difficulties of writers who were working out a contract theory in terms of Roman Law had been that the product of a contract of individual persons would be a *societas*, but that this strictly had no personality of its own, while even the fictitious personality of the Roman *universitas* could only come into existence through concession by the state, and hence was not strictly applicable to the state itself.[3] Pufendorf and other seventeenth-century lawyers evaded this obstacle by substituting for the older terminology their conception of 'moral personality'. By this they meant what we should probably call legal personality, as opposed to natural personality. The legal world was a 'world not of physical, but of mental factors—or rather, in view of the fact that it was the moral aspect of these mental factors which was really in question, it was a world of moral factors, or *entia moralia*'.[4] In effect Pufendorf meant by moral personality the capacity to be the subject of rights and duties in the sphere of natural law; and as this capacity could be possessed either by individuals or by corporations, we arrive at the distinction, within the sphere of moral personality, between the *persona moralis simplex* (the individual in his capacity as a legal person) and the *persona moralis composita* (the group or corporation in the same capacity).[5] In this sense, therefore,

---

[1] *De J. N. et G.* VII. ii. 5, 6.

[2] Ibid., § 7. *Singuli* must be understood here as heads of households, for Pufendorf did not mean literally all individuals, irrespective of status, age, or sex. Cf. p. 123, n. 3.   [3] See p. 45, above.

[4] Gierke, *Nat. Law* (tr. Barker), i. 118, q.v. for a fuller discussion of Pufendorf's thought in this connexion.

[5] Ibid., p. 121; see Pufendorf, *De J. N. et G.* I. i. 12, 13. This distinction

a group, the state included, could be regarded as possessing personality for legal (i.e. contractual) purposes, if not psychologically.

Individuals having thus contracted themselves into a community, the next stage is the creation of a government, though a greater or lesser period of time may elapse between these stages. For this a second contract is necessary, and for some political theorists this completed the process. Pufendorf and his followers, however, intercalated between the two contracts a *decretum* to determine what form of rule was to be established. This involves the idea that the whole body of the people as united by the social contract forms for the time being a kind of democratic assembly;[1] but as yet this is only the *rudimenta* of a state, and not a proper democracy, for only after the contract of submission has established a regular government, whose will all have thereby promised to obey, can individuals be coerced against their private will.[2] Yet even in this inchoate stage Pufendorf holds that individual liberty is not incompatible with the necessity of abiding by the decision of the majority, for if a minority dissents, it must not expect to be allowed to remain with the rest.[3]

Finally we come to the contract of submission itself, by which

between simple and composite moral persons came to be replaced by a distinction, found also in Pufendorf (op. cit. vii. ii. 6, where separate *personae physicae* become one *persona moralis*, by a contractual union), between the *persona physica* (the individual) and the *persona moralis*, a phrase which, with the adjective *composita* omitted, became merely a technical term for a group. This sense of the word is also found in Suarez (cf. the sentence from him quoted above, p. 70; and compare with this the meaning of the English phrase 'a moral certainty', on which see the article in *O.E.D.*). It was in this form that the expression was inherited by Rousseau; the danger then was that a new and unwarranted ethical connotation might be imported into the phrase, and encourage the theory that the 'moral person' of the community cannot err. Writers of the natural law school could not conceive of a group as capable of any action except through the agency of some representative individual. Hence their insistence on the necessity of a contract of subjection following the contract of union. (Cf., e.g., the theory of Hert, below, p. 153.)

[1] Cf. *De J. N. et G.* vii. v. 6, where he says that when a 'multitudo liberorum hominum' come together 'pactum initura circa conjunctionem sui in unam civitatem, jam tum coetus iste instar aliquod democratiae obtinet', because every one is free to express his own opinion.   [2] Ibid.

[3] *De J. N. et G.* vii. ii. 7. The ground for this is, presumably, that by remaining they give tacit consent, though he does not actually use this phrase here. Later (§ 20) he does in fact apply the phrase *pacto tacito* to children born into a state, and further remarks that the consent of wives and servants is accounted for through their husbands and masters. As we have seen, the first formation of state was a contractual union of patriarchal households, in which the patriarchs alone acted freely.

all promise to obey the government (be it monarchy, aristocracy, or democracy) which it has been decided to establish, on condition that in return the government will afford protection.[1] Previous writers had found themselves in difficulties when they tried to make the theory of a contract of submission, which works easily with a king or an oligarchical senate, apply to a democracy, and Pufendorf becomes equally entangled. For how can the people contract with itself; or, otherwise, who are the parties to the contract of government? It might be suggested that the parties are the minority and the majority, for by the contract of submission the minority is bound to accept the decisions of the majority; but this is a very far from plausible expedient, and apart from the likelihood that the majority and minority will be numerically different on every occasion, it makes the institution of democracy differ in principle from the institution of monarchy, in which the popular party to the contract is the whole people. After a long discussion Pufendorf finally propounds the solution that the parties are the *populus* collectively on the one hand, and distributively (*singuli*) on the other, for in these senses they have different wills and are different persons. Even so there is an inconsistency, for the people who contract with a monarchical ruler are not individuals but the collective moral person created by the social contract.[2] But if unsuccessful here, Pufendorf was fairly successful (granting his contractarian principles) in solving the problem of combining

[1] *De J. N. et G.* VII. ii. 8. In §§ 9–10 he attempts a detailed reply to Hobbes's refusal to admit the existence of a contract between ruler and subjects. 'Dum ultro principi me subjicio, obsequium ipsi promitto, defensionem mihi stipulor. Princeps dum me civem recipit, defensionem mihi promittit, obsequium a me stipulatur. Ante eam promissionem neque ego ipsi obsequi, neque iste me defendere, saltem ex obligatione perfecta, tenebatur. Quis ejusmodi actum ex classe pactorum velit excludere?' He proceeds to deny that this *pactum* is *supervacuum* because there was a previous *conventio* among those who thus voluntarily submit to the king, nor will he admit the validity of the objections felt by Hobbes to a pact between ruler and subjects.

The phrase *ex obligatione perfecta* above is significant. Hume later on was to show that it is unnecessary to base allegiance on a promise to obey, because the same reason that explains the obligation to keep promises also explains the obligation to obey the law. But the juristic contractarians would not rest content with anything short of a *perfect* obligation, which to their minds meant an obligation sealed by a contract. They were apparently willing to sacrifice both historical truth and logical consistency in order to secure this formal legality.

In *De Off.* II. vi. 7–9 Pufendorf summarizes his account of the formation of the state by *duo pacta et unum decretum*, remarking that these are required 'ut civitas *regulari modo* coalescat'. This seems to imply a recognition that a state might be formed, irregularly, by other means.

[2] On this point see Gierke, *Nat. Law* (tr. Barker), ii. 335.

individual liberty in the state of nature with the necessity of the minority submitting to the will of the majority in the state. His clear distinction of the two contracts, which enabled him to escape Hobbes's conclusions, served him again here, for he secured the individualist principle by making the social contract unanimous, and then one of the terms of the contract of submission, in case a democratic constitution were chosen, was that the will of the majority should henceforward prevail.

A completed state is now in existence, with a *summum imperium*,[1] and much of the rest of Pufendorf's work is occupied with the discussion of the scope of positive law and the internal arrangements of government, with which we are not concerned here.[2] Under the necessity of meeting Hobbes's doctrines, the contract theory had now reached its fullest elaboration, and subsequent writers, while they differed in details and emphasis, did little more than repeat in essentials what was now the accepted political theory of the whole contractarian school. All believed in the historical truth of their theory, subject to certain qualifications, and undoubtedly one of its functions was to explain the genesis of the state, though the elaborate succession of contracts, or of contracts and decree, made it historically even less plausible than before. Their main purpose, however, was philosophical—to explain the necessity of political obligation, while keeping it within the framework of the moral principles that were embodied in the tradition of the law of nature.

---

[1] *De J. N. et G.* VII. iii. 1.

[2] Once contractually established, Pufendorf's government enjoys large powers over its subjects. The contract theory, in fact, though often an introduction to a liberal type of government, was by no means always so; as Jellinek remarks (*Allgemeine Staatslehre*, p. 187), the practical effect of Pufendorf's theory was to bring Hobbes's absolutism into a *schulgerechte Form*. His system rested ultimately on the foundations laid by Althusius, but he modified them in the light of Hobbes's work, and adapted them to a unitary type of state.

IX

LOCKE AND THE ENGLISH REVOLUTION

POLITICAL theory in England in the second half of the seven-teenth century was divided between two main schools—the Anglican Royalists who believed in the divine hereditary right of kingship, and their Whig opponents, who maintained the cause of popular rights[1] and a limited monarchy. The contract of govern-ment, between king and people, became a cardinal principle for the Whigs, and their belief in it continued for many years apparently unshaken either by the historical scepticism of the Tories or by the more logical attacks of Hobbes. Hobbes was potentially their more dangerous opponent, and a whole series of writers felt im-pelled to undertake the task of refuting him. Most of them were unoriginal, and while they differed in the effectiveness with which they stated their case, their work scarcely amounted to more than repetition and elaboration, with variations, of the standard themes of natural law, limited or mixed monarchy, and the contract of government,[2] and it seems doubtful if they all fully understood the significance of Hobbes's position. Though an upholder of abso-lutism, Hobbes was equally obnoxious to the Tories as to the Whigs, for his theory seemed to justify obedience to any successful *de facto* government, such as the military dictatorship of Oliver Cromwell; and the legitimist principles of the Royalists naturally led them to repudiate any doctrine which attributed even the origins of power to the people. Royalists and churchmen were as prominent therefore as Whigs or freethinkers among the antagon-ists of Hobbes. Clarendon himself was one of those who wrote a book for the express purpose of denouncing the *Leviathan*;[3] and

---

[1] The rights of landlords would be nearer the real Whig philosophy (cf. Defoe; p. 134, note 2, below), but at any rate they were opposed to royal absolutism.

[2] Particulars about some of these writers may be found in J. E. Bowle, *Hobbes and his Critics* (1951).

[3] *A Brief View and Survey of the Dangerous and Pernicious Errors to Church and State in Mr. Hobbes's Book, entitled Leviathan*, by Edward, Earl of Clarendon (1670). His argument is in the main historical and practical: an assembly such as Hobbes describes 'was never heard of, nor can be conceiv'd practicable', and 'it cannot be imagin'd possible in nature' that an assembly of equals should ever agree to set up one man with such absolute jurisdiction. But his chief objection to Hobbes is on the ground that kings and subjects were born, not made. 'In

when, on 21 July 1683, the University of Oxford demonstrated its loyalty to Church and King by solemnly condemning in Convocation a series of subversive propositions, and burning the books that contained them on a bonfire in the Schools Quadrangle, Hobbes's *Leviathan* and *De Cive* found themselves in a mixed company along with the works of Buchanan and Cartwright, Milton and Baxter, John Knox and Cardinal Bellarmine.[1]

By this time, however, Hobbes's works were almost forgotten, and they remained relatively unheeded until, late in the eighteenth century, Jeremy Bentham and others came to appreciate the significance of his doctrine of legal sovereignty. Meanwhile, in the late seventeenth century, the vital question in practical politics was the succession to the throne. It was this which came to a head in the controversy over the Exclusion Bill, and the same issue was at stake a few years later in the Revolution itself. These crises were the occasion for the issue, or reissue, of a great flood of controversial pamphlets and treatises, prominent among which was Sir Robert Filmer's chief work, *Patriarcha*.[2] This was a thoroughgoing defence of the legitimacy of absolute monarchy on the grounds of its inheritance of the powers conferred by God on Adam and his successors. Whig writers immediately recognized it as a formidable weapon in the hands of their Tory opponents, and as many set themselves to answer it as in the previous generation had sought to refute Hobbes. Among them was Locke himself, but his *Two Treatises of Government*, the first of which is a direct reply to Filmer, while the second also contains numerous allusions to his work, were not published until 1690, by which time

truth,' he declares, 'all power was by God and nature invested into one Man, where still as much of it remains as he hath not parted with and shar'd with others.'

[1] For an account of the bonfire see A. Clark, *Life and Times of Anthony Wood*, vol. iii (Oxford Hist. Soc., 1894), p. 63. 'The scholars of all degrees and qualities', he tells us, who stood and watched the fire, 'gave severall hums whilst they were burning.' First among the propositions condemned was: 'All civil authority is derived originally from the people', and second: 'There is a mutuall compact, tacit or express, between a prince and his subjects, and that if he perform not his duty, they are discharged from theirs.' The third proposition was to the effect that lawful governors on becoming tyrants forfeited their right to govern. Altogether twenty-seven propositions were condemned: see *Somers Tracts* (ed. Scott), viii. 420.

[2] Though first published in 1680, no doubt as a contribution to the dispute about Exclusion, it had actually been written about thirty years previously, and had circulated for a time in manuscript. Filmer himself died in 1653. See the Introduction by Peter Laslett to his edition of Filmer's *Patriarcha and other Works* in Blackwell's Political Texts.

the successful accomplishment of the revolution had put the controversy in a new light.

We cannot and need not deal with more than a few samples of these Whig opponents of divine hereditary right. They continued to base their arguments on what were by now a standard set of assumptions, prominent among which was the contract of government between king and people, though they differed widely in the lengths they were prepared to go in the practical conclusions they drew from it. A fairly extreme position, though not as radical as some of the Puritan doctrines of the Commonwealth period, is illustrated by the *Discourses concerning Government* of Algernon Sidney.[1] Like Locke, he makes Filmer his main object of attack, repudiates the idea that royal authority is derived from paternal or patriarchal power, and ranges himself with Buchanan, Calvin, and Bellarmine in the belief that the people can depose princes and need not endure tyranny.[2] Government, however, is a necessity, for though men were born free and equal, they could not remain in the state of nature, in 'the perpetual and entire fruition' of the liberty given by God, since 'the Liberty of one is thwarted by that of another'. But 'whilst they are all equal, none will yield to any, otherwise than by a general consent. This is the ground of all just governments'. Societies originate in the 'free resolve of free men' to join together and establish laws which they oblige themselves to observe'[3] and the formation of the state involves the 'general consent of all to resign such part of their Liberty as seems to be for the good of all'.[4] Governments may differ in form, but all must originate in consent,[5] and in good governments changes are possible in the superstructure while the foundations remain unshaken.[6]

Sidney does not trouble to make the careful distinctions between the social contract and the contract of submission that characterized his contemporaries abroad,[7] but his theory of society is

---

[1] Like Filmer's *Patriarcha*, this was a posthumous work, for although written in 1681 it did not appear in print until 1698. Sidney was executed in 1683.

[2] c. i, §§ 2, 9.   [3] c. ii, § 5.   [4] c. ii, § 20.

[5] c. i, § 10. In § 11 he admits that government may in fact originate in force, but all just power is derived from the consent of the people.

[6] c. ii, § 17. This is an allusion to a point frequently raised in the dispute about the nature of fundamental law. It occurs in the pamphlets of Ferne and Herle (above, p. 91), Hunton, Filmer, and elsewhere.

[7] It was not only in England, it may be remarked, that the theory of the contract of government was still maintained, as distinct from the social contract, as an argument against despotism. The French Protestant writer Pierre Jurieu,

essentially contractual. Instead of a formal social contract we have a 'free resolve' of individuals to unite together and obey laws, and this, if not actually called a contract, is a contract in effect: it is an agreement of each to surrender some of his liberty on condition that all the rest do likewise. Once society has come into existence, and a government has been established, even if it is not made clear whether these were separate events, or formed a single operation, Sidney leaves no doubts about the contractual relationship between magistrates and 'the Nations that created them'. Contracts of government are 'real, solemn and obligatory'; even if not plainly expressed, and only 'implicit, and to be understood', they are nevertheless 'not dreams but real things, and perpetually obliging'.[1]

Sidney's political doctrine, like that of all the Whigs, rested on his belief that the ordinary man was born not simply as the subject of a reigning dynasty, but as the possessor of 'native rights', of which the laws should confirm the enjoyment. 'The Liberty of a people', he writes, 'is the gift of God and Nature',[2] and this doctrine leads him to take up a definitely republican position: his government consists not of an hereditary dynasty, however much restricted in power, but of magistrates appointed by the people. And though the relationship between people and magistrates is one of contract, the scales are weighted on the popular side. 'The People for whom and by whom the Magistrate is created can only judge whether he rightly perform his office or not',[3] and in effect popular resistance to government is justifiable provided it is sufficiently concerted. 'The general revolt of a nation cannot be called a rebellion',[4] says Sidney; and though Locke and the Whig politicians of 1688 repeated much the same doctrine, Sidney's statement of it, which resembles Milton's,[5] reveals him to have been more radical than the majority of his Whig contemporaries.

The views of the practical Whig politicians of the Revolution may be illustrated by the debates that took place on the exact definition of the means whereby James II was to be held to have ceased reigning and given place to the new monarch. The Revolution was accompanied by a large output of pamphlets, in which all the issues at stake were debated, and all the familiar arguments

for example, used it in the latter part of the seventeenth century against Bossuet, who upheld the divine right of kings. See R. Lureau, *Les Doctrines Politiques de Jurieu* (Bordeaux, 1904), pp. 42 ff., and G. H. Dodge, *The Political Theory of the Huguenots of the Dispersion* (New York, 1947), pp. 34–93.

[1] c. ii, § 32. Cf. c. iii, § 19. [2] c. iii, § 33. Cf. c. ii, § 31.
[3] c. iii, § 41. [4] c. iii, § 36. [5] Cf. above, p. 101.

marshalled anew, first to encourage one side or the other in their respective policies, and then to excuse or justify what had actually taken place. A good example of the latter is Robert Ferguson's *Brief Justification of the Prince of Orange's Descent into England.* The author of this pamphlet combines the two current Whig doctrines, fundamental law and a contract of government, and identifies both with the constitution itself. 'No government is lawful', he writes, 'but what is founded upon compact and agreement between those chosen to govern and those who condescend to be governed.' Accordingly, 'the articles upon which they stipulate the one with the other become the fundamentals of the respective constitutions of nations, and together with superadded positive laws are both the limits of the rulers' authority and the measure of the subjects' obedience'.[1] There was nothing new in this theory,[2] but it was obviously useful as a basis for the Whig contention that a king who had broken the original contract and violated the fundamental laws had *ipso facto* annulled 'all the legal rights he had to govern', and absolved all his former subjects 'from the legal engagements they were under of yielding him obedience'.[3] Note the word *legal*, twice repeated. The point was that this was no mere revolt or rebellion, which might perhaps have been justified by an appeal to the law of nature; the Whigs tried to make out that their action was legally covered by the provisions of the constitution itself.

In the debates in the Convention there was much discussion of the questions whether James II had 'abdicated' or 'deserted' the government, and whether the throne was vacant or not, but as the Commons had resolved that he had 'broken the original contract between king and people', a good deal was also heard, on both sides, of the line of argument we have just noticed. Sir Robert Howard, for instance, had been told 'that the king has his crown by divine right', but he maintained that the people had a divine right too, and that the king could forfeit his crown 'if he break that pact and covenant with his people', for 'the constitution of the government is actually grounded upon pact and covenant with the people'.[4]

The Bishop of Ely and the Earl of Clarendon criticized[5] the idea

---

[1] *State Tracts* (1689), i. 136.
[2] Cf., e.g., the views of Herle, Hunton, and Baxter, above, pp. 91, 92, 102.
[3] *State Tracts* (1689), i. 138.
[4] *Parly. Hist.* v. 46.   [5] i.e. the second earl.

of an original contract. The Bishop did not deny the contract outright, but insisted that it must have been 'made at the first time, when the government was first instituted, and the conditions that each part of the government should observe on their part'. Among these were the respective shares in Parliament of king, lords, and commons in making and altering the laws, including the laws governing the succession. He argued, accordingly, that in the case of 'an abdication in a successive kingdom . . . the compact being made to the king, his heirs and successors, the disposition of the crown cannot fall to us, till all his heirs do abdicate too'. Only 'the person that broke the Contract', therefore, could be set aside, and his forfeiture of the throne could not 'break the line of succession, so as to make the crown elective'.[1]

The Earl of Clarendon went farther than this, and voiced the historical objections of constitutional Tories to the whole idea of contract. 'This breaking the Original Contract', he urged, 'is a language that hath not been long used in this place; nor known in any of our law-books, or public records. It is sprung up, but as taken from some late authors, and those none of the best received, and the very phrase might bear a great debate, if that were now to be spoken to.' In particular, while agreeing that 'the king is bounded by law', he refused to admit that 'his obligation there-unto' proceeded from his coronation oath. By English law, 'he is as much king before he is crowned as he is afterwards, and there is a natural allegiance due to him from his subjects immediately upon the descent of the crown upon him'. The oath put a further obligation upon his conscience, but as king he was equally bound to observe the laws before he took the oath, 'and no body will make that Oath to be the Original Contract, as I suppose'.[2]

Sir George Treby replied to these objections by evading them. 'We are gone too far,' he pleaded, 'when we offer to enquire into the Original Contract, whether any such thing is known or understood in our law or constitution, or whether it be new language amongst us.' The only positive remarks he made in its favour were that 'it is a phrase and thing used by the learned Mr. Hooker . . .,

---

[1] *Parly. Hist.* v. 73.

[2] Ibid. v. 76, Hunton, whose *Treatise of Monarchy* was reissued at this time, recognized the same objection to the view that the king's prerogative was limited by the coronation oath (*Treatise of Monarchy*, part II, c. i, § 4). Cf. also the denial that the coronation oath is a contract in Eliot's *De Iure Maiestatis* (quoted in G. P. Gooch, *Political Thought from Bacon to Halifax*, p. 66). But cf. below, p. 134, n. 1.

whom I mention as a valuable authority, being one of the best men, the best churchman, and the most learned of our nation in his time. . . . He alloweth, that government did originally begin by Compact and Agreement.'[1] In referring to Hooker, Sir George Treby (like Locke) was appealing to an authority who might be expected to impress the Tories; but the actual phrase 'original contract' does not occur in Hooker's work, and it is doubtful how far he would have approved of the use that the Whigs were making of his name.

However that may be, the Whigs won their point in 1689. By a small majority they carried the famous phrase in the Lords, and though it did not appear in the Declaration of Rights itself, the original contract remained firmly embedded in Whig political theory. A number of writers took it for granted, and it became a commonplace to refer the liberty of Englishmen to the embodiment of the contract in their constitution. The original contract played a conspicuous part in that 'Whig Saturnalia', as it has been called,[2] the trial of Dr. Sacheverell. Mr. Lechmere, for example, one of the Whig managers of the prosecution, maintained that the terms of the constitution 'do not only suppose, but express an Original Contract, between the Crown and the People, by which that supreme power was (by mutual consent, and not by accident) limited and lodged in more hands than one', and that 'the continuance of the same Contract' was demonstrated by 'the uniform preservation of such a constitution for so many ages, without any fundamental change'.[3]

This contention did not pass unchallenged, and Mr. Phipps, for the defence, composed a new set of variations on the customary theme of historical unreality. 'When the Original Contract was made that learned gentlemen did not think fit to inform us. Was it before Magna Charta?' Yet, if Magna Charta (as was then commonly believed) included 'all the Liberties the Subjects then laid claim to', and was 'the Source and Spring of all their Liberties', it was odd that the contract was never mentioned in it. Again, was it made before the statute of 25 Edward III?[4] Counsel had never heard of the contract being pleaded to any indictment for high treason, 'nor objected to enervate or take off the force of that Statute. . . . Till the Legislature have declared', he continued,

---

[1] *Parly. Hist.* v. 79.   [2] R. W. Lee, *The Social Compact*, p. 82.
[3] *The Trial of Dr. Henry Sacheverell* (printed by order of the House of Lords, 1710), p. 22.   [4] The great Treason Statute of 1352.

'what the Original Contract is, and determined what Act of the Supreme Executive Power shall amount to a Dissolution of that Original Contract, and discharge the Subjects from their Allegiance, I must beg pardon if I think that as to resistance in general, the Law stands still upon the Foot of the 25th of Edward III.'[1]

These thrusts seem to have caught the Whigs unprepared, and all Mr. Lechmere could do was to refer to the coronation oath and the oath of allegiance, and assert in vague and magniloquent terms that if he chose 'to go over the several Branches that make up the ancient Frame of our government', and 'draw together some of the many incontestible Evidences of its Original Freedom', he could prove (but prove it he never did) 'the truth and certainty of that position of an Original Contract between the king and the people'.[2] That a creed could survive such an exposure by the mere repetition of party clichés may suggest to the modern reader that politicians in the seventeenth and eighteenth centuries were as deaf to reasoned argument as they are today, unless it suited their own programme.

It would be a mistake, however, to suppose that the Whig creed was nothing more than a fabrication of abstractions. Even if Mr. Lechmere gave no historical details, the Whigs could and did frequently refer to history. They believed that their version of history was as good as the Tories', if not better, and numerous pamphlets and treatises were written to adduce historical evidence in support of the contention that the constitution embodied an original contract.[3] There was, in fact, more to be said, both for and against the original contract, than appeared explicitly in the speeches of either Tories or Whigs at the Sacheverell trial. The Tories had a strong legal and historical case for arguing that the king was the mainspring of the government, and that from him every organ in the realm drew its motive power. On the other hand

---

[1] *Trial*, p. 152.   [2] Ibid., p. 285.

[3] Thus in *The Fundamental Constitution of the English Government, proving King William and Queen Mary our Lawful and Rightful King and Queen* (1690), W. Atwood quoted the Laws of Edward the Confessor, Bracton, and various other authorities to prove the existence of an original contract, and cited a series of historical incidents, from the time of the Anglo-Saxons to the reigns of Edward II and Richard II, to demonstrate the consequences of its being broken by the king. An even more elaborate attempt to substantiate the Whig doctrine of contract by historical examples was made by James Tyrrell in a lengthy treatise entitled *Bibliotheca Politica*. Tyrrell was a close friend of Locke's, and like Locke wrote an answer to Filmer's *Patriarcha*, with the title *Patrarcha non Monarcha*.

there was an equally strong historic tradition, to which the presumptions of the common law were active witnesses, that the monarchy was not unlimited, and that subjects had rights, notably of liberty and property, which were frequently spoken of as fundamental. On several famous occasions, in the distant as well as the more recent past, drastic steps had been taken against kings whose rule was condemned as tyrannical. As we have seen, the relationship between a feudal monarch and his vassals was essentially contractual, and it was not in fact uncommon in the Middle Ages for the coronation oath, which was meant to be a guarantee that the king would respect the constitutional rights of his subjects, to be referred to as a compact.[1] It might indeed be argued that with the obsolescence of feudalism, and the evolution of sovereignty, which was coming to be located in the hands of Parliament, there was really no longer any place for talk of an original contract in a description of the English constitution. But this was as yet only imperfectly realized, and both the contract and fundamental law long continued to be part of the stock-in-trade of the upholders of constitutional principles.[2] So far, in fact, was the original contract from losing ground that it was even adopted by the Tories under the House of Hanover, possibly because they came to the conclusion that otherwise they could never cast off the stigma of Jacobitism and hope to regain office.[3] So firmly established did the idea

[1] Cf. Henry of Huntingdon, quoted in Stubbs, *Select Charters* (9th edn.), p. 137: 'Inde perrexit rex Stephanus apud Oxeneforde, ubi recordatus est et confirmavit pacta quae Deo et populo et sanctae Ecclesiae concesserat in die coronationis suae.' Cf. also *pactio*, confirmed *mutuo iuramento*, made with the city of London on his election (*Gesta Stephani*, quoted ibid., p. 136).

[2] Cf., e.g., Daniel Defoe's *The Original Power of the Collective Body of the People of England* (1701), where he argues that the people, interpreted in the course of the pamphlet as the freeholders (cf. p. 138, n. 4, below), are the source of all power, and delegate it to king and government, whence they may resume it if their governors become tyrants. He quotes the example of the Revolution in England, and remarks that 'the present happy restoring of our liberty and constitution is owing to this fundamental maxim,

That kings, when they descend to tyranny,
Dissolve the bond, and leave the subject free'.

[3] In joining the Whigs in 1688 the Tories had already virtually abandoned their old principles of non-resistance. Cf. Bolingbroke, *A Dissertation upon Parties* (1733–4), letter xiii, where after quoting Hooker with approval and commiserating most nations on the illiberality of their governments, he proceeds to congratulate his fellow countrymen. 'Our original contract hath been recurred to often, and as many cavils as have been made, as many jests as have been broke about this expression, we might safely defy the assertors of absolute monarchy and arbitrary will . . . to produce any one point of time, since which we know anything of our constitution, wherein the whole scheme of it would not

of the original contract become that even Hume, who was shortly
to demolish much of the ground on which it stood, could not bring
himself to abandon the phrase itself.[1]

It is often supposed that Locke did most to erect the Whigs'
theory of government into the Palladium of English liberty which
they all believed it to be. His *Treatises of Government*, it is true,
were published after the Revolution was over, but Whig opinion
welcomed his work as a philosophical exposition and justification
of the principles by which they were proud to have been guided.
Locke was an undoubted contractarian, and believed, like every
Whig, in constitutional rights and the need for limited monarchy;
yet the 'original contract' of the Whigs was a pure contract of
government, whereas Locke's theory was worked out on somewhat
different lines. According to Locke, while the people agree by
compact to establish a 'civil government', they do not enter into
a contract with their rulers, but, as we shall see presently, make the
government trustees on their behalf. In this respect Locke appears
to have been widely misunderstood,[2] and if the Whigs adopted
him as their political philosopher, he really occupies that position
by virtue of his general political attitude and conditional justification of revolution rather than by his adherence to the particular
contractual formula adopted at the Revolution.

have been one monstrous absurdity, unless an original contract had been supposed.' A contract is implicit in the very nature of our constitution, which 'is in
the strictest sense a bargain, a conditional contract between the prince and the
people, as it always hath been, and still is, between the representative and collective bodies of the nation'. The idea of a contract between the House of Commons
and the electorate seems to be a new element in the theory.

[1] See below, p. 186.

[2] Cf., e.g., *A Treatise concerning Civil Government*, by Josiah Tucker, Dean of
Gloucester (1781), where he attacks Locke for supposing that there was a contract between king and subjects, and repeats the usual objections about the
occasion when the contract was made in England (was it at the coronation,
&c.). These difficulties, Tucker argues, are insoluble on Locke's principle of an
actual contract between king and people, but vanish if one regards government
as based on a *quasi-contract*. 'In all human *Trusts* . . . where is a *Duty* to be
performed, which is not actually expressed, specified, or contracted for—but
nevertheless is strongly implied in the Nature of the Trust:—the Obligation to
perform that implied Duty is of the Nature of a Quasi-Contract:—a Contract
as binding in the Reason of Things, and in the Court of Conscience, as the most
solemn Covenant that was ever made' (pp. 141–2). But Locke never said that
there was a contract between king and people; on the contrary, his position was
really the same as what Tucker suggests as an alternative, but without the
additional and unnecessary complication of the quasi-contract. By this Tucker
evidently meant an implied agreement which resembled but was not actually
a contract; but on its possible implications see below, pp. 225 ff.

Locke's account of civil society begins, as was customary, with the state of nature. It is a state of freedom and equality (as 'the judicious Hooker' had maintained), but one in which men are bound by real obligations. 'The state of nature has a law of nature to govern it, which obliges everyone, and reason, which is that law, teaches all mankind . . . that being all equal and independent, no one ought to harm another in his life, health, liberty or possessions.'[1] Force and fraud, in fact, are not, as in Hobbes, the cardinal virtues.[2] In the state of nature a man who transgresses the law of nature 'declares himself to live by another rule than that of reason and common equity, which is that measure God has set to the actions of men for their mutual security, and so he becomes dangerous to mankind'. Every man, therefore, 'by the right he hath to preserve mankind in general, may restrain or, where it is necessary, destroy things noxious to them, and so . . . hath a right to punish the offender, and be executioner of the law of nature'.[3] It is the 'want of a common judge with authority' that distinguishes the state of nature from civil society, and the state of nature is not necessarily a state of war.[4] 'Force without right upon a man's person makes a state of war both where there is, and is not, a common judge', whereas 'men living together according to reason without a common superior on earth, with authority to judge between them, is properly the state of nature'.[5]

Man was not intended, however, to live a solitary life.

God, having made man such a creature that . . . it was not good for him to be alone, put him under strong obligations of necessity, convenience and inclination, to drive him into society, as well as fitted him with understanding and language to continue and enjoy it. The first society was between man and wife, which gave beginning to that between parents and children, to which, in time, that between master and servant came to be added.[6]

There are thus natural societies in the state of nature, but the family falls short of 'political society', which exists only when every man has given up the power which he had in the state of nature to defend himself and his property, and surrendered it to the community. In civil society a common law and judicature

---

[1] *Second Treatise*, § 6.
[2] Cf. § 14: 'Keeping of faith belongs to men as men, and not as members of society.' Hobbes had said that men must perform their covenants, but by this he meant only that they would do so if they were reasonable and prudent.
[3] § 8.   [4] § 19.   [5] Ibid.   [6] § 77.

are established, in order to perform the function of deciding disputes and punishing offenders, which in the state of nature had been exercised by private individuals.[1]

The change from a state of nature to civil society can only take place by consent, since men by nature are 'all free, equal and independent'. Civil society is formed by each 'agreeing with other men, to join and unite into a community'. For this 'original compact, whereby he with others incorporates into one society, the individual consent of all who join it is necessary, and any who prefer not to join the society may be left out, and remain in the state of nature. Once the society is formed, however, 'the majority have a right to act and conclude the rest'; for in forming a community 'they have thereby made that community one body, with a power to act as one body', and this must of necessity (for there is no other way) be by the will of the majority. The compact, in fact, involves the consent of every one 'to submit to the determination of the majority'; it would, indeed, be meaningless if a man were 'left free and under no other ties than he was in before in the state of nature'.[2]

Locke is aware of the historical objections to the social contract —'that there are no instances to be found in story of a company of men, independent and equal one amongst another, that met together, and in this way began and set up a government'.[3] He pleads in reply that 'government is everywhere antecedent to records';[4] and though he admits that 'if we look back as far as history will direct us towards the original of commonwealths, we shall generally find them under the government and administration of one man',[5] this does not disprove the thesis that political society began by the consent of the individuals who united to establish it.[6] Reason, after all, is 'plain on our side that men are naturally free';[7] Locke, in fact (like Hobbes), is not primarily concerned with historical origins, and therefore is not seriously distressed if his theory is historically improbable. Similar objections could be raised to the state of nature as an historical condition, but he replies that 'all princes and rulers of "independent" governments all through the world are in a state of nature', and the state of nature

[1] § 87.
[2] §§ 95–97. Locke also allows for the possibility that it may be agreed that the votes of more than a bare majority shall be required.
[3] § 100.   [4] § 101.   [5] § 105.   [6] § 106.
[7] § 104. Cf. § 171: political power 'has its original only from compact and agreement and the mutual consent of those who make up the community'.

exists today between man and man in the absence of civil society, for instance 'between a Swiss and an Indian in the woods of America'.[1] Just as Hobbes's state of nature signified his view of the lawlessness of human character apart from the bonds of government, so Locke by the same means seeks to show that in his opinion man is not naturally lawless, but the subject of rights and obligations which are really binding and which, moreover, he is naturally inclined to respect.

In expressing his theory, however, in an historical form, as an account of the origin of society, Locke, like the other contractarians, was involved in difficulties, not the least of which was the familiar problem how to account for the position of the descendants and successors of the original founders of the state. Even if we pass over the theory that one of the terms of the original contract was that all who joined the community should consent to be ruled henceforward by the majority, there still remains the question of how to accommodate the doctrine that every man is 'naturally free, . . . nothing being able to put him into subjection to any earthly power, but only his own consent',[2] with the fact that subsequent generations were born into the state through no volition of their own. Locke suggests that sons who claim to inherit their fathers' possessions do in fact give consent at the age of twenty-one, because 'the son cannot ordinarily enjoy the possessions of his father but under the same terms his father did, by becoming a member of the society, whereby he puts himself presently under the government he finds there established, as much as any other subject of that commonwealth'. But as this consent is 'given separately in their turns, as each comes to be of age, and not in a multitude together, people take no notice of it, and . . . conclude they are naturally subjects as they are men.'[3]

The modern reader is unlikely to regard this as a satisfactory solution of the difficulty, especially when he reflects on its implication that only property-owners and sons with expectations count as full members of the state. To Locke and his contemporaries, however, this no doubt seemed a reasonable and natural point of view[4] and from propertyless labourers, like foreign visitors, a lower degree of consent was enough. He recalls 'the common distinction of an express and a tacit consent' and maintains that

---

[1] Second Treatise, § 14.   [2] § 119.   [3] § 117.
[4] Cf. the interesting chapter entitled 'Freehold and Status' in D. Ogg, England in the Reigns of James II and William III (Oxford, 1955), pp. 54–98.

'every man that hath any possessions or enjoyment of any part of the dominions of any government doth thereby give his tacit consent'. Everybody, therefore, is equally obliged to obey the laws: not only the landowner, but even a man who has 'a lodging only for a week, or whether it be barely travelling freely on the highway'. In fact, he concludes, tacit consent, and hence the obligation of obedience, 'reaches as far as the very being of anyone within the territories of that government'.[1] We can only reply that if consent could be watered down like this, it would lose all value as a guarantee of individual liberty, and the most outrageous tyrant could be said to govern with the consent of his subjects. Locke indeed goes on to suggest that a man who has given only tacit consent to a government is not obliged to remain under it if he does not like it, but 'is at liberty to go and incorporate himself into any other commonwealth, or agree with others to begin a new one *in vacuis locis*'.[2] There may have been more possibilities of so doing in the seventeenth century than there are today, when the whole world is mapped out under governments, and freedom of movement is restricted by quotas and immigration laws,[3] but, as Hume pointed out,[4] even in Locke's time such liberty must have been largely imaginary.

The contract theory, in fact, is faced with an awkward dilemma. It may, on the one hand, be regarded as a purely historical theory to explain the origins of the state, in which case it is untrue, and having no bearing on the rights of subsequent generations, it is useless as an explanation of political obligation. If, on the other hand, we are to treat it, as I think we must, as primarily an analysis of political obligation, the position of present-day citizens is the crux of the question. But in this case the theoretical individualism, which holds that no one need obey any government which he has not personally undertaken to obey, is incompatible with any government at all. We are really confronted with the problem of liberty in as insoluble a form as that in which J. S. Mill stated it, when he complained that self-government turned out in practice to be not 'the government of each by himself', but only the government 'of each by all the rest'—or even by a bare majority of the rest.[5]

---

[1] *Second Treatise*, § 119.   [2] § 121.
[3] Some of our modern would-be refugees, incidentally, encounter obstacles not only in entering a new country but in leaving their own.
[4] See below, p. 187.   [5] J. S. Mill, *On Liberty*, c. i.

Most contractarians agreed that the reason why men were willing to exchange the liberty of the state of nature for obedience to the laws of civil society was that this liberty was at best precarious, and men preferred to surrender some of it in order to safeguard the remainder. Locke goes farther than this, for he recognizes that a government, to be effective, must have full powers. On becoming a citizen, therefore, a man surrenders all his natural rights, and 'puts himself under an obligation to everyone of that society to submit to the determination of the majority, and to be concluded by it'.[1] He 'must be understood to give up all the power necessary to the ends for which they unite into society';[2] and 'political power', Locke has already told us, is 'a right of making laws with penalties of death, and consequently all less penalties, for the regulating and preserving of property, and of employing the force of the community, in the execution of such laws, and in the defence of the commonwealth from foreign injury.'[3] He adds, however, an important proviso: 'and all this only for the public good'. Furthermore, natural law obliges rulers as much as it does ordinary people, so that the government to be established will be no arbitrary sovereign after Hobbes's pattern,

> as if when men, quitting the state of nature, entered into society, they agreed that all of them but one should be under the restraint of laws; but that he should still retain all the liberty of the state of nature, increased with power, and made licentious by impunity. This is to think .that men are so foolish that they take care to avoid what mischief may be done them by polecats or foxes, but are content, nay, think it safety, to be devoured by lions.[4]

Locke also made an important innovation in his doctrine that the natural rights of man before the formation of society included the right of property. Most previous writers had maintained the traditional assumption of a primitive community of property, defining this as a *communio negativa*, by which they meant not a positive communism but the non-existence of property altogether in the state of nature. From this they were led to the idea of a special contract of property; according to some writers this might be included in the social contract, but in any case it was maintained, by contractarians as well as absolutists, that private property only came into existence with the state.[5]

[1] *Second Treatise*, § 97.   [2] § 99.   [3] § 3.   [4] § 93.
[5] Cf. Pufendorf, *De J. N. et G.* iv. iv. 4: God gave the world to men in common, and the state of nature involved 'omnium rerum communionem, non quidem

Locke, however, while starting from the assumption that God gave the earth and the lower animals to men in common, declared that 'every man has a property in his own person. This nobody has any right to except himself. The labour of his body and the work of his hands . . . are properly his.' From this assumption he argues that whatever a man 'removes out of the state that nature hath provided and left it in, he hath mixed his labour with it, and joined it to something that is his own, and thereby makes it his property'.[1] While there was 'still enough and as good left' for others, this principle applied equally to the appropriation and improvement of land as to movable property,[2] and the only limit to appropriation was that a man might not take from the common store more than he could 'make use of to any advantage of life before it spoils'.[3] This limitation, however, only applied in primitive conditions, for the invention of money, which can be hoarded indefinitely without 'spoiling', opened the door to the unrestricted (and unequal) accumulation of capital.

Locke thus brought the economic structure of the society of his own age within the bounds of natural law. Our modern industrial age has become conscious, whereas Locke was oblivious, of the social consequences of an uncontrolled capitalist system, but we should not blame Locke for accepting without question the outlook and values of his own time. Apart from this, however, it may be argued that while Locke's doctrine might perhaps be accepted as a description of the method by which primitive men in fact acquired property, it provides no real explanation of the creation of a *right* of property. The only guarantee of the immunity of a man's person or possessions in the state of nature is the respect of his neighbours for the law of nature, which is only another name for a moral obligation, and which wicked men will ignore. But private property in the state is safeguarded in fact by the laws and government of the state, and can only be held on such conditions as the state imposes. The same principle holds good of a man's 'person', which in the state of nature would be as much open to natural perils and the designs of wicked men as his possessions. Whatever

illam quam positivam diximus, sed negativam, i.e. res omnes fuisse in medio positas, et non magis ad hunc quam ad illum pertinuisse'. Private property 'praesupponit factum humanum, et pactum aliquod tacitum vel expressum', the 'prima conventio' being that what one man appropriated from the common stock for his own use the others would refrain from seizing from him. Cf. Gierke, *Nat. Law* (tr. Barker), i. 103–4.

[1] *Second Treatise*, § 26.   [2] § 33.   [3] § 31.

security, therefore, of life or limb as well as of goods, a man enjoys in society, he owes to the protection of society. Locke's right of property is open, in fact, to the same objections as can be raised against all pre-social natural rights of any kind; the most that we can claim is that the government of a state, if it is well ordered, will respect the moral obligations which enlightened opinion believes to be binding. Locke, however, was anxious to secure that the natural rights which the state, as he believed, was formed to safeguard should include a right of property, and his argument, untenable as it was, was of great influence on the theories of property of subsequent contractarian thinkers.

The first step, after the decision by compact to form a civil society, was to establish the legislative power. This was 'not only the supreme power of the commonwealth, but sacred and unalterable in the hands where the community have once placed it'.[1] Locke, it will be observed, avoids Hobbes's word *sovereign*, and his 'supreme power' is not 'nor possibly can be absolutely arbitrary over the lives and fortunes of the people'. It is no more than 'the joint power of every member of the society given up to that person or assembly which is legislator', and 'nobody has an absolute arbitrary power over himself, or over any other, to destroy his own life, or take away the life or property of another'. The legislative power is 'limited to the public good of the society', and it must observe the rules of the law of nature.[2] Locke also suggested positive safeguards against the risk of the government becoming arbitrary and tyrannical. One lay in the structure of government itself, the legislature being distinguished and kept separate from the executive,[3] and he also enumerated several specific limitations to the extent of the legislative power.[4]

The erection of the latter, though distinctly separate from and subsequent to the contract of union, is not described as a contract

---

[1] *Second Treatise*, § 134. The executive power may also be called supreme in certain circumstances (§ 151), but 'placed anywhere but in a person that has also a share in the legislative is visibly subordinate and accountable to it' (§ 152).

[2] § 135.

[3] In the eighteenth century the separation of powers was widely advocated as the most effective method of securing constitutional government. It owed its vogue largely to Montesquieu, who professed to discern in it the guiding principle of the English constitution. The powers which Locke distinguished (and which he no doubt drew from his own observation of the government of England) do not correspond exactly with Montesquieu's, but the principle he had in mind was essentially similar. See my *John Locke's Political Philosophy*, c. v.   [4] *Second Treatise*, c. xi.

of government.[1] It is rather an act, the first common act, of the newly united society, though Locke refrains from giving details of how it took place.[2] We may infer its character, however, from his later remarks that the members of the legislature must act 'pursuant to their trust',[3] and that the legislative is 'only a fiduciary power to act for certain ends', so that 'there remains still in the people a supreme power to remove or alter the legislative, when they find the legislative act contrary to the trust reposed in them'.[4] Locke was here borrowing a conception peculiar to English law, which had been used by several previous writers.

A trust in English law [to quote Sir Ernest Barker] is not a contract, and the trustee does not enter into relations of contract with the trustor— or with the beneficiary. Roughly, he may be said to consent to incur a unilateral obligation—an obligation to the beneficiary which, if it implies the trustee's possession and vindication of rights against other parties on behalf of the beneficiary, implies no rights for the trustee himself on his own behalf.[5]

If we describe political relations on the analogy of trusteeship, the people as trustor creates the legislature as trustee on its own behalf, and is therefore both trustor and beneficiary of the trust; but in neither capacity is it in any contractual relationship with the trustee. This conception fitted Locke's intention admirably, for unlike the contract of government, in which rights and duties were reciprocal, it left the duties on the side of the government, and the rights on the side of the people.[6] The supreme power of the people, however, comes into action 'not as considered under any form of government, because it can never take place till the government be dissolved'.[7] This, he insists against Hobbes, does not involve the dissolution of society[8] (this was the moral he drew

---

[1] Still less as a contract of subjection. Locke did not hold the view that the people subjected themselves to a government; they erected a government for their own convenience, and ultimately the government was subordinate to them, not they to it (c. xiii).

[2] Locke's theory, in this and other respects, involves a position closely resembling that described by Pufendorf (above, p. 123), where the people in the interval between the social contract and the contract of government are in a kind of imperfect democracy.

[3] § 134.   [4] § 149.

[5] In Gierke, *Nat. Law* (tr. Barker), ii. 299.

[6] The people collectively, of course; an individual, as we have seen, must obey the will of the majority when he enters the community.

[7] *Second Treatise*, § 149.

[8] c. xiii.

from the Revolution of 1688), and therefore revolution is justified whenever the government acts contrary to its trust.[1] Unfortunately he gives no satisfactory answer to the question how in practice the people are to decide whether such action has occurred, and how in that case they are to procure the downfall of the government. The analogy of trusteeship, however, was free from many of the faults of the contract theory, and was a neat way of expressing the principle that governments were responsible to their subjects.

Though it continued to find support, the political trust by no means superseded the contract theory. Whig politicians still spoke of the original contract, until it finally lost ground before the attacks of a series of writers in the eighteenth century, while abroad the contractual school of Pufendorf and his followers continued to hold the field. With Rousseau, indeed, the people ceased to enter into contractual relations with the government, but he went farther than Locke, and made the government not a trustee but a mere delegate of the sovereign general will. In more recent years the idea of political trusteeship has come to find a fresh sphere of usefulness as a guide to the relationship between states and their colonial dependencies, particularly when these are inhabited by backward peoples. This idea, largely an English contribution to modern political thought, probably derives much of its vogue from Burke,[2] but he in turn was adapting to fresh

[1] Strictly speaking, according to Locke (and cf. above, p. 130), it was not *revolution*, nor were the people *rebelling* against their government. A government which broke its trust automatically dissolved itself, and the people then simply erected a new government in the vacuum. Locke would only justify such action if it were done by the society acting as a whole (i.e. through a majority at least), and it is clear from c. xix that he did not contemplate this happening frequently.

[2] Notably from his statement of the principles governing the relations between Great Britain and India, in his *Speech on Mr. Fox's East India Bill* (1783), in *Works* (1826 edn.), iv. 11: 'All political power which is set over men ... ought to be some way or other exercised ultimately for their benefit. If this is true with regard to every species of political dominion, and every species of commercial privilege, none of which can be original, self-derived rights, or grants for the mere private benefit of the holders, then such rights, or privileges ... are all in the strictest sense a *trust*; and it is of the very essence of every trust to be rendered *accountable*; and even totally to *cease*, when it substantially varies from the purposes for which alone it could have a lawful existence.' Cf. also p. 20, where he alludes to 'the company's abuse of their trust'.

As Professor Coupland remarks, this idea—one of the fruits of the recent disaster in America—marked the abandonment of mercantilist ideas and the beginning of a new imperialism. In 1800 the servants of the East India Company were instructed to regard themselves no longer as 'the agents of a commercial concern' but as 'the ministers and officers of a powerful Sovereign' charged with

purposes a theory to which Locke and his English and American predecessors had first given currency.

Locke has come to be thought of as one of the principal exponents of the social contract theory, and there can be no doubt that the popularity of his work, both in England and abroad (and notably in North America) did much to spread its vogue and influence. Yet there is little that is original in his work. There is an obvious resemblance between his political theory and that of Pufendorf, whose work we know he admired,[1] and critics have pointed out parallels between Locke's ideas and those of various English predecessors.[2] Locke was a scholar who had read widely, and the importance of his contribution to political thought lay not in its novelty but in its timeliness and its mode of expression. He summed up, and published in an easy, readable style, the accepted commonplaces of the political thought of his generation, at a moment when the successful accomplishment of the Revolution of 1688 made the government of England seem a model to be envied. The defects of the contract theory—its artificiality, its neglect of the deeper psychological factors underlying the cohesion of society, the logical inconsistencies involved in trying to reconcile individual consent with obedience to government by

'sacred trusts' for the 'good government' of British India, and the 'prosperity and happiness' of its people. (Quoted in R. Coupland, *The American Revolution and the Brit. Empire* (1930), p. 194.) For further details about the history of the trust concept as a political metaphor see my *John Locke's Political Philosophy*, c. vii.

[1] He recommended the study of Grotius and Pufendorf as part of a gentleman's education.

[2] e.g. Philip Hunton (cf. p. 91, above). See also A. H. Maclean, 'Lawson and Locke', in *Cambridge Historical Journal*, ix (1947), pp. 69–77. If Locke was unoriginal, still less original were the eighteenth-century writers who followed him. Thus Bishop Hoadly virtually copied Locke, though scarcely acknowledging his debt. He attacked the derivation of government from Adam and the patriarchs, quoted Hooker, and, by equating consent with a tacit contract, argued that an original contract, tacit if not expressed, was always to be found at the inauguration of the state (B. Hoadly, *The Original and Institution of Civil Government Discussed*, 1710, in *Works*, ed. J. Hoadly, 1773, ii. 182 ff.).

Bishop Warburton was one of the more colourful of eighteenth-century divines, but his political theory was commonplace. He described the institution of government as a remedy for the injustice which prevailed in the state of nature (a condition in which the strongest appetite was that of self-preservation, and the consequent violence and excesses would have been as bad as the Hobbists describe were it not for the restraining principle of religion), and declared that 'in entering into Society it was stipulated, between the Magistrate and the People, that Protection and Obedience should be the reciprocal conditions of each other' (W. Warburton, *The Alliance between Church and State* (1736), i, cc. 2, 3).

majority-rule—are as obvious in Locke as in any writer, and have often been emphasized by critics. They are no reason for singling out Locke for special attack, since they are common to the whole contractarian standpoint, and there is much in Locke, apart from them, that is sound and reasonable.

X

THE CONTRACTUAL SCHOOL OF THE LATE SEVENTEENTH AND EARLY EIGHTEENTH CENTURIES

UNDER the influence of Puritan and Whig traditions the contract theory in England (if we except Hobbes) remained essentially the doctrine of a party which espoused the cause of constitutional liberty against the claims of absolute monarchy and the alternative theory of divine right and non-resistance. Abroad, on the other hand, the contract theory became less propagandist and more juristic, and was accepted by practically every political lawyer; some were more inclined towards monarchical absolutism, others towards popular sovereignty, while others again kept to a kind of *via media*, but by appropriate manipulation of the contract of submission, which was supposed to be the foundation of the power of every government, all types of state, whether monarchy, aristocracy, or democracy, could be explained by a uniform contractual theory of political obligation. We have already examined the work of Pufendorf, who was the virtual founder of this whole school of systematic political science, and it would take too long to discuss anything approaching the whole output of the many writers who adopted his juristic approach to politics. But it was in their hands, in the late seventeenth and early eighteenth centuries, that the social contract reached its heyday, and it will be worth while in this chapter, by examining a selection of their works, to note what modifications the theory underwent before it began to decline in favour altogether.

To a nineteenth-century German like Gierke, looking back on this previous phase of the political philosophy of his nation, the whole 'natural law' school appeared to be open to two principal objections. One was that its individualism was inconsistent with an adequate theory of the real nature of political obligation, or, in effect, of the majesty of the state; the other that its contractualism, by its inevitable antithesis of two parties, ruler and people, rendered impossible a satisfactory account of the unity of the state.[1]

[1] Cf. Gierke, *Nat. Law* (tr. Barker), i. 44–52. The natural-law school was also bound to be unsatisfactory in its account of the state, if only because it reduced

The older tradition of the unity of society still survived, but was as yet powerless to make much impression against the prevailing contractarian school.[1] Only in the nineteenth century, with the decline of the contract and natural law, and their replacement by the historical school of German law, and the philosophy of Hegel, could an acceptable system of political theory be constructed. But if we value the political liberty of England, for which the individualist assumptions of English law are in large measure responsible, and view totalitarian theories of the state with misgiving, we may feel that greater disadvantages and dangers result from an over-emphasis of the metaphor of organism than of contract, and that even if the contract theory itself be logically inconsistent and historically unsound, that does not necessarily invalidate the individualism of which it was only a particular manifestation. In that case the natural-law writers of the seventeenth and eighteenth centuries are full of interest, for their fundamental principles were essentially sound, even if their modes of expression were faulty; and part of the task of a modern political theorist will be to construct a system which, while avoiding their logical and historical errors, will safeguard the principles which some of their nineteenth-century successors tended to neglect.

One of the earliest after Pufendorf of these political jurists was Ulrich Huber, professor of law at Franeker in Dutch Friesland, whose work *De Jure Civitatis* appeared in 1682; in Germany Christian Thomas (Thomasius), professor at Leipzig and afterwards at Halle, completed his *Institutionum Jurisprudentiae Divinae Libri Tres* in 1687, to be followed in 1705 by his *Fundamenta Juris Naturae et Gentium*. Huber agrees with Hobbes that the state of nature was a state of war, but at the same time he maintains, with Pufendorf, that the reason for political organization was a *desiderium societatis naturale*,[2] though he admits that besides this desire, and its accompanying *odium confusionis*, another cause was men's ill will, against which those who were well-disposed could protect themselves only by a combination, in which all their wills

---

public law to a mere complex of elements (contract, &c.) derived from private law. This would not matter much to an Englishman, whose own law makes no formal distinction between public and private law; but to the nineteenth-century German publicist the affairs of the state stood on a separate plane, altogether higher and nobler than the private affairs of individuals.

[1] Gierke, *Nat. Law* (tr. Barker), i. 110–11.

[2] Huber, *De Jure Civitatis*, I. i, c. 3.

should become one (*conjunctione multorum . . . per quam omnium voluntas una fieret*).[1]

This account of the origin of the state, beginning with a number of free individuals, but ending in their subordination to the will of a single sovereign, might well be taken as typical of the whole contractarian school in Europe in the seventeenth century. The sovereign ruler, however, does not make his appearance at once, for first of all the state was formed as a democracy, which is closest to the state of nature,[2] and this took place by a *foedus* establishing the prevalence of the will of the majority (*ut majoris partis voluntas sit omnium voluntas*).[3] Hobbes held that the people do not constitute a *unum* even when they are *congregati*, still less when they are separate, and that all they do is to make a compact individually with one another to obey the sovereign; but according to Huber the people can and do form a whole, and are not necessarily dissolved into their component units even when they have no ruler.[4] This primitive democracy, however, did not last indefinitely, and Huber puts forward the hypothesis that the people, *taedio confusionis*, conferred sovereignty either on one man or on a few.[5] This *delatio imperii*, however, does not take place (as in Hobbes) through the direct acknowledgement of their allegiance by individuals: votes are indeed collected individually (*viritim*), but the result is a single *decretum* which is truly a unity (*fit unum quid e multis*).[6] Hobbes was wrong, therefore, in maintaining that sovereignty was the outcome, not of a contract of submission, either to a majority or to the rulers, but simply of a contract of individuals with one another, and that therefore the sovereign is under no contractual obligation.[7] On the contrary, there is a *foedus* between

---

[1] Ibid. I. ii. I.

[2] I. ii. 4. Here Huber differs somewhat from Pufendorf, according to whom the result of the social contract was only the *rudimenta* of a state which, though like a democracy, *democratia proprie vocari nondum poterunt* (*De J. N. et G.* VII. v. 6: cf. above, p. 123).

[3] I. ii. 3. This is further explained as a 'foedus omnium cum omnibus, ut quae consensu majoris partis statuuntur, ea cunctos obligent'.

[4] I. iii. 4. Huber's argument is directed mainly against Hobbes, who denied the existence of a contract of submission between people and ruler; but absolutist versions of the contract of submission maintained that while the monarch was confronted with a corporate people in the act of making the contract, the community itself expired in that very act, leaving the sovereign as the complete personification of the state, which then consisted, as far as the possession of rights and duties was concerned, simply of the ruler face to face with a collection of individual subjects. Huber's argument is also aimed against this view (cf. Gierke, op. cit. i. 145).

[5] I. ii. 5.   [6] I. iii. 4.   [7] I. ii. 4.

ruler and subjects, which governs their mutual relations, and in virtue of which tyrants may be resisted and punished.[1] Huber thus steers a middle course between the conclusions of Hobbes, according to whom the people surrendered the whole of their liberty to the sovereign, and those of writers such as Sidney or Althusius, who made the rulers merely the servants of the people. Huber held that there was a real surrender of authority, but that the people retained certain rights by which the exercise of the ruler's authority was limited.

The main principles of Thomasius' political theory follow closely those of Pufendorf and Huber, but he begins on much more 'organic' lines. Society (*societas*), he explains, is either equal, unequal, or mixed (*mixta*): human societies are either equal or mixed, the only *societas inaequalis* being that between men and God.[2] Men may form artificial societies for particular purposes, but there is also a natural human society to which men are urged by divine command or for the common benefit of the whole human race;[3] furthermore, man is never for a moment entirely isolated and cut off from society (*in statu integro absque societate*); he is from the beginning in relationship with God,[4] and in this *societas*, unequal though it is, there is greater love and trust than in any human relationship, even that of the family. The state of nature is not a state of war;[5] it denotes the common condition of all men in respect of the qualities which distinguish them from the brutes —the faculty of reason and the ability to acknowledge a supreme Lawgiver, and to regulate their actions in accordance with his rules.[6] Reason, he continues, involves speech, and speech is impossible apart from society; if we call a man rational, therefore, it is equivalent to calling him social, and *socialitas* is defined as a common inclination, planted by God in the whole human race, which makes men desire a happy and peaceful life with other men —peaceful because we cannot reason in a state of unrest.[7]

[1] Cf. I. ix. 3, 4. C. 5 ('De fide et perfidia Summarum Potestatum in contractibus') states that rulers are constituted *conventionibus* and are bound by promises, reinforced by oath. This contract of submission is possible because the people can be treated as a juristic unity in relation to the other party, the ruler.

[2] C. Thomasius, *Inst. Jur. Div.* I. i. 93, 94. The state, in which there are ruler and subjects, but some rights on both sides, is 'mixed': free associations within the state are examples of a *societas aequalis*.

[3] Ibid., § 95.   [4] I. ii. 27.

[5] In I. ii. 49 he quotes Pufendorf against Hobbes's theory.

[6] Ibid., § 50; in § 52 he gives an express warning against confusing his own senses of the words *naturalis* and *socialis* with those in Hobbes.

[7] I. iv. 54, 55. 'Ipsi misanthropi,' he adds in § 60, 'si extra societatem constituti forent, essent miseri.'

This analysis of human nature and society incorporates a good deal of Aristotelian doctrine; in fact, Thomasius accepts Aristotle's *dictum* that man is φύσει πολιτικὸν ζῷον,[1] and his remarks about man's unfitness for a solitary life, God's gift of Eve to Adam, and the subsequent development of the life of the family,[2] might lead one to expect a purely historical account of the origins of the state. Yet, although he had maintained that man is naturally social, and by equating the law of nature with the will of God, the supreme Lawgiver, and insisting that man is never independent of God, had laid a surer foundation than Pufendorf for the genuinely legal force of natural law, his conclusion was a contractarian system practically identical with Pufendorf's. For although the state itself is a *societas naturalis*,[3] yet man's natural *socialitas* is merely an *inclinatio* for a life in society, which is only called *societas* when it has been *in actum deducta*.[4]

Following Scholastic tradition, in fact, Thomasius maintains that it is not inconsistent with acceptance of Aristotle's doctrine to hold that man is brought into the state not by nature alone, but also by external agencies. The state differs from wedlock and the family, which result from the operation of a natural instinct, in that men are driven into political society by the fear of harm from other men.[5] Man, if naturally sociable, is also naturally a lover of freedom; he dislikes subordination to others, and the fear of punishment is hardly enough to compel him to obey his rulers. Yet the man who becomes a citizen must sacrifice his natural liberty, and submit to the commands of an authority which holds the powers of life and death over him, and by whose orders he may be bidden to do things he naturally finds distasteful.[6] For all the natural sociability of the elements which compose it, the state, in fact, involves an artificial union of wills and forces[7] which naturally belong to free individuals. As in Pufendorf, there are two *pacta* and a *decretum*: the first contract is between individuals, hitherto living in natural freedom, by which they agree to form a perpetual union as fellow citizens; and this contract must be unanimous, for any one who disagrees remains outside the state which is to be formed.[8] Then comes the *decretum*, in order to

---

[1] III. vi. 7.　　[2] I. i. 28–34.　　[3] III. vi. 7.　　[4] I. iv. 56.

[5] Owing to the fall of man and the appearance of sin; there is an echo of Augustinian doctrine here.　　[6] III. vi. 22–23.

[7] § 28. What Thomasius is here trying to express is, in effect, the distinction between society and the purely legal organization of the state.

[8] Unanimity is required in the original contract of union, but majority rule

decide on the form of government to be introduced, and thirdly the second contract, by which the government, whether of one man or of a plurality of men, promises to protect and defend its subjects, who on their part promise obedience and submission.[1]

In his later work Thomasius seems to be aware of the difficulties that beset his political theory, and he tends to shift his ground in a more definitely individualist direction. The state of nature is the crux of the question. If, as Thomasius declares, it is really social, there seems to be no use at any rate for the first contract (the social contract of union); yet if we omit this, and (waiving historical improbabilities) imagine men, already living a social existence, but under no government, proceeding direct to the contract of submission, there immediately arises the problem of the dissentient minority. It is also open to question whether the *socialitas* of the state of nature, in which men's actions are governed by obedience to the laws of nature or of God,[2] is consistent with the individual liberty also ascribed to the state of nature, in which men follow their own discretion in all things.[3] It may be replied that the law of nature is distinct from the laws of the state, and that it is only from the latter that men are free in the state of nature; but this weakens the status of natural law as genuine law, and if it can be disregarded in practice with impunity (and men must be able to disregard it if they are to be called free, unless their freedom is of the special kind that is equivalent to compulsion, like that in Winthrop[4] or Rousseau), it is reduced to mere moral obligation.[5]

At any rate, in his *Fundamenta Juris Naturae et Gentium* Thomasius insists much less on the *socialitas* of the state of nature, and while claiming to pursue a *media via inter Hobbesianos et Scholastico-Aristotelicos*, he declares that the state of nature is strictly speaking neither a condition of war nor a condition of peace, but a *confusum chaos ex utroque*, which has more the character of war than of peace.[6] Consistently with this decided shift in an individualist direction, he raises the further question, if man is

---

is defended where the governing body is a *concilium* on the ground that 'commodior alia litium et dissensuum evitandorum ratio haberi non potest, nisi statutum est, quota pars concilii consentiens requiratur ad repraesentandam voluntatem universitatis' (*Inst. Jur. Div.* III. vi. 64). This at least recognizes that the majority principle (as Burke later pointed out; see below, p. 194) is an arbitrary one.

[1] §§ 29–31.
[2] *Inst. Jur. Div.* I. ii. 50.
[3] Ibid. III. vi. 22.
[4] Cf. above, p. 88.
[5] On this weakness of Thomasius cf. Gierke, *Nat. Law* (tr. Barker), ii. 288.
[6] *Fund. J. N. et G.* I. iii. 55.

impelled towards a political existence by natural desire, how this natural desire is distinguished from external fear; in answer to this he concludes that the *causa primaria* of the state is fear, and reasserts his doctrine that states are *exstructae per duplex pactum et unum decretum.*[1] At the same time he is aware of the historical uncertainty of the contract theory; it is doubtful, he admits, whether states were first formed *ita subito et uno quasi continuo actu* by the innocent taking deliberate action to safeguard themselves against the wicked. It may well have been the wicked themselves (as in the theory of Thrasymachus) rather than the innocent who formed the first state; but if the origin of the state is monarchical and founded in violence, *cadunt ista duo pacta et decretum!*[2] In the end, therefore, we get the impression that Thomasius began by constructing an elaborate formal theory of the state, but that then, though he realized both its internal inconsistency and its inapplicability to reality, he was incapable of the reconstruction, if not the total abandonment of his original principles that the situation really required.

The work of Hert (Hertius), an eminent jurist in Germany in the late seventeenth and early eighteenth centuries, and professor of law at Giessen, may perhaps be taken as a sample of the many secondary figures in the history of contractarian thought during this period. His argument is largely derivative; some pages, for example, are taken up with quotations from Grotius, Pufendorf, and other authorities on the subject of *socialitas*, which is upheld against Hobbes's theory of the state of nature as a state of war, and is said to be the foundation of the rules of the law of nature.[3] Farther on the state is defined as a society composed of many men, joined together by their mutual compacts (*societatem multorum hominum, mutuis eorundem pactis conflatam*) and provided with power to make use of the force of individuals for the sake of a quiet and happy life.[4] The terms of the pact which is the necessary origin of society can be known, Hert continues, if we imagine the state of nature outside civil society. First of all there must be a compact between individuals by which they agree to live together and join

[1] Ibid. III. vi. 2.

[2] Ibid, §§ 3, 6. We cannot imagine a place for the contracts, he adds, *in constitutione Reipublicae Nimrodianae et Romanae.*

[3] J. N. Hertius, *Commentationum atque Opusculorum de . . . Argumentis* (Frankfort, 1737, but written some years previously), I. i, pp. 61 ff., 78 ff. On p. 71 we are told that 'socialitas fons est notionum in natura positarum'.

[4] Ibid., p. 286.

their wills and forces. The effect of this contract is that they become as it were one person or one body (*ut paciscentes fiant una quasi persona seu unum corpus*). A number of quotations are given in support of this, but Hert goes less far than Pufendorf, much less far than Huber, in ascribing real personality to the product of the social contract, which he says would be a mere imperfect and formless embryo if there did not supervene the second contract, of government, which is the force that holds it together.[1] Between the two contracts comes a *consultatio et decretum de forma regiminis*; the second contract transfers the wills and forces of all to one man or assembly. Formless as was the intermediate stage between the two contracts, everybody could then take part in the decision about the future government; but in case of disagreement, he adds, the opinion of the majority carries the day, for it was so agreed by the first pact, though apparently this was only a tacit agreement.[2] Hert's theory is clearly more biased in the direction of absolutism than that of some of his contemporaries, and perhaps its main interest to us today is as an illustration of the varying conclusions which could be drawn, by slight alterations of emphasis, from the same basic presuppositions. This is not surprising, considering that the whole contractarian apparatus was an imaginary construction, and that the state of nature, which lay at the root of all theories of this type, was constant only in the negative quality of difference from civil society and the absence of positive laws and sanctions. Of positive attributes (war, peace, sociability, or what not) it could with almost equal plausibility be given whatever suited the purposes of the writer.

The theory of J. H. Boehmer, another eminent jurist of the early eighteenth century, and like Thomasius professor of law at Halle, is of some interest in this connexion, because in him we have a man of even more definitely absolutist tendencies, who seems to have found the contract theory awkward and improbable, yet was unable to get rid of it, and so endeavoured to explain away or water down many of its customarily libertarian implications. He declares at the outset that the proper function of men is to live together in peace and tranquillity, and that the rule, or *norma*, by which men are naturally cemented together (*qua homines inter se naturaliter sunt conglutinati*),[3] is called the law of nature. It is a real

---

[1] Hertius, op. cit., p. 287. [2] p. 288.
[3] J. H. Boehmer, *Introductio in Ius Publicum Universale* (1709), *Pars Generalis*, i. 23.

and binding obligation to preserve peace, recognized by intuition (*in hominum cordibus scripta*);[1] and consequently, though men are naturally free, there are limits to natural liberty, in that no one may infringe the rule that binds them to respect each other's peace.[2]

From this Boehmer passes to consideration of the foundations of the state. The law of nature itself, he maintains, involves no absolute necessity for men to live in states; the law of nature would favour political life, especially if there were no other way of securing peace, but he cannot admit that nature itself is the *causa principalis* of the formation of civil society: an examination of human nature shows the contrary. Even within states peace is often broken, and heavy penalties are necessary to keep men obedient to the laws of the state. Still less is the origin of states to be found in *indigentia humana*. Hobbes and Pufendorf, different though their theories were, were probably right, he concludes, in making the state artificial in origin.[3]

In proceeding to an examination of the implications of the state, Boehmer adopts the current individualist tradition of treating it as on a par with any other *societas*, which is formed by the union of a number of wills for a common purpose, thus producing a *nexus* or *vinculum* which holds together and preserves the resulting *corpus morale* and directs it to its appointed end.[4] This union of wills is made by agreement (*consensu*), which may be express or tacit; the *societas* thus created, he adds, may be either equal or unequal.[5] In applying these principles to the formation of political societies, Boehmer adopts a less doctrinaire attitude than many contemporary contractarians, and his political theory as a whole is marked with touches of realism which make it fit less neatly into the formal structure of the contract theory. He recognizes, for example, that states may be formed by the descendants of a common stock who live together, and while maintaining that they are united *tacito aliquo pacto*,[6] he admits that a body of primitive men must have been *admodum rudis*, so that it is hardly possible to pretend that they can everywhere have made explicit social contracts. The fact remains that they apparently did unite together,

---

[1] Ibid., § 29.   [2] Ibid., § 38.

[3] Ibid., *Pars Specialis*, I. i. 3–7, 8 ff.

[4] Ibid. ii. 1, 2. On the word *morale* cf. above, p. 123; it will be observed that it has now become a mere technical expression for a corporate body, without any reference to the idea of moral personality with which it was associated in Pufendorf.   [5] Ibid., §§ 3, 4.   [6] Ibid., ii. 7.

so that we must assume some contract; but it can only have been a tacit one, and a very weak one at that (*valde inerme*), because nobody who wanted to withdraw from the community could be prevented from doing so.[1] It is also unlikely that they proceeded to create more stable conditions by erecting a government through any express compact, because the turbulent freedom of the state of nature in which they were living as individuals is incompatible with the formality of such a compact.[2]

The real origins of *imperium*, the *vinculum arctius* by which political states are controlled, are to be found, Boehmer continues, partly in violence, when some one broke in on the community, and having won the support of some, compelled the rest to submit because resistance was impossible, and partly in the gradual acquiescence in and confirmation of the sovereignty of the man who thus obtained supreme control.[3] Those who say that God confers sovereignty immediately on rulers, he continues, lay a more solid foundation for government, but they show ignorance of morals, for government is of human origin, though God approves of its institution.[4] Boehmer cannot agree with Hobbes, then, that there is not even a tacit contract between ruler and people,[5] nor, on the other hand, can he accept Huber's theory that the original contract of individuals results in the immediate production of a democracy.[6] In defining the state Boehmer provides, as alternatives, for either tacit or express pacts;[7] the powers of a government, he says, may be limited by express pacts, and it can also be determined *ex pactis* whether a monarchy be elective or hereditary.[8] One gets the impression, however, that he added these clauses largely for formal completeness, and that it was only the dominance of the current apparatus of contractarian phraseology, which was

[1] J. H. Boehmer, *Introductio in Ius Publicum Universale, Pars Specialis*, ii. 10.

[2] § 13; cf. § 10: 'vix est ut expressum pactum ubique fingi possit, ob tantam animorum dissensionem.' This suggests that the law of nature which enjoined peace was seldom heeded, or, more probably, that Boehmer never thought of the state of nature as an historical era, but adopted the conception of the law of nature to express what he believed to be the implications of human nature and its faculty of reason.

[3] § 14. Government rests on consent (*ex condicto*), he admits in § 17, but this does not consist of a formal contract of subjection, but is *magis ex patientia et taciturnitate longi temporis*.

[4] Ibid., §§ 24–26.   [5] § 21.   [6] § 23.

[7] c. iii, § 1. His definition of a state is 'coetus seu complexus hominum sub imperio pactis vel expressis vel tacitis unitus, tutioris vel tranquillioris vitae gratia'.

[8] Ibid., §§ 30, 31.

common to the whole school of natural law, that made him conceive of the state as an artificially and contractually constructed
compound. Every one agreed that its construction involved one
or more contracts, but Boehmer's keener sense of historical reality
prevented him from accepting the idea that these were formal or
actual, and he fell back, therefore, on the idea of tacit contract.

It must have been difficult, if not impossible, for any one
brought up in the contractarian traditions that were current all
over Europe in the seventeenth and eighteenth centuries to rise
clear of its characteristic individualist attitude to politics. Leibniz,
for instance, though he started in principle from the idea of the
community as a whole, nevertheless argued that allegiance was
based on a pact—a promise made by every subject of the state to
obey its laws and legal decisions—and that this was the justification
for punishment.[1] Even Montesquieu, the oft-proclaimed herald
of the historical school which was to sweep away the fictions of the
social contract,[2] though it is true that he does not say in so many
words that the state is founded in contract, conforms to the same
notion that the individual is prior to the community, and that the
state is created by a union of particular wills.[3]

Frederick the Great himself, who was no believer in democracy,
wrote at some length on the errors of princes, and their mistaken
idea that God created men simply to be the instruments and
ministers of their unregulated passions. Rather, he maintained,
men submitted themselves to a fellow citizen not 'pour être les
martyrs de ses caprices et les jouets de ses fantaisies: mais qu'ils
ont choisi celui d'entre eux qu'ils ont cru le plus juste pour les
gouverner, le meilleur pour leur servir de père, . . . enfin l'homme
le plus propre à représenter le corps de l'État, et en qui la souve-
raine puissance put servir d'appui aux lois et à la justice, et non de
moyen pour commettre impunément les crimes et pour exercer la

---

[1] G. W. Leibniz, *Methodi Novi Discendae Docendaeque Jurisprudentiae*, ii.
19 (in *Opera Omnia* (ed. Dutens, Geneva, 1768), IV. iii. 186). Cf. also ibid.,
§ 71 (p. 211). The same individualist assumption that the state is an artificial
construction is implied in his definition in *Caesarini Fürstenerii Tractatus de
Jure Suprematus*, c. x (in *Opera*, IV. iii. 357). Cf. Gierke, *Nat. Law* (tr. Barker),
i. 104, ii. 296.

[2] Cf. Sir F. Pollock, *History of the Science of Politics* (new edn. 1911), p. 86.

[3] Cf. *De L'Esprit des Lois*, i, c. 3, where we read that *l'état civil* is a *réunion
des volontés*. 'Les forces particulières ne peuvent se réunir sans que toutes les
volontés se réunissent.' In c. 2 he speaks of the sway of the law of nature 'avant
l'établissement des sociétés'; at the same time he condemns Hobbes's theory as
unreasonable, on the ground that men have a natural attraction for as well as fear
of one another.

tyrannie'.[1] He expressed the same sentiments in a work written forty years later, where, after describing the condition of primitive men as one of 'abrutissement', he suggested that 'violences' and 'pillages' led to a union of families, which was the origin of laws, 'qui enseignent aux sociétés à préférer l'intérêt général au bien particulier'. He uses the very phrase 'social compact' itself, saying that the 'grande vérité, qu'il faut agir envers les autres comme nous voudrions qu'ils se comportassent envers nous, devient le principe des lois et du pacte social'.[2]

By the middle of the eighteenth century, when even hereditary despots had become benevolent, political theorists were beginning to insist more and more on the rights of man and the popular side of the contract of government. While contractual absolutists maintained that at the formation of the state the people made a total surrender of their freedom, others had always insisted that when men entered the state they only surrendered what was necessary for the safety of the whole. Much of the history of the contract theory, in fact, is concerned with the struggle to secure from the power of the government either freedom of conscience, as with the *Monarchomachi*, or, as in Locke, the rights of property. In time there grew up the idea that some, at any rate, of the rights of man were inalienable and inviolable, so that the people, instead of making a simple contract of submission to their ruler, were described as free to choose between a variety of alternatives in disposing of the authority over their members constituted by the contract of union.

Formal and doctrinaire as is much of his system, this is very apparent in the political theory of Christian Wolff. It will be remembered that *societas* (partnership) was one of the consensual contracts of Roman Law:[3] Wolff, defining *societas*, repeats this, adding that the word is used not only of the contract but also of

---

[1] Frederick II, *Considérations sur l'état présent du corps politique de l'Europe* (1738), in *Works* (Berlin, 1848), viii. 25–26.

[2] *Essai sur les formes de gouvernement et sur les devoirs des souverains* (1777), in *Works*, ix. 196. If, in accordance with the title, sovereigns have duties as well as rights, the contract of government is implied in his further remarks that as laws cannot be maintained without an executive government, 'ce fut l'origine des magistrats, que le peuple élut et auxquels il se soumit'. The social contract is also alluded to several times (e.g. in phrases such as 'citoyens auxquels nous lie le pacte social') in his *Lettres sur l'amour de la patrie* (ibid., p. 221).

The Encyclopaedist Baron d'Holbach similarly argued (1773) in favour of a *pacte tacite*; cf. P. Janet, *Histoire de la Science Politique* (3rd edn., Paris, 1887), ii. 490.　　　　　　　　　　　　　　　　　　　　[3] Cf. above, p. 45.

the men themselves who are thus associated together for some purpose, and that those who enter into the contract of association are called *socii* or members of the society (*qui societatem contrahunt, socii, vel membra societatis, vocantur*).[1] Among the attributes of a *societas* is the right that belongs to its members to compel a fellow member to observe his obligations, and this right of the whole to enforce the obedience of individuals, which arises out of the contract or quasi-contract of association, is *imperium*.[2] It is the contract which determines the rights and duties of individuals, and its terms may vary in a number of ways. There may be a simple contract (*si societas simpliciter contrahitur*), in which case the *societas* is *aequalis*; all have the same rights and duties, and are therefore equal, and nobody has any special privilege (*praerogativa*). Or it may be expressly agreed that one of the members is to have special duties not binding on the others, or special rights not enjoyed by the others; in this case the members are unequal and the *societas* is called *inaequalis*.[3]

The state for Wolff is simply a species of the genus *societas*, so that when he comes to deal with political questions he applies to the state the distinctions and conclusions already arrived at for *societas* in general. The particular purpose for which states are formed is to obtain *vitae sufficientia*, peace and security, which are unobtainable by individuals; the method, a pact entered upon by free individuals.[4] The resulting *imperium*, or *potestas civilis*, is a product of the pact (*ex pacto oritur*) by which the state was constituted, and originally, he adds, is in the hands of the people (*penes populum*).[5] When a state is to be formed, therefore, the people, that is to say all the members collectively (*populus sive universi*), must agree among themselves on the course to be followed. A number of alternatives are open to them: they may either retain sovereignty themselves, or hand it over to a single person, or to several jointly; they may hand it over entire, or only in part, conditionally or unconditionally, revocably or irrevocably, for a fixed period of time, or for life, or indefinitely, and so on.[6] Fundamental laws and other stipulations may or may not be laid down, and various forms of constitution are possible in accordance with the various alternative dispositions of political authority.[7]

[1] C. Wolff, *Institutiones Juris Naturae et Gentium* (Halle, 1750), part III, sect. i, c. i, § 836. He says that *societas* is a *pactum, vel quasi pactum*, by which he presumably intends to cover what other writers treated as a 'tacit contract'.
[2] Ibid. x, § 838.   [3] Ibid., § 839.   [4] Ibid. III. ii, c. i, §§ 972, 977.
[5] Ibid., § 979; cf. § 982.   [6] Ibid., § 982.   [7] Ibid., §§ 984, 990 ff.

Wolff's treatment of all this is dispassionate and formal, and his political theory does not differ fundamentally from that of Pufendorf or Thomasius or any other of the contractarian jurists of the previous fifty or a hundred years. Nevertheless there is far more emphasis than before on the part of the people in the institution of government, and the consequences of reducing the state to the level of a contractual association of free individuals are brought out with uncompromising and systematic thoroughness. If such doctrines of popular sovereignty were laid down as legal dogmas by professional jurists, and even hereditary monarchs acknowledged their responsibilities to their subjects, there is little wonder that political propagandists were soon ready to issue whole lists of the rights of man, and demand that all government should respect them.

We have dealt so far mainly with German writers, but the ideas they developed were widely current in other countries in the eighteenth century. The French-Swiss thinker Vattel, for instance, who was largely a follower of Wolff, was of great influence in spreading the doctrines of the natural-law school of political theory, in America as well as in Europe.[1] The characteristic individualism of the contractual school of thought is apparent at the very outset of his work, when he defines nations or states as 'Sociétés d'hommes unis ensemble pour procurer leur salut et leur avantage, à forces réunies'.[2] Man, he continues, is not self-sufficient; moreover, his faculties of reason and speech indicate that intercourse is natural to him. 'Voilà d'où l'on déduit la société naturelle établie entre tous les hommes.'[3] There is, then, a natural society among men, which arises apart from any deliberate action; but circumstances make it necessary to establish a government, and the state is created by a definite 'acte d'association civile ou politique'. This is in effect a social contract, although individuals were already living a kind of social existence; its terms are that 'chaque citoïen se soumet à l'autorité du corps entier, dans tout ce qui peut intéresser le bien commun. Le Droit de tous sur chaque membre appartient donc essentiellement au Corps Politique, à l'État.'[4]

---

[1] Cf. Sir E. Barker's Introd. to Gierke, *Nat. Law*, i, pp. xi, xlvii.

[2] E. de Vattel, *Le Droit des Gens ou Principes de la Loi Naturelle* (1758; facsimile edn. pub. by Carnegie Institution of Washington, 1916), Introd., § 1. In § 2 he adds that such a society, having its own affairs and interests, deliberating and making decisions in common becomes 'une Personne morale, qui a son Entendement et sa volonté propre, et qui est capable d'obligations et de droits'.

[3] Ibid., § 10.

[4] Ibid. 1. i. 2.

This done, the people as a whole can choose between a variety of alternative forms of government, either retaining sovereign authority themselves, and so constituting a democracy, or entrusting it to one man or a few.

Vattel is here a close follower of Wolff, and it will be observed how the contract of government, which was as essential to the schemes of Pufendorf or other more absolutist contractarians of the seventeenth century as the preliminary contract of union, has by now practically dropped out of sight, and the erection of government has become in effect an act of the sovereign people. It is only a short step from this position to that of Rousseau.[1] In other ways also there is visible an increasing readiness to accept to the full the consequences of a thoroughgoing individualism. Vattel held, for example, that the children of citizens become citizens by *consentement tacite*, but every man is naturally free, and when he comes of age he can consider whether or not he will join the society into which he was born. He has the right to expatriate himself, though Vattel urges that he should exercise it sparingly, for he owes a debt of gratitude to his country and should remain a member of it if possible.[2] This closely resembles Locke's theory, but Locke had insisted that a full member of a community was 'perpetually and indispensably obliged to be and remain unalterably a subject to it'.[3]

[1] The more orthodox system was still holding its ground, however. Only a few years before Vattel another Swiss jurist, Burlamaqui, had propounded a system of politics which was closely based on the Pufendorf tradition. Civil society arose 'par le moyen des conventions', which consist of the usual three stages: (*a*) the first *convention*, by which individuals unite and form a single body, (*b*) an *ordonnance* which determines the form of government, (*c*) another *convention* between the government decided on and the subjects. The resulting state is to be regarded 'comme un Corps, comme une Personne morale, dont le souverain estl e Chef, ou lat ête, et les particuliers les membres'. (J. J. Burlamaqui, *Principes du Droit Politique*, 1751, ii. 1–3; iv. 3–6, 10, 15.)

About the same time the Irishman Francis Hutcheson, who became Professor of Moral Philosophy at Glasgow, expounded an essentially similar doctrine, in which legitimate civil power is founded on consent or convention, under the usual form of two contracts and an intervening decree. Hutcheson admits that it is not probable that 'these three regular steps' were actually taken in creating the constitutions of existing states, 'yet 'tis plain that in every just constitution of power there is some such transaction as implicitly contains the force of all the three'. He also defends at some length the resulting tacit contract by which posterity is bound. (F. Hutcheson, *System of Moral Philosophy* (Glasgow, 1755), ii. 4; iii. 4, 5.) Hutcheson is commonly regarded as a pioneer of the 'Scottish school' of philosophy, and in ethics was a precursor of the Utilitarians; but his politics are mainly derivative, and he seems to have ignored the arguments of Hume (which Bentham subsequently adapted to the utilitarian standpoint; see below, Chap. XII).

[2] Vattel, op. cit., §§ 212, 220.   [3] *Second Treatise*, § 121.

It is difficult to decide clearly how far the contractarian writers of the seventeenth and eighteenth centuries believed that their theories were literally true. The whole method and approach of the juristic writers is often so remote from reality that one seems to be threading the ramifications of a formal system rather than an account of the origins of any actual states; yet their qualifications and reservations, their tacit contracts or quasi-contracts, their replies to possible historical objections, undoubtedly suggest that they were anxious to persuade their readers that their theories were compatible with history. At the same time their contracts were primarily deduced from their individualist presuppositions, and these in turn were the consequences of their adaptation to political purposes of the terminology of Roman private law, by which the state became a *societas*, or contractual partnership of individuals, and the contract of government was equated with the Roman contract of *mandatum*.

This mixture of history and logic is well illustrated in the work of the eighteenth-century Frenchman Goguet.[1] The condition of primitive men 'au sortir du déluge', he writes, resembled that of the animals, in that different families lived separately from one another.[2] When in course of time families united, 'quelle qu'en soit la cause', this can only have occurred 'par un accord de volontés sur certains objets'. If one regards society from this point of view, it logically follows that it must have been based on agreements,[3] which formed its first laws, and were in turn the origin of all subsequent regulations. But while contract is the necessary logical basis of a society formed by a union of individuals, we need not suppose that the first states arose through express contracts formally solemnized.

Il n'a pas été nécessaire que ni les premières conventions, ni les conditions qui leur servoient de fondement, fussent expresses. Il a suffi . . . qu'elles aient été tacites. Telle aura été, par exemple, la règle, de ne point enlever à autrui ce dont il avoit l'usage et la possession. . . . Il n'a pas fallu de solemnités pour établir ces règles et ces maximes. Elles doivent leur origine à ces sentiments de justice et d'équité, que la Providence a gravés dans le cœur de tous les hommes.[4]

[1] The reader will note the resemblance of what follows to the political theory of Boehmer discussed above.
[2] A. Y. Goguet, *De l'Origine des Loix, des Arts et des Sciences* (Paris, 1758), Introd.   [3] Ibid., bk. i, *ad init.*
[4] Ibid. The first laws, he continues, were therefore not the result of deliberation confirmed by solemn acts, but arose naturally 'par l'effet de conventions

We return, in fact, to the moral principles of which the law of nature was the embodiment; but if the actual origins of states are to be sought in natural growth, and the social contract is demanded not by history but by logic, for which (in defence to history) a tacit contract will suffice to preserve the contractual principle; then, it must be confessed, the contract theory has already lost much of its force. It was on these lines, indeed, that it fought a rearguard action all through the nineteenth century against the attacks of the historical school; but if the contract is reduced to a mere implication, we may well inquire whether the principles from which it is supposed to follow cannot be stated better in some other way, which will not involve its undeniably unhistorical associations, or whether indeed the contract is in fact a necessary consequence of those principles at all.

tacites. . . . L'autorité politique n'a été elle-même établie que par une convention tacite entre ceux qui s'y sont soumis et ceux à qui on l'a déférée.'

XI

ROUSSEAU, FICHTE, KANT, HEGEL

THE social contract is popularly connected with the name of Rousseau above all other writers, largely no doubt on account of the title of his most famous work. In a sense, as we shall see, he was the great popularizer of the ideas which had been worked out by the contractarian lawyers who preceded him, but in the end he was far from being an apostle of an individualist theory of the state. Like Hobbes, with whose principles, different though they were from his own, he had close affinities, he introduced a new and disturbing element into the stream of contractual theory, which it would hardly be going too far to say contributed most powerfully to its ultimate extinction.

In his early *Discourse on the Origin of Inequality among Men* (1755) he gives us a quasi-historical account of the development of political organization, though he admits that it is hypothetical and may indeed be imaginary. The original state of nature, according to Rousseau, was neither a Hobbesian war of all against all, nor a Lockian abode of peace and goodwill; it was just a condition of brutish isolation, in which men were physically much stronger than they are today. Society developed by the family widening into the tribe, a nomadic existence giving place to fixed residence, and the consequent acquisition of property.[1] Inventions and the arts followed, but with them grew passions and needs, and then came vices and disorders, vanity, jealousy and self-assertion, violence and outrage. States and civil government were created by the adroitness of the rich, who imposed upon the poor. They pretended that if instead of turning their forces against each other, men collected them in a supreme power to govern by wise laws, the weak would be guarded from oppression, the ambitious would be restrained, and all would be defended in peace from the attacks of their common enemies. The rich thus safeguarded their possessions, but they did so at the expense of the poor, who were virtually enslaved.

---

[1] 'The first man', says Rousseau, 'who, having enclosed a piece of ground, bethought himself of saying *This is mine*, and found people simple enough to believe him, was the real founder of civil society' (*Discourse*, ii).

Though such have been the effects of the establishment of government, yet government did not begin with arbitrary power; 'this is the depravation, the extreme term, of government, and brings it back, finally, to just the law of the strongest, which it was originally designed to remedy'. Rousseau disagrees with Pufendorf's idea that men may divest themselves of their liberty in favour of other men, and it would be 'unreasonable to suppose that men at first threw themselves irretrievably and unconditionally into the arms of an absolute master, and that the first expedient which proud and unsubdued men hit upon for their common security was to run headlong into slavery'. On the contrary, there is a 'fundamental compact underlying all government', and we may 'regard the establishment of the political body as a real contract between the people and the chiefs chosen by them: a contract by which both parties bind themselves to observe the laws therein expressed, which form the ties of their union'. Thus, while the people 'concentrated all their wills in one', 'the magistrate, on his side, binds himself to use the power he is entrusted with only in conformity with the intention of his constituents, to maintain them all in the peaceable possession of what belongs to them, and to prefer on every occasion the public interest to his own'.

Such a constitution, unfortunately, led to unavoidable abuses, and in various ways legitimate power was converted into arbitrary tyranny, until at length 'despotism, gradually raising up its hideous head and devouring everything that remained sound and untainted in any part of the State, would . . . trample on both the laws and the people, and establish itself on the ruins of the republic'. Inequality is now complete: it involves a 'return to the law of the strongest, and so to a new state of nature, differing from that we set out from: for the one was a state of nature in its first purity, while this is the consequence of excessive corruption'. The despot is now in power 'only so long as he remains the strongest', for 'the contract of government is . . . completely dissolved by despotism', and he has no right to complain if his subjects rise against him.[1]

Insurrection, in fact, is the only remedy for this last phase of human misery; and if Rousseau has gained the reputation of being an advocate of revolution, it rests on his early *Discourse*, assisted, no doubt, by the famous sentence at the beginning of the *Contrat Social*, that 'Man is born free; and everywhere he is in chains'.[2] This, indeed, reflects the same attitude—that man has sacrificed

[1] *Discourse*, ii.   [2] *Contrat Social* (1762), i. 1.

his natural liberty and been defrauded of the advantages he
expected to gain in return; but in the *Contrat Social* Rousseau
proceeds to advocate, not revolution, but a particular form of
political organization which can make government legitimate.
There are great differences, therefore, between the conclusions of
the *Contrat Social* and those of the *Discourse*. One of the striking
features of Rousseau's political philosophy is that while he employs
the terminology he inherited from the school of natural law, he
abandons much of the doctrine it enshrined. In the *Contrat Social*,
indeed, he distinguishes between force and right,[1] but in the
Preface to the *Discourse* he rejects the whole tradition of natural
law as unintelligible and useless, and discovers in the human soul
'two principles prior to reason, one of them deeply interesting us
in our own welfare and preservation, and the other exciting a
natural repugnance at seeing any other sensible being, and particularly any of our own species, suffer pain or death. It is from the
agreement and combination', he continues, 'which the understanding is in a position to establish between these two principles,
without its being necessary to introduce that of sociability,[2] that
all the rules of natural right appear to me to be derived'. Natural
right, then, means no more to Rousseau than it did to Hobbes; it
is merely another name for natural instinct. 'Man's first feeling
was that of his own existence,' Rousseau tells us, 'and his first care
that of self-preservation';[3] and observation of the behaviour of
other men taught him that for them as well as for himself the sole
motive was the love of well-being.[4]

These principles are retained in the *Contrat Social*, but they lead
in a new direction. The natural man's 'first law', we now read, 'is
to provide for his own preservation, his first cares are those which
he owes to himself';[5] and it is only when the state of nature has

---

[1] *C.S.* i. 3.

[2] This is clearly aimed at the natural-law school (cf. p. 121, above). At the
same time it will be observed that Rousseau differs from Hobbes (and agrees
with Spinoza) in recognizing the existence of natural sympathy in man. Rousseau
sometimes appears, like Hobbes, to treat man as essentially self-regarding, but
he also admits the existence of an altruistic element which conflicts with this
natural selfishness. According to Rousseau, a man's repugnance at seeing others
suffer is not, as for Hobbes, only a disguised form of selfishness, but he can feel
'a genuine impulse of compassion', which leads him never to 'hurt any other
man, nor even any sentient being, except on those lawful occasions on which
his own preservation is concerned and he is obliged to give himself the preference'. His own interest, however, comes first. (*Discourse*, Preface.)

[3] *Discourse*, ii.   [4] Ibid.

[5] *C.S.* i. 2.

been changed into the civil state that justice is substituted for instinct and the 'voice of duty' takes the place of 'physical impulses and the right of appetite'.[1] Greek sophists had used similar language, and concluded that justice and morality were merely conventional—an artificial (and intolerable) imposition on man's natural freedom. Rousseau, however, while recognizing that justice and duty are essentially social products—they are meaningless except in the context of social relationships between man and man—is now far from maintaining that life in organized society marks a decline from a primitive 'natural' existence. On the contrary, society opens for men the prospects of an altogether preferable and nobler life.

Hobbes, starting from a similar basic view of human nature, proceeded to advocate submission to the power of a despot, because this was the only way to obtain security. For Rousseau, however, 'civil tranquillity' is an insufficient reward for the loss of natural liberty, since the miseries men will probably have to suffer at the hands of the despot and his ministers 'press harder on them than their own dissensions would have done. . . . Tranquillity is found also in dungeons', he remarks, 'but is that enough to make them desirable places to live in?'[2] Whatever the motive, he rejects entirely the theory that civil society was founded by an absolute surrender to arbitrary government. 'To renounce liberty is to renounce being a man, to surrender the rights of humanity and even its duties. . . . Such a renunciation is incompatible with man's nature', and 'it is an empty and contradictory convention that sets up, on the one side, absolute authority, and, on the other, unlimited obedience.'[3] Grotius says that a people can give itself to a king, but 'the gift is itself a civil act, and implies public deliberation', so that we must first know how a collection of individuals becomes a people. This involves the recurrent problem of the minority, and proves, he urges, that there must have been a 'prior convention'; for since each man is free in the state of nature, 'where, unless the election were unanimous, would be the obligation on the minority to submit to the choice of the majority? . . . The law of majority voting is itself something established by convention, and presupposes unanimity on one occasion at least.'[4]

To begin with, then, there must be a social contract, by which the state of nature is brought to an end; for we must suppose that men somehow reached the point at which they realized that in

[1] *C.S.* i. 8.   [2] *C.S.* i. 4.   [3] Ibid.   [4] *C.S.* i. 5.

isolation they were not strong enough to overcome the obstacles to survival, and that the only way to create a greater force was by aggregation. But 'the force and liberty of each man are the chief instruments of his self-preservation'; how, then, 'can he pledge them without harming his own interests? . . . The problem is to find a form of association which will defend and protect with the whole common force the person and goods of each associate, and in which each, while uniting himself with all, may still obey himself alone, and remain as free as before'.[1]

It was perhaps unfortunate that Rousseau stated his problem in these terms, for they seem to make it inherently insoluble,[2] and have misled a number of critics. If the self which is obeyed is the same as the self which obeys, and a man's freedom is to be literally the same after as before the contract, clearly there can be no government at all; there can be nothing but anarchy.[3] Yet, according to Rousseau, the answer to this problem is provided by a social contract which consists of 'the total alienation of each associate, together with all his rights[4] [i.e. natural powers] to the whole community'. Men will be prepared to make this surrender, whereas they would never voluntarily submit to a Hobbesian monarch, because 'as each gives himself absolutely, the conditions are the same for all; and, this being so, no one has any interest in making them burdensome to others', while 'each man, in giving himself to all, gives himself to nobody; and as there is no associate over whom he does not acquire the same right as he yields others over himself, he gains an equivalent for everything he loses, and an increase of force for the preservation of what he has'. If Rousseau had stopped short at this point, the problem as he stated it would still remain unsolved, for only if there were constant unanimity would every individual feel that he had gained more than he had surrendered. Some contractarians had been content with a contract by which individuals unanimously consented to submit for the future to the will of the majority, but for Rousseau (though this is in fact what his system amounts to in the end) this course was

---

[1] *C.S.* i. 6.

[2] But cf. below, p. 172, n. 1.

[3] We are confronted, in fact, with the same fundamental self-contradiction of extreme individualism as appears in J. S. Mill's remark quoted above (p. 139).

[4] In *C.S.* ii. 4 he says that 'Each man alienates . . . by the social contract only such part of his powers, goods and liberty as it is important for the community to control': but this amounts to the same thing, because 'the Sovereign is the sole judge of what is important'.

blocked by the stipulation that after the contract as well as before it every man should obey himself alone; this condition would obviously not be fulfilled in the case of a member of a minority who was coerced by the will of the majority.

Accordingly Rousseau translates the social contract into a submission by which 'each of us puts his person and all his power in common under the supreme direction of the general will'.[1] For 'at once, in place of the individual personality of each contracting party, this act of association creates a moral and collective body, composed of as many members as the assembly contains votes, and receiving from this act its unity, its common identity, its life and its will'. This notion, as the phraseology clearly shows, Rousseau borrowed from the natural-law philosophers who preceded him, but what exactly he meant by it is by no means clear,[2] and widely divergent interpretations have been put upon it. One school of thought, following the system of politics developed by Hegel, and in England by Bernard Bosanquet,[3] finds in the general will and its associated ideas a conception of great value, and maintains that Rousseau was essentially the forerunner of Hegelian idealism in politics, though his expression of it was hampered by the contractarian and individualist phraseology which was current in his age, and from which he was unable wholly to extricate himself. Other commentators, however, such as Mr. E. F. Carritt,[4] have found in the general will only a confused idea to which no precise meaning can be attached, and which in Rousseau only served to cloak his failure to solve the problem that he had set himself. According to Mr. Carritt, Rousseau's fundamental standpoint throughout was psychological hedonism, but he was a psychological hedonist 'of the altruistic or inconsistent type, like Mill', so that while what he ought to have tried to prove (though, of course, to prove it would have been impossible) was 'that it is always to my private advantage to obey the general will, . . . he spends his energy in establishing a different point, that the general will always leads to the "common good"'.[5]

---

[1] He had previously developed this idea in the *Discourse on Political Economy* (1755).

[2] If, as the post-Kantian idealists maintained, he meant that the state is as much a psychological reality as an individual person is (or even more so), he was really adapting the natural-law concept of a 'moral person' to new uses.

[3] Cf. *The Philosophical Theory of the State* (4th edn., 1923), esp. pp. 99 ff.

[4] In *Morals and Politics* (Oxford, 1935).

[5] Op cit., pp. 68, 69.

Rousseau is obliged to admit that, even after the contract has been made,

each individual, as a man, may have a particular will contrary or dissimilar to the general will which he has as a citizen. His particular interest may speak to him quite differently from the common interest. . . . In order, then, that the social compact may not be an empty formula, it tacitly includes the undertaking, which alone can give force to the rest, that whosoever refuses to obey the general will shall be compelled to do so by the whole body. This means nothing less than that he will be forced to be free.[1]

But if the basic motive of everybody is desire for his own pleasure, we are immediately confronted once more with the question of the minority: why are dissentient individuals obliged to obey—that is, why is it to their interest to do so? Rousseau's answer, according to Mr. Carritt, is that the general will 'only speaks when interests do not differ. It tells no lies because it can be asked no questions'.[2]

The general will is always in the right [says Rousseau] [because] to be really such, it must be general in its object as well as its essence; . . . it must both come from all and apply to all, and . . . it loses its natural rectitude when it is directed to some particular and determinate object. . . . Indeed, as soon as a question of particular fact or right arises . . . the matter becomes contentious. It is a case in which the individuals concerned are one party, and the public the other. . . . In such a case, it would be absurd to propose to refer the question to an express decision of the general will, which can be only the conclusion reached by one of the parties, and in consequence will be, for the other party, merely an external or particular will, inclined on this occasion to injustice and subject to error.[3]

In other words, the general will never damages individual interests because it never decides anything but non-contentious questions. When a conflict arises, and a disobedient citizen is 'forced to be free', force is applied by the 'prince' or executive government, to whom the general will delegates the decision in private disputes. Then why must we obey the executive? Apparently because it was appointed by the general will, which is a man's own will acting in his own interests; but this is just to push the difficulty one stage back, and then beg the question in the end.

[1] C.S. i. 7. Cf. his admission in iv. 1 that it is only 'as long as several men in assembly regard themselves as a single body' that they 'have a single will which is concerned in their common preservation and general well-being'.
[2] Morals and Politics, p. 70.   [3] C.S. ii. 4.

Moreover, a further difficulty is involved. The sovereign people can decree that there shall be an executive, but the general will is confined to general questions; how then can it make the particular decision to appoint certain persons to office? Rousseau's solution is simply a conjuring trick; on the analogy of the English House of Commons, which can resolve itself into Grand Committee, and thus 'from being at one moment a sovereign court, becomes at the next a mere commission', so 'without sensible change, and merely by virtue of a new relation of all to all, the citizens become magistrates and pass from general to particular acts, from legislation to the execution of the law'.[1]

The upshot of Rousseau's theory, then, according to this interpretation, is that he ultimately and inevitably fails to solve the insoluble problem he set himself at the outset. Instead of being 'as free as before', the citizen is compelled to obey the will of the majority, and although Rousseau paradoxically calls this making him free, the concept of the general will only confuses instead of clearing up the problem of the potential conflict between general and particular interests. If they clash, he is as helpless as if he were at the mercy of Leviathan, or even more so, for a popular may be even more tyrannical than a personal despotism, and Rousseau's specious language is calculated to encourage its pretensions.

Some of these charges go home, but to interpret Rousseau on these lines is to misunderstand his whole purpose. The mistake lies, I think, in taking too literally the wording of his statement of the problem—'to find a form of association . . . in which each . . . may still obey himself alone, and remain as free as before'. The implication of this is that Rousseau's primary object was to preserve the liberty enjoyed by individuals in the state of nature, and that he thought of the social contract as an historical event. On the contrary, with Rousseau, as with Hobbes, the contract was only a supposition, or assumption, whose function was to justify the existence of government. His starting-point, it is true, was individualist, but in the *Contrat Social* the whole emphasis is on the superiority of social life over the state of nature. And it turns out that in society a man is not simply 'as free as before': he loses his natural liberty, Rousseau tells us, and gains civil liberty instead,[2] and with it a right of property, guaranteed by the law, instead of

[1] *C.S.* iii. 17.
[2] Locke made the same point when he said that 'the end of law is not to abolish or restrain, but to preserve and enlarge freedom' (*Second Treatise*, § 57).

mere precarious possession, dependent on his own strength. More than this, the citizen gains 'moral liberty', which alone makes him his own master, whereas if a man is a prey to his appetites he is nothing but a slave. There can be no doubt that what Rousseau stresses is the benefit conferred by social life, not the need to try and preserve in society the values of the state of nature. Society emancipates and civilizes man, whereas in the state of nature he was only a limited and stupid brute.[1]

Rousseau, in fact, faces two ways. He begins with the individualist assumptions and phraseology of the school of natural law, but his conclusion is collectivist. The transition is effected by the concept of the general will, which on any interpretation is the crucial question in Rousseau. It is different from a man's individual or particular or private will.[2] It is different also from the will of all, which is only the sum of particular wills.[3] It is 'always right' (*droite*: perhaps 'direct' or 'straightforward' would be a more accurate translation) 'and always tends to the public advantage';[4] it is 'constant, unalterable and pure'.[5] How, then, can it be arrived at? In one place Rousseau seems to identify it with the will of the majority, for he tells us that though individual wills conflict, the plusses and minuses cancel out, and the resultant sum of these differences is the general will.[6] Elsewhere, however, we are told that when the people vote they should not consider whether they approve of a proposal or not, but only whether they judge it to be in accordance with the general will;[7] and that when the people deliberate, the general will only emerges if they are adequately informed, and are not influenced by being grouped in parties.[8] Rousseau also condemns representative government,[9] and maintains that the general will can only find expression in a small city-state where all the citizens meet and vote directly in a popular

---

[1] *Contrat Social*, i. 8. In the state of nature, after all, man's liberty was not by any means complete. Not only were his activities restricted by the extent of his own capacities, but he had to live under the inescapable conditions imposed by the laws of inorganic nature. He would not, however, have felt such natural restrictions as a loss of liberty, because they were impersonal and necessary. In a civil society governed in accordance with the *Contrat Social* a man will likewise accept human laws, because, applying equally to all alike, he will recognize that they also are impersonal and necessary. In his *Rousseau* (Cambridge, 1955), p. 288, Professor F. C. Green has recently suggested that, interpreted in this way, the phrase 'as free as before' need not present an insoluble contradiction. 'The true object of the *Contrat*', as he puts it, 'is to imitate by art what Nature has done so well.'   [2] *C.S.* i. 7.   [3] *C.S.* ii. 3.
     [4] Ibid.   [5] *C.S.* iv, 1.   [6] *C.S.* ii. 3.
     [7] *C.S.* iv. 2.   [8] *C.S.* ii. 3.   [9] *C.S.* iii. 15.

assembly. Even then, while 'the general will is always right, . . . the judgement guiding it is not always well informed', and there is no possibility of the people framing their own laws for themselves. They can do no more than ratify what is put before them by the Legislator.[1]

So, although there are places where Rousseau seems to be an ultra-democrat, attributing infallibility to the majority, on closer scrutiny it seems that the general will, while it springs from the people, is not necessarily a democratic idea at all. What makes the will general, he remarks, is not so much the number of voices as the common interest uniting them.[2] This is the clue to what lay in Rousseau's mind, and it points forward to Kant's conception of a rational will. Though he did not succeed in formulating it clearly, it seems that Rousseau was struggling to express the idea of a will for our own real interest, which may conflict with what we actually will at any particular moment. 'Our will is always for our own good, but we do not always see what that is',[3] and this is the reason why the will of all differs from the general will, and that men in their own interests are compelled to obey. We need not attribute to Rousseau the Hegelian metaphysic which, going farther than Kant, and equating the real with the rational, enables compulsion by any existing state to be identified with real liberty. Nevertheless, the ultimate significance of Rousseau in the history of political thought is as a precursor of a collectivist attitude to man's place in society rather than as a vindicator of individual liberty. Historians are less inclined than they used to be to emphasize Rousseau's importance as a source of inspiration for the French Revolution, but in any case one of its results was the dogma that nothing must stand in the way of the sovereign people, and the plebiscitary dictatorship of Napoleon foreshadowed the totalitarian régimes of the twentieth century.

Thus the significance of Rousseau's famous treatise belies the title he gave it. His social contract is no guarantee of the individual's natural rights; it leads instead to the sovereignty of the general will. In this, as in other respects, Rousseau resembles Hobbes,[4] and (again as in Hobbes) there is no second contract in Rousseau. In the course of history it was the governmental contract,

---

[1] *C.S.* ii. 6, 7.   [2] *C.S.* ii. 4.   [3] *C.S.* ii. 3.

[4] The social contract must be unanimous, dissentients being simply left outside, but once the state is established Rousseau repeats the old theory that residence implies consent (*C.S.* iv. 2).

rather than the social contract proper, which had acted as a check
on those in authority. For Rousseau, as for other collectivists,
there is no need to check the powers in the hands of the general
will. Provided it can find expression (and this, admittedly, is a
cardinal difficulty in Rousseau), it is infallible. It need give no
guarantees; it cannot hurt anyone;[1] it cannot even wish to lay on
anyone a burden not necessitated by the well-being of the community.[2] So, like Leviathan, it is sovereign, and cannot be divided
or alienated. It is true that an executive government, or magistracy,
must be established, but this is a mere delegation of functions,
not a separation of powers.[3] Its institution, he states definitely, is
not a contract, but an act of the sovereign people.[4] The contract
of government is thus jettisoned altogether, and through his
influence on Kant and Hegel Rousseau contributed powerfully
to the development of the idealist theory, which combined with
the historical school to discredit the social contract itself, and with
it the individualist theory of liberty. If Rousseau had been told
that he was sacrificing the individual to the state, he would, I feel
sure, have repudiated such a charge,[5] and in his *Discourse on
Political Economy* there is an eloquent passage in which he protests
against such a notion. Nor would he himself accept the view that
men's real interests are best secured by an enlightened dictatorship, although this is in fact what his doctrine was apt to lead to.

For some years, however, Rousseau's real significance was misunderstood. Burke regarded him as essentially a revolutionist, and
in the late eighteenth century the social contract continued to find
favour, and was associated with an even more extreme individualism. The Italian law-reformer Beccaria, for instance, after remarking that 'laws, which are or ought to be covenants between
free men, have generally been nothing but the instruments of the
passions of some few men, or the result of some accidental and
temporary necessity',[6] propounds the theory that men are naturally
free and that no one would gratuitously part with any of his own
liberty with a view to the public benefit. What a man would

---

[1] *C.S.* i. 7.   [2] *C.S.* ii. 4.   [3] *C.S.* ii. 2.   [4] *C.S.* iii. 16, 17.

[5] He might also say that the charge was 'wrongly put', which was his answer
to the question 'how a man can be free and yet constrained to conform to a will
which is not his own' (*C.S.* iv. 2). He added, in a characteristic paradox, that
'the citizen consents to all the laws, even to those which have been passed in
spite of his opposition, even to those which will punish him if he dares to break
them'.

[6] C. Beccaria, *Crimes and Punishments* (1764; tr. J. A. Farrer, 1880), c. 1.

naturally wish, if it were possible, would be a condition (like that to which some of the Greek sophists aspired) in which 'the covenants which bind others should not bind himself'.[1] Men grew 'tired of living isolated lives in a perpetual state of war, and of enjoying a liberty which the uncertainty of its tenure rendered useless'. Therefore they joined together in society, and sacrificed a part of their liberty 'in order to enjoy the remainder in security and quiet. The sum-total of all these portions of liberty . . . constitutes the sovereignty of a nation, and the sovereign is the lawful trustee and administrator of these portions. . . . Each would only place in the general deposit the least possible portion', just enough, that is, 'to protect it from the encroachment of individuals whose aim it ever is not only to recover from the fund their own deposit, but to avail themselves of that contributed by others'. Hence those who break the social contract incur punishment, the right to which is constituted by 'the aggregate of these least possible portions', and which becomes 'an abuse and not justice' if it goes beyond this limit. In particular, no government can rightly inflict capital punishment, because in the first place no one would surrender to others the right to kill him, and secondly, suicide being wrong, no one possesses such a right to surrender even if he would.[2]

Beccaria was avowedly a propagandist, but he rested his case for penal reform on an unqualified theory of enlightened selfishness which can have few equals in the history of political thought. Yet one can find parallels in the late eighteenth century to his idea of the state as essentially an aggregation of right-possessing individuals, and of government as a kind of liberty-fund or banking account in which they had all made deposits. Justus Möser, for example, a popular German author of the time, compared civil society (*bürgerliche Gesellschaft*) to a joint-stock company in which each citizen was a shareholder, and suggested that the state was formed by a social contract, explicit or tacit, by which the landowners united themselves into a company.[3]

The doctrines of the French Revolution, in its early stage at least, were symbolized in the Declaration of the Rights of Man, but

---

[1] Ibid., c. 2.   [2] Ibid., c. 16.

[3] J. Möser, *Patriotische Phantasien*, vol. iii (Berlin, 1778), § 63 (*Der Bauerhof als eine Actie betrachtet*). Cf. also the idea of the Physiocrats (following Locke) that the state exists to protect individuals and their property. One is inevitably reminded of the often-quoted passage of Burke's, reproduced below, p. 196. Yet it is an historical fact that the East India Company, which began as a trading concern, grew by stages into no less a state than British India.

the social contract itself, though now closely associated with the revolutionary movement, does not seem to have played a very important or novel part, directly at any rate, in the formulation of the political programmes of the revolutionary leaders. According to Atger, indeed, the only avowed contractarian among them was Babeuf,[1] but this is a rather misleading statement, for all the essence of contractarianism, if not the contract itself, is clearly revealed in Sieyès.

Liberty and property, according to Sieyès, are anterior to society, and men, 'en s'associant', can have had no other object than protection for their rights and security for the development of their faculties.[2] A nation is 'un corps d'associés',[3] and his theory of the state is fundamentally individualist. One can only understand 'le mécanisme social', he tells us, if we analyse a society into its component elements 'comme une machine ordinaire'. Societies are formed in stages, in the first of which 'on conçoit un nombre plus ou moins considérable d'individus isolés qui veulent se réunir. . . . Cette première époque est caractérisée par le jeu des volontés *individuelles*. L'association est leur ouvrage. Elles sont l'origine de tout pouvoir.' The next stage consists of the creation of 'la volonté commune', and for this purpose 'ils confèrent donc, et ils conviennent entre eux des besoins publics et des moyens d'y pourvoir'. They then confer on some of their own number the exercise of such portion of their will and power as is necessary to guard and provide for the public needs, and thus a government is established.[4] Sieyès thus accepted all the individualist preconceptions of Rousseau, but without his quasi-Hegelian conclusions.

In Babeuf, who was one of the earliest French communists, we find a mixture of hedonism and altruism which also must have been suggested by Rousseau. On entering society, he tells us, every one, 'en quelque sort', made two pronouncements, which are the foundation of all justice: 'Je ne veux plus souffrir' and 'Je ne veux plus qu'aucun de mes associés souffre'. Happiness (*bonheur*, explained a little farther on as *le bonheur commun*) is

---

[1] F. Atger, *Essai sur l'histoire des doctrines du Contrat Social* (Nîmes, 1906), pp. 316–57.

[2] E. Sieyès, *Essai sur les Privilèges* (1788), printed with his *Qu'est-ce que le tiers état?* (1789), ed. Champion (Paris, 1888), p. 2.

[3] *Qu'est-ce que le tiers état?* (ed. Champion), p. 31.

[4] Ibid., pp. 65–66; cf. p. 85, where 'la volonté d'une nation' is defined as 'le résultat des volontés individuelles, comme la nation est l'assemblage des individus'.

'le seul but de la société': this is 'le contrat primitif' and 'la clause fondamentale du pacte social', whose violation involves breach of the pact. 'C'est là en entier la loi et les prophètes. Je défie qu'on me dispute que les hommes, en se réunissant en association, aient pu avoir d'autre but, d'autre volonté que celle d'être tous heureux.'[1]

Apart from these sentimental opinions, however, the social contract was really implicit in the whole apparatus of the rights of man. Thomas Paine, for example, repeats the familiar theory that man by virtue of his existence possesses natural rights, including the right to judge in his own cause, 'but what availeth it him to judge, if he has not power to redress? He therefore deposits this right in the common stock of society, and takes the arm of society, of which he is a part, in preference and in addition to his own.' He does not owe anything to society, for 'every man is a proprietor in society, and draws on the capital as a matter of right'. Every civil right, therefore, 'grows out of a natural right, or, in other words, is a natural right exchanged'. 'Civil power', similarly, 'is made up of the aggregate of that class of the natural rights of man, which becomes defective in the individual in point of power, . . . but when collected to a focus, becomes competent to the purpose of every one.' It 'cannot be applied to invade the natural rights which are retained in the individual'. Like Rousseau, Paine rejects the theory of a contract between government and subjects. This, he remarks, 'has been thought a considerable advance towards establishing the principles of Freedom', but men existed before governments, and the original compact, therefore, was between individuals themselves, 'each in his own personal and sovereign right', thereby deciding to create a government. 'This is the only mode in which governments have a right to arise, and the only principle on which they have a right to exist.' It was embodied, according to Paine, in the French National Assembly.[2]

Amid these polemics the German legal writers of the school of Pufendorf and his successors continued to expound their traditional contractarian theory, but with some modifications, mainly, in accordance with the spirit of the age, in the direction of a more pronounced individualism. Thus A. L. von Schlözer tells us that the first men, or rather, the patriarchs at the head of their families,

---

[1] Quoted by A. Espinas from 'Défense Générale de Babeuf, présentée devant la Haute-Cour de Justice', in his 'Babeuf et le Babouvisme', in *La Philosophie sociale du XVIIIe Siècle et la Révolution* (Paris, 1898), pp. 310, 311.

[2] T. Paine, *The Rights of Man* (2nd edn., 1791), pp. 52–58.

united their forces (but not their wills) by a social contract, but though they ought to have respected this, in practice they failed to do so; dissensions therefore arose, and a government was established to stop them. The *pactum unionis virium*, in fact, was insufficient (*unzulänglich*) without the addition of a *unio voluntatum*, which took the usual form of a *pactum subjectionis*, by which men, for the sake of public safety, renounced their private wills and transferred them to a sovereign (who might be one or few or many). The influence of Rousseau may be seen here, for although Schlözer retains the Pufendorfian framework of two contracts, their contents are different; in fact, the terms of Rousseau's social contract appear to be distributed between them. Unlike Rousseau, however, Schlözer maintains the traditional German view that there is a contract between ruler and subjects.[1]

C. von Schlözer, son of the last writer, agreed with his father that the patriarchs, originally living at enmity in the woods, came to recognize that a claim to possessions was useless without the strength to secure them, and so united their forces by a contract of union, followed later by a contract of subjection, in which they surrendered their wills also to a sovereign. He goes farther in an individualist direction, however, by insisting not only on the equality of all in the state of nature, but on the consequent need for unanimity in both pacts. Some writers held that in the pact of subjection a majority vote sufficed to bind all, because society was a 'person'. But society in the sense of the bare product of a social contract is not yet a *persona moralis*, and cannot bind its members, since the social contract is a mere *unio virium*. There must follow the *unio voluntatum*, for which a new pact is necessary, and in which each individual surrenders his private will, and is obliged henceforth to recognize the will of the sovereign as his own. Only then is it permissible to compare society to a person.[2] How in fact men could unite their forces without also uniting their wills is not explained.

The division of the contractual basis of the state into two contracts, however, was now practically obsolete, in spite of this modification of their contents, and, as in Rousseau, it was the social contract alone which still carried weight. The individualist principle

---

[1] A. L. von Schlözer, *Allgemeines Staatsrecht* (Göttingen, 1793), pp. 48–49, 63–76, 95.
[2] C. von Schlözer, *Commentatio de Jure Suffragii* (Göttingen, 1795), §§ 9–11. Cf. also his *Anfangsgründe der Staatswirthschaft* (Riga, 1805), i, §§ 5–8.

it embodied reached its zenith in Germany in the earlier writings of Fichte. No man, he declares, is bound to obey anybody but himself, and rightly a civil society can be founded only by a contract between its members.[1] This contract of all with all secures to men an inalienable right to alter the constitution of the state,[2] and on this rests a justification of revolution; moreover, it is an inalienable right of man to rescind (*aufheben*) his contracts, and this is equally true of the *Bürgervertrag*.[3] Individuals can retire at will from the state they have contractually entered,[4] and what one can do several can do also. These stand to one another, and to the state they are leaving, under pure natural law; if they please, they can reunite, enter upon a new social contract on any conditions they choose, and form a new state. The Jews, according to Fichte, are an example of such a state within the state, and the same is partly true of the army, the nobility, and the Church.[5]

In his later years, however, Fichte receded markedly from this extreme if not anarchical individualism. At the outset he had admitted that historically states have not been formed by cool deliberation, but by force, although *rechtmäßigerweise* the only ground of political obligation is contract;[6] in his *Grundlage des Naturrechts* (published in 1796)[7] the original rights of man are admittedly only a fiction, though a fiction necessary for the purposes of science, and in reality men only attain to rights in a community with others. Yet as an explanation of the structure of rights and duties within the state the contractual apparatus is retained, in an even more highly elaborate form than before. Three contracts are involved, according to Fichte, in the construction of the state, of which the first is the property contract (*Eigenthumsvertrag*), by which each individual agrees with all the others on what property, rights, and liberties he is to have, and what he is to cede to the others. (There is no natural right of property, according to Fichte, but all have an equal claim to everything: private property is only

---

[1] J. G. Fichte, *Beiträge zur Berichtigung der Urtheile des Publicums über die französische Revolution* (1793), in *Sämmtliche Werke* (Berlin, 1845), vi. 81. On Fichte see the Introduction by H. S. Reiss to *The Political Thought of the German Romantics* in Blackwell's Political Texts (Oxford, 1955).

[2] Ibid., pp. 103 ff.

[3] Ibid., p. 159. 'Unabänderlichkeit und ewige Gültigkeit irgend eines Vertrages', according to Fichte, 'ist der härteste Verstoß gegen das Recht der Menschheit an sich. . . . Nämlich, im Vertrage ist die gegenseitige freie Willkür (arbitrary will) Grund der Rechte und der Verbindlichkeit.'

[4] Ibid., p. 115.   [5] Ibid., pp. 148–53.
[6] Ibid., p. 81.   [7] In *Sämmtliche Werke*, vol. iii.

possible when men have renounced this.) This agreement must be made individually, and in person with all the others, each being the one party, and all the others as individuals (for only as individual free beings does he agree with them) the other party.[1]

The property contract leads on necessarily to the second, or protection contract (*Schutzvertrag*), in which each individual similarly agrees with all the others to protect their specified property and rights, provided they will likewise protect his. The 'negative will' (i.e. the promise to abstain from invading) established by the first contract is thus converted into a positive will.[2] At the same time, in order that these contracts may be fulfilled, a protective authority must be established, and to this each member must contribute, and thus fulfil his promise to protect the rights of the others. The creation and direction of this authority involves the conception of a whole, which is formed by the third stage, or union contract (*Vereinigungsvertrag*). This 'secures and protects the two previous contracts, and in union with them forms the fundamental contract of state organization'. The effect of this is that each individual becomes 'a part of an organized whole (*ein Theil eines organisirten Ganzen*) and melts (*schmilzt*) into one with it'.[3]

This kind of language might lead one to expect that in spite of all these contractual preliminaries the conclusion would be an absolutist state in which the individual was completely submerged; but Fichte still maintains, against Rousseau, that it is only one part of a man's being and nature which is so woven into the state: otherwise he remains a free individual. But when the social contract has admittedly been reduced to an imaginary hypothesis, which has no relation to historical truth, and is intended only as a kind of logical postulate, its content can be manipulated at will, and there is no reason why it should not lead in the end to the totalitarian state. This is in fact what happened with Fichte, who in his later writings insisted more and more on the 'higher' aspect of the state, and finally reduced the individual to the level of a mere instrument for the service of its ends.[4]

---

[1] *Sämmtliche Werke*, iii. 196. Cf. his remarks on p. 178 on the necessity of individual consent and the inability of the majority to bind the minority. Yet, he adds, when it comes in due course to the 'Berathschlagung über die Wahl der Magistratspersonen', conditions are different, and only 'relative unanimity' is required.

[2] Ibid., p. 197.   [3] Ibid., p. 204.

[4] Cf. his *Grundzüge des gegenwärtigen Zeitalters* (1804–5), in *Sämmtliche Werke*, vii. 146. In his last work, *Die Staatslehre* (1813), the contract is dropped altogether.

Rousseau himself had already pointed the way towards this conclusion, and Fichte's great contemporary Kant followed in the same direction. It is more than doubtful whether Rousseau meant his social contract to be taken as literally true;[1] for Kant, at any rate, who, like Rousseau, had inherited the theory and was never able to abandon it altogether, it avowedly lost all pretence of historical reality. Arguing that the only will competent to make a public law is that of the whole people, 'as it is only when all determine about all that each one in consequence determines about himself', he enunciates the principle of an 'original contract', which is a fundamental law arising 'out of the universal united will of the people'. It is 'the only condition upon which a civil, and therefore, wholly rightful constitution can be founded among men'. Whether called an 'original contract' or a 'social contract', it 'may be viewed as the coalition of all the private and particular wills of a people into one common and public Will'.[2]

But there is no reason, he continues, to suppose this contract to have been actually a fact; indeed, it is impossible that it should have been. We need not, therefore, try to prove from history that any people ever did execute such a contract. 'In short, this is merely *an Idea of Reason*; but it has undoubtedly a practical reality.' It is a principle in the light of which legislators should enact only 'such laws as might have arisen from the united will of a whole people', and the citizen should 'regard the law as if he had consented to it of his own will. This is the test of the rightfulness of every public law'.[3] It does not follow, however, that the people have any right to resist by word or deed the ruler of a state who enacts wrongful laws.[4]

In his *Perpetual Peace* Kant declared that 'the Republican Constitution is . . . the only one which arises out of the idea of the

---

[1] Cf. his opening remarks that he does not know how the change from freedom to political subordination came about, but that the question he thinks he can answer is, 'What can make it legitimate?' (*C.S.* i. 1.) For Rousseau, in fact, the contract is no more than a device to bridge the gap between the liberty of the individual and the authority of the general will. For the controversy among German critics on the question whether Rousseau believed in the historical truth of the contract see Gierke, *Althusius* (additional matter in 3rd edn.), pp. 347–50.

[2] I. Kant, *On the Saying 'That may be right in theory but has no value in practice'* (1793), tr. W. Hastie, *Kant's Principles of Politics* (Edinburgh, 1891), pp. 43, 46.

[3] Ibid. Cf. p. 49, where he says that in judging whether a law agrees or not with a principle of right a legislator 'has an infallible criterion in the idea of the "original contract" viewed as an essential idea of reason'.

[4] Ibid., p. 55.

Original Compact, upon which all rightful legislation of a people is founded',[1] but his general political doctrine was strongly authoritarian. The origin of sovereignty, he remarks, is *practically inscrutable* by the People who are placed under its authority. . . . The question has been raised', he continues, 'whether an actual Contract of Subjection originally preceded the civil government as a fact. . . . But such questions, as regarding the People actually living under the Civil Law, are either entirely useless, or even fraught with subtle danger to the State.'[2]

But if the people must unquestioningly obey, philosophers may examine the grounds on which this necessity rests. Kant begins with the idea of a lawless state of nature in which, in the absence of restraint, men do violence to each other; but this is not a 'particular historical condition or fact', nor is our formation of this idea the result of 'any experience prior to the appearance of an external authoritative Legislation'. The state of nature is revealed, in fact, in what had always been its true colours, though in many writers they were obscured by quasi-historical trappings: it is just a logical abstraction from the state of society, reached by imagining man stripped of everything which he owes to society. Even although human nature may in reality be 'well-disposed or favourable to Right', yet for the purposes of formulating a logical theory we must begin, according to Kant, with 'the rational Idea of a state of Society not yet regulated by Right'. This need not be represented as 'a state of absolute Injustice', but, if it ever existed, it must be regarded as an unregulated condition (*ein Zustand der Rechtlosigkeit*), in which there was no authoritative judge to settle disputes. But considering that 'every one of his own Will naturally does *what seems good and right in his own eyes*', it is evident that in the state of nature none can be safe from violence.

---

[1] *Perpetual Peace* (1795), tr. Hastie, op. cit., p. 89. It was also, he added, the necessary condition of perpetual peace among nations. Similarly in his *Rechtslehre* (1796, in *Gesammelte Schriften* (Berlin, 1914), vol. vi), tr. Hastie, *Kant's Philosophy of Law* (Edinburgh, 1887), p. 210, he says that 'every true republic is and can only be constituted by a representative system of the people'.

[2] Ibid., p. 174. When we say all authority is 'from God', he adds, we do not refer to the historical origin of the constitution, but are expressing 'an Ideal Principle of the Practical Reason'. What we mean is that it is a duty to obey the law. Cf. ibid., pp. 208 ff., where he remarks that 'it is vain to inquire into the historical origin of political mechanism, for it is no longer possible to discover historically the point of time at which civil society took its beginning. . . . To prosecute such an inquiry', he continues, 'in the intention of finding a pretext for altering the existing constitution by violence is no less than penal.'

The next stage, then, is a union in which men leave the state of nature and all obey public laws,[1] and the act by which the people 'is represented as constituting itself into a State' is called the original contract (*der ursprüngliche Contract*). 'This is properly only an outward mode of representing the idea by which the rightfulness of the process of organizing the Constitution may be made conceivable.' Kant thus interprets the contract once more as an 'idea of reason', and its terms show the meaning which he attributed to Rousseau. 'All and each of the people give up their external freedom (*ihre äußere Freiheit*) in order to receive it immediately again as Members of a Commonwealth', which is 'the people viewed as united altogether into a State.' The current contractarian theory of natural rights, therefore, by which an individual who joins the state is held to have sacrificed a part of his native freedom for a particular purpose (e.g. protection), is wrong; rather 'he has abandoned his wild, lawless freedom wholly (*er hat die wilde gesetzlose Freiheit gänzlich verlassen*) in order to find all his proper Freedom again entire and undiminished, but in the form of a regulated order of dependence, that is, in a Civil State regulated by laws of Right'.[2] This disposes of Beccaria's theory that capital punishment must be wrong because it could not be contained in the original contract.[3] 'No one wills to be punished, but in submitting himself along with all other citizens to the laws, he knows that if there are criminals among the people, the laws will include penal laws.'[4]

If the contract has only a pragmatic reality, and is merely a supposition to explain the obligations of citizens and rulers, who are to behave 'as if' it were real, we may well wonder whether it is anything but a useless fiction. For Kant, indeed, it was altogether superfluous, since political obligation could quite well be founded directly, without any interpolation of a contract, on the moral obligations which he already recognized as universally binding.[5] Kant, in fact, brings us within sight of the end of the history of the contract theory. Political philosophy, now no longer entangled with the question of the origin of the state, could devote itself wholly to the problem of political obligation (*Rechtsgrund*, as Gierke calls it), and with the abandonment of the individualist

---

[1] *Rechtslehre*, § 44.   [2] Ibid., § 47.
[3] Molina's solution of this problem may be remembered; see above, p. 68.
[4] *Rechtslehre*, § 49.
[5] Cf. Hume's argument, discussed in the next chapter.

presuppositions of the contract theory, the way lay open to Hegel's exaltation of the majesty of the state.

According to Hegel, just as it is impossible to 'subsume marriage under the concept of contract', so it is equally far from the truth to 'ground the nature of the state on the contractual relation, whether the state is supposed to be a contract of all with all, or of all with the monarch and the government.[1] The intrusion of this contractual relation, and relationships concerning private property generally, into the relation between the individual and the state', he continues, 'has been productive of the greatest confusion in both constitutional law and public life.' This confusion of political rights and duties with the rights of private property was characteristic of feudalism, but it is wrong to regard the rights of the monarch and the state today as being 'grounded in contract'. Men who thought thus 'have transferred the characteristics of private property into a sphere of a quite different and higher nature.'

Hegel proceeds to attack Beccaria's notion that the state has no right to inflict capital punishment, because it cannot be presumed that 'the readiness of individuals to allow themselves to be executed was included in the social contract, and that in fact the contrary would have to be assumed'. But the state is not a contract at all, he repeats, 'nor is its fundamental essence the unconditional protection and guarantee of the life and property of members of the public as individuals. On the contrary, it is that higher entity which even lays claim to this very life and property and demands its sacrifice.'[2]

It is quite wrong, therefore, to think of the state as existing specifically to secure and protect property and personal freedom, or of 'the interest of the individuals as such' as 'the ultimate end of their association'. If that were so, membership of the state would be optional, whereas, as he explains later, 'it does not lie with an individual's arbitrary will to separate himself from the state, because we are already citizens by birth. The rational end of man is life in the state. . . . Permission to enter a state or leave it must be given by the state', and the notion that membership of

---

[1] *Hegel's Philosophy of Right*, tr. T. M. Knox (Oxford, 1942), p. 59. On p. 242 he appears to confuse the social with the governmental contract, for he says 'it has recently become very fashionable to regard the state as a contract of all with all. Everyone makes a contract with the monarch, so the argument runs, and he again with his subjects.' For the comparison with marriage cf. above, p. 69.

[2] Ibid., p. 71.

the state is something optional, depending on 'arbitrary will' and contract, is false. In Hegel's words, 'the state is mind objectified', and so 'it is only as one of its members that the individual himself has objectivity, genuine individuality, and an ethical life'.[1]

We may take exception to Hegel's phraseology, and the philosophy that underlies it, yet we can hardly deny that in some ways his portrait of human life is closer to history and reality than the abstractions of the contractarian school. It is open, however, (metaphysics apart) to two serious objections, one theoretical, the other practical. The theoretical objection is that it fails to distinguish between society and the state, and attributes to citizenship what is more truly due to membership of society. The practical objection lies in the terrible consequences which have resulted in the last hundred years from the exaggeration of Hegel's claims for the state as against the 'arbitrary will' of individuals. Perhaps we should not blame Hegel for this, and it is true that the Nazis repudiated a Hegelian parentage. Instead, perhaps we should remember that when he wrote Prussia was still only on the brink of assuming the leadership of the movement to create a united national state out of the fragments into which Germany had been divided for centuries. In such circumstances exaggeration ought not to surprise us. Yet its consequences have undoubtedly contributed something to the discredit into which Hegel's philosophy has fallen in recent years.

[1] Ibid., p. 156.

XII

THE CONTRACT THEORY IN DECLINE

OVER seventy years before Hegel abandoned the social contract and enunciated a political philosophy totally at
variance with everything it had stood for, a shrewd
attack had been launched against it by David Hume.[1] The gist of
his argument was that the contract theory is illogical; he did not
like Hegel (or Aristotle), deny the premises themselves from
which it was supposed to follow, by maintaining that man is
essentially only a part of a political whole, but accepted the idea
that the free individual is the natural unit and the state only an
aggregation of individuals. Men are so nearly equal in bodily and
mental powers, according to Hume, that

nothing but their own consent could, at first, associate them together,
and subject them to any authority. The people, if we trace government to its first origin in the woods and deserts, are the source of all
power and jurisdiction, and voluntarily, for the sake of peace and order,
abandoned their native liberty, and received laws from their equal and
companion. The conditions upon which they were willing to submit
were either expressed, or were so clear and obvious, that it might well
be esteemed superfluous to express them.

If this is what is meant by the original contract, 'it cannot be denied
that all government is, at first, founded on a contract, and that the
most ancient rude combinations of mankind were formed chiefly
by that principle'.[2]

It does not follow, however, according to Hume, that because
government was contractual in origin, it remains contractual 'in
maturity'. No 'regular administration' could be formed on the
basis of this primitive consent; in fact, though he has just agreed
that it may be called a contract, he proceeds to say that early
chieftains 'ruled more by persuasion than command', and that the

---

[1] Hume's Essay 'Of the Original Contract' was first published in the third
edition (1748) of his *Essays Moral and Political*, in which it was Essay xxv. It
later became Essay xii in Part ii of *Essays, Moral, Political and Literary*. He had
already stated the same arguments more briefly in his *Treatise of Human Nature*
Bk. iii (of Morals), part ii, §§ 7 ff. This appeared in 1740.

[2] In the next paragraph, however, we shall see that he denies the historical
validity of the contract too.

idea of a 'compact and agreement . . . expressly formed for general submission' was 'far beyond the comprehension of savages'. At any rate, the real foundation of government, he maintains, is the fact that popular acquiescence in government led in time to 'habitual obedience'. Examination of the world today, he continues, affords no support for the view that government rests on a contract. 'On the contrary, we find, everywhere, princes who claim their subjects as their property, and assert their independent right of sovereignty from conquest or succession', and subjects who similarly acknowledge their subordination. If it is urged that the contract is so ancient that the present generation does not know it, his reply is that apart from the dubious assumption that the consent of the fathers binds their children, the theory is not justified by experience in any age or country, and in this sense it is unhistorical. 'Almost all the governments which exist at present, or of which there remains any record in story, have been founded originally either on usurpation, or conquest, or both, without any pretence of a fair consent, or voluntary subjection of the people.'

To the plea that continuing to live under a government implies 'tacit consent' he replies that this is only reasonable where there is a real possibility of departure. 'Can we seriously say, that a poor peasant or artizan has a free choice to leave his country, when he knows no foreign language or manners, and lives from day to day by the small wages he acquires? We may as well assert that a man, by remaining in a vessel, freely consents to the dominion of the master, though he was carried on board while asleep, and must leap into the ocean and perish, the moment he leaves her.' We might attribute 'tacit consent' to a foreigner who settles in a country whose government and laws he knows beforehand, 'yet is his allegiance, though more voluntary, much less expected or depended on than that of a natural born subject. On the contrary, his native prince still asserts a claim to him.'

These, however, are relatively superficial objections, and he passes on to 'a more philosophical refutation'. Moral duties, he suggests, are of two kinds: (a) those to which men 'are impelled by a natural instinct or immediate propensity . . . independent of all ideas of obligation', such as parental love, gratitude, or pity, and (b) those performed 'from a sense of obligation, when we consider the necessities of human society and the impossibility of supporting it if those duties were neglected'; such is the source of justice or fidelity. The 'political or civil duty of allegiance' rests on precisely the same footing. Experience shows that we cannot indulge our natural instincts in unlimited freedom, and that society cannot be maintained without the authority of magistrates. It is absurd, therefore, to found allegiance on fidelity, or regard to promises, since both alike arise from the interests of society. If it be asked why we must obey the government, the answer is 'because society could not otherwise subsist'. The contractarian maintains that it is because we have promised to obey, but he is embarrassed if it is asked why we are bound to keep our promise, and cannot 'give any answer, but what would immediately, without any circuit, have accounted for our obligation to allegiance'. Even though we cannot accept Hume's reduction of obligation to interest,[1] or his qualified acceptance of the contractual origin of government, this does not affect the cogency of his argument against contract as the explanation of political obligation. We may hold that we have a duty to keep promises and to obey the laws, not only because it is to our interest to do so, but because we believe that such action is right, in the sense that it is the best means of attaining what we regard as good; but Hume's point is still valid, that there is no reason to explain the one as a consequence of the other.

Hume thus argued that in practice government rested not on consent but on habit, and that in theory political obligation could be satisfactorily explained without recourse to any contract. The contract was therefore not only fictitious but unnecessary. In attacking the doctrine from this angle Hume differed from most anti-contractarians, who generally impugned the historicity of the contract and advanced instead a theory of divine right; but damaging though his criticism was as far as it went, it missed the root of the matter. In eighteenth-century Britain, at any rate, upholders of the contract were not primarily interested in the philosophical problem of political obligation: they were more concerned as practical politicians to ensure that the obligation of citizens to obedience, irrespective of its origin, should not be unlimited or unconditional. This the contract theory secured, at the same time stipulating that the powers of government were likewise conditional and limited. Whether the terminology of contract is

[1] Cf. *Treatise*, III. ii. 11, where we are told that experience shows that life without society is impossible, and that the maintenance of society is incompatible with the unlimited gratification of appetite. 'So urgent an interest quickly restrains their actions, and imposes an obligation to observe those rules which we call the laws of justice.' It further 'gives rise to the moral obligation of duty'.

a suitable mode of expressing this constitutional reciprocity of obligations between ruler and subject is still an arguable question, and we need not be surprised that as long as the constitution was still thought of in terms of the Revolution settlement, the contract theory survived Hume's attack on it.

Moreover, though Hume rejected the contract itself, he retained the individualist presuppositions which are really its weakest feature, and his history was at fault when, at the conclusion of his essay, he argued that government cannot 'in general' have a contractual foundation, because 'new discoveries are not to be expected' in political matters, and 'scarce any man, till very lately, ever imagined that government was founded on compact'. In England itself the vogue of the original contract was indeed a relative novelty, but the theory in general, as this book bears witness, was far older and more universal.[1]

In the second half of the eighteenth century the contract theory, though by no means defunct, suffered a noticeable decline in popularity, to which Hume's arguments undoubtedly contributed something, as may be gathered from the writers who quoted him; but for some time the favourite line of attack remained historical, sometimes made all the easier by setting up a travesty of the theory as a target. Thus Blackstone ridiculed the picture of individuals assembling 'in a large plain', entering into an original contract, and choosing 'the tallest man present to be their governor'. The notion 'of an actually existing unconnected state of nature', he continued, 'is too wild to be seriously admitted', besides being contradicted by all we know of the primitive condition of mankind. In reality civil society was formed and preserved by the development of families, which 'formed the first natural society among themselves'.

This kind of criticism was cheap and easy enough, but missed the mark, and Blackstone was prepared to swallow the main implications of the contract theory as an analysis of present-day society. For 'though society had not its formal beginning from any convention of individuals, actuated by their wants and fears', yet, he maintains, these wants and fears are 'the only true and natural foundations of society'. It is 'the *sense* of their weakness and imperfections that *keeps* mankind together', and this is what we mean

---

[1] Hume refers to the occurrence of the contract in Plato's *Crito* (cf. above, p. 18, but he seems to think that apart from this the theory was invented by the Whigs.

by 'the original contract of society; which, though perhaps in no instance it has ever been formally expressed at the first institution of a state, yet in nature and reason must always be understood and implied, in the very act of associating together'.[1] Blackstone, in fact, though he professes to know better, is essentially a contractarian, but he upholds only an 'implicit' contract.[2]

Jeremy Bentham, whose *Fragment on Government*[3] had Blackstone for its chief target, eagerly fastened on this inconsistency, by which the contract was 'by turns embraced and ridiculed', and devoted a number of pages to a discussion of it, though he had hoped 'that this chimera had been effectively demolished by Mr. Hume'. His criticism of the contract is really no more profound than Blackstone's own, and though spun out to considerable length, amounts in effect to no more than this: that the original contract is a fiction, which may have been useful once; but the age of fiction is now over. It is impossible to construe the coronation oath or any other element in the constitution as a contract; and even supposing a contract had been made in times past, promises exchanged between the king and my great-grandfather mean nothing to me today. The principle of utility is a sufficient explanation of political duty, apart from any contract; 'the obligation of a promise will not stand against that of utility: while that of utility will against that of a promise'.[4]

While Bentham believed that in utility he had found a better key to political (and every other) obligation than any original contract, he had by no means extricated himself from the whole contractarian environment. He maintained that civil society did not originate in a contract, but for all that it was preceded by what he called 'natural society', which exists 'when a number of persons are supposed to be in the habit of conversing with each other without paying habitual obedience to any one person or set of persons'. This 'passes into a political society when its members begin to pay such obedience', but according to Bentham the line parting natural from political society is invisible, and the only distinguishing mark is the establishment of certain 'names of office'. Though Bentham rejected the social contract, therefore, and also the idea of natural rights, he retained the correlative idea of a state of nature,

[1] Sir W. Blackstone, *Commentaries on the Laws of England* (1765–9), i. 47.

[2] Blackstone's position closely resembles that of his French contemporary Goguet; cf. above, p. 162.

[3] 1776 (ed. F. C. Montague, 1891).

[4] *A Fragment on Government*, i. 36–47.

in a form practically equivalent to Locke's, and his utilitarianism
was essentially individualist.[1]

The late eighteenth century was a period when men were losing
their belief in the older, naïve contractarianism, which accepted
the contract as literally true, yet they had not succeeded in finding
a new theory of government to take its place. The result was an
apparently half-hearted and often inconsistent rejection of some
and acceptance of other parts of the contractarian system; and in
England, at least, the contract was so much the protégé of Revolutionary Whiggism that its survival depended more on the fortunes
of its patrons than on the effects of logical argument, either for or
against it. Joseph Priestley, for example, the political spokesman
of nonconformity, claimed in his *Essay on the First Principles of
Government*[2] to have availed himself 'of a more accurate and ex-
tensive system of morals and policy than was adopted by Mr.
Locke and others who formerly wrote upon this subject'.[3] What
was new in Priestley's work seems to have come from Rousseau,
but he cast it into a form which anticipated the utilitarianism of
Bentham. So he insisted that property, or any kind of right, 'is
founded upon a regard to the general good of the society under
whose protection it is enjoyed; and nothing is properly *a man's
own*, but what general rules, which have for their object the good
of the whole, give to him'.[4] There is no explicit social contract in
Priestley, but he adopted the traditional individualist assumption
that men once lived independent and unprotected lives, and that
in order to obtain security and the opportunity to participate in
common enterprises they 'must voluntarily resign some part of
their natural liberty[5] and submit their conduct to the direction of
the community'. He did not positively assert that any governments

---

[1] As F. C. Montague remarked, in Bentham 'we trace the last fading characters
of the *a priori* philosophy which invented the social contract' (op. cit. (ed.
Montague), Introd., pp. 83, 84). In Appendix III to the first volume of *La Formation du Radicalisme Philosophique* (Paris, 1901), É. Halévy prints from a University College, London, manuscript a fragment of Bentham's on the original
contract, written probably twenty years later than *A Fragment on Government*. In
this he draws a contrast between Rousseau and Locke, whom he calls 'the inventor
of the system of the original contract, or at least the first man of great name whom
it is customary to consider as the author of it', and to whom he wrongly attributes
the idea of a contract between king and people. In both Locke and Rousseau
it is a fiction, he considers, and a bad one. The actual origins of government are
quite different, and Filmer's account was much nearer historical truth.
[2] 1768.   [3] Op. cit., preface.
[4] Ibid., p. 41.   [5] Ibid., pp. 9, 10. Not the whole of their natural liberty,
as in Rousseau.

had actually been so formed: he admitted, indeed, that all governments 'have been in some measure compulsory, tyrannical and
oppressive in their origin', but such a voluntary surrender of
natural liberty 'must be admitted to be the only equitable and fair
method of forming a society'. And since nobody can without his
consent be deprived of his natural right of relieving himself of
oppression, the people have an inalienable right to bring their
governments into conformity with this model. Following Locke,
he argued that if magistrates abuse their trust the people have the
right to depose and punish them, and, again like Locke, he denied
that this meant 'opening a door to rebellion'. Granted the possibility that the people, as well as their governors, might abuse their
power, it was improbable that in large societies the people would
be easily driven to extremities.[1]

A somewhat similar basis underlies the political theory of Richard
Price, whose name is often linked with Priestley's. He cites Locke
in support of the view that all government is 'in the very nature
of it, a trust'. It is created by the people, 'is conducted under their
direction, and has nothing in view but their happiness'.[2] One
consequence he deduces from this is that as members were elected
for a limited period, Parliament has no power to perpetuate itself,
or even to prolong its own duration.[3] 'If omnipotence can, with any
sense, be ascribed to a legislature, it must be lodged where all
legislative authority originated; that is, in the People.' Another
consequence, which he urged in the second part of his work, was
that England had no right to govern the American colonies. As in
Priestley, there is no explicit contract in Price. The contract was,
in fact, more appropriate to the Whiggish belief in mixed or
limited government than to the radicalism which, in spite of his
acknowledgements to Locke, Price frankly espoused.

If we return to statements of more moderate views, we shall still
find contractual foundations hidden beneath a structure purporting
to have got rid of them, and contractual phraseology still serving
as a means of expressing ideas which have really outgrown it. It
would be a mistake to look for a formulated political system in
Burke, but this inconsistency is nowhere better illustrated than in
his pages. It is in his *Appeal from the New to the Old Whigs*[4] that

---

[1] Priestley, *First Principles*, pp. 16, 23, 30.
[2] R. Price, *Observations on the Nature of Civil Liberty* (1776), § 2.
[3] Yet it was sixty years since the Septennial Act was passed!
[4] 1791; in *Works* (1826 edn.), vol. vi.

we shall find the nearest approach to an explicit statement of his political principles. Here he argues against the contention, maintained by the French Revolutionists and the 'New Whigs', that the people have a supreme authority to change the foundations of government, and upholds against it the 'Old Whig' principles of the English Revolution settlement—'the original contract, implied and expressed in the constitution of this country, as a scheme of government fundamentally and inviolably fixed in king, lords, and commons'. James II had attempted to subvert this constitution, and the Revolution was justified by necessity, as being the only means left 'for the recovery of that ancient constitution, formed by the original contract of the British state; as well as for the future preservation of the same government'.[1]

In support of this contention Burke quotes large excerpts from the speeches of the Whig managers at the trial of Dr. Sacheverell. At the same time he is no believer in the rights of man; if society confers benefits, it also imposes duties.

> Though civil society might be at first a voluntary act (which in many cases it undoubtedly was), its continuance is under a permanent, standing covenant, co-existing with the society; and it attaches upon every individual of that society, without any formal act of his own. . . . Men without their choice derive benefits from that association; without their choice they are subjected to duties in consequence of these benefits; and without their choice they enter into a virtual obligation as binding as any that is actual.[2]

It seems, then, that whatever may have happened originally, the contract is now 'virtual'. There are some duties, he continues, 'which are not in consequence of any special voluntary pact. They arise from the relation of man to man, and the relation of man to God, which relations are not matter of choice. On the contrary, the force of all the pacts which we enter into with any particular

---

[1] Ibid., p. 148. Cf. p. 201: 'The constitution of a country being once settled upon some compact, tacit or expressed, there is no power existing of force to alter it, without the breach of the covenant, or the consent of all the parties. Such is the nature of a contract.' The old Whigs defended the constitution against its breach by James II; Burke defends it from an attack on the other side by the advocates of a popular revolution. Cf. also his phrase in *Reflections on the Revolution in France* (1790; the work in defence of which he wrote his *Appeal from the New to the Old Whigs*) in *Works* (1826 edn.), v. 57: 'The engagement and pact of society, which generally goes by the name of the constitution.' He went on to describe the authority of law as 'emanating from the common agreement and original contract of the state, *communi sponsione reipublicae*' (ibid. v. 58).

[2] *Works*, vi. 205.

person, or number of persons, . . . depends upon those prior obligations.'[1] In fact, there are real moral obligations, and man's place in society is determined not by contract, even implicit, but by 'the ancient order into which we were born'.[2]

He then considers what is meant by 'the people', to whom the revolutionists attributed sovereign power, and he appears to stand forth as not only a contractarian but an individualist; at the same time he delivers a shrewd blow at what had always been a weakness of many systematic contractarians—the claim of a majority to decide and act in the name of all. 'In a state of *rude* nature', he writes, 'there is no such thing as a people. A number of men in themselves have no collective capacity. The idea of a people is the idea of a corporation. It is wholly artificial; and made like all other legal fictions by common agreement. What the particular nature of that agreement was, is collected from the form into which the particular society has been cast.' It is 'the original compact or agreement which gives its corporate form and capacity to a State', and apart from it men do not form a people. 'They are a number of vague, loose individuals, and nothing more.'[3]

At the French Revolution, he implies, when the government (i.e. the contract) was dissolved, the people returned to this state of dissolution, and it is absurd, therefore, for a majority of them to claim to bind the rest.

We are so little affected by things which are habitual that we consider this idea of the decision of a *majority* as if it were a law of our original nature: but such constructive whole, residing in a part only, is one of the most violent fictions of positive law. . . . Out of civil society nature knows nothing of it; nor are men, even when arranged according to civil order, otherwise than by very long training, brought at all to submit to it. . . . This mode of decision [he continues] '. . . must be the result of a very particular and special convention, confirmed afterwards by long habits of obedience, by a sort of discipline in society.[4] [Majority-rule] [he suggests] must be grounded on two assumptions: first, that of an incorporation produced by unanimity; and, secondly, an unanimous agreement, that the act of a mere majority (say of one) shall pass with them and with others as the act of the whole.

---

[1] *Works*, vi. 206.   [2] Ibid. 207.   [3] Ibid. 210, 211.

[4] The wisdom of these reflections of Burke's is strikingly confirmed by the breakdown of representative institutions in many countries of Europe in recent years, where parties which have not learned the habit of accepting the vote of an adverse majority resort to violence instead of argument to make their views prevail.

That majority-rule is 'a matter of positive arrangement' is confirmed by the fact 'that several States, for the validity of several of their acts, have required a proportion of voices much greater than that of a mere majority'. The old constitution of Poland, in which unanimity was required in the Diet, approached 'much more nearly to rude nature than the institutions of any other country'.

Upon the dissolution of government 'each man has a right, if he pleases, to remain an individual. Any number of individuals, who can agree upon it, have an undoubted right to form themselves into a State apart, and wholly independent. If any of these is forced into the fellowship of another, this is conquest and not compact.' 'In the abstract, it is perfectly clear that, out of a state of civil society, majority and minority are relations which can have no existence; and that, in civil society, its own specific conventions in each corporation determine what it is that constitutes the people, so as to make their act the signification of the general will.' Finally, 'neither in France nor in England has the original, or any subsequent compact of the State, expressed or implied, constituted *a majority of men, told by the head*, to be the acting people of their several communities'.[1]

All this seems to involve an extreme individualism in which all men are free and equal; yet Burke proceeds to write of a 'natural aristocracy', declares that 'the state of civil society, which necessarily generates this aristocracy, is a state of nature; and much more truly so than a savage and incoherent mode of life', since 'man is by nature reasonable' and 'art is man's nature';[2] and pours scorn on the rights of man, which 'the Abbé John Ball understood . . . as well as the Abbé Grégoire'.[3] His final conclusion is that revolution is alarming and dangerous, and that 'the foundation of government is . . . laid, not in imaginary rights of men . . . but in political convenience, and in human nature; either as that nature is universal, or as it is modified by local habits and social aptitudes, . . . in a provision for our wants, and in a conformity to our duties'. He claims to stand at 'a middle point', urging that 'a certain portion of liberty' is 'essential to all good government', but that 'this liberty is to be blended into the government, to harmonize with its forms and rules; and to be made subordinate to its end'.[4]

A similar mingling of contractual phraseology with a profound appreciation of the historical solidarity of a nation appears in

---

[1] Ibid., pp. 212–16.   [2] Ibid., pp. 217, 218.   [3] Ibid., p. 220.
[4] Ibid., p. 258.

the well-known passage in his *Reflections on the Revolution in France*:

Society is indeed a contract. Subordinate contracts for objects of mere occasional interest may be dissolved at pleasure—but the State ought not to be considered nothing better than a partnership agreement in a trade of pepper and coffee, calico or tobacco, or some other such low concern, to be taken up for a little temporary interest, and to be dissolved by the fancy of the parties. It is to be looked on with other reverence; because it is not a partnership in things subservient only to the gross animal existence of a temporary and perishable nature. It is a partnership in all science; a partnership in all art; a partnership in every virtue, and in all perfection. As the ends of such a partnership cannot be obtained in many generations, it becomes a partnership not only between those who are living, but between those who are living, those who are dead, and those who are to be born. Each contract of each particular State is but a clause in the great primaeval contract of eternal society, linking the lower with the higher natures, connecting the visible and invisible world, according to a fixed compact sanctioned by the inviolable oath which holds all physical and all moral natures, each in their appointed place.[1]

Here Burke almost seems to be playing a rhetorical game with the familiar contractarian phraseology; or rather, to be reading into it such new depths[2] of meaning as to transform it out of all recognition. If such are the real truths of politics, could they not be better expressed, we might wonder, by frankly abandoning the contract altogether, and openly adopting an 'organic' theory of the state? But Burke, we must remember, was addressing an audience accustomed to think in terms of the original contract, and he deliberately intended to direct their thoughts away from some of the errors usually advocated by its adherents. This may have led him into apparent inconsistencies, but after all he never meant to enunciate a systematic political philosophy. The truth seems to be that what Burke abhorred was abstract reasoning in politics,[3] and he repudiated (in a manner supposed to be characteristic of Englishmen) all those who drew practical conclusions from general principles. Party sympathy and dislike of revolutionary radicalism led him to defend the Whig settlement of 1689, and with it the idea of the original contract; but in identifying it (as indeed the Whigs had done) with the laws and usages of the con-

[1] *Works*, v. 183–4.
[2] Not really new, of course: cf. Hooker, above, p. 74.
[3] Cf. L. Stephen, *Hist. of Eng. Thought in the Eighteenth Century* (1876), ii. 225.

stitution, he made it a matter of practical politics rather than of
theoretical speculation. But in this form it was unlikely to outlive
the Whig theory of the constitution, and of the place of the Revolution as a permanent definition of its principles. The immediate
effect of Burke's rhetoric was to elicit Paine's *Rights of Man*,
which horrified all but the Radicals; in the long run the contract
theory seemed inappropriate and superfluous when the sovereignty of the people, advocated by Paine as a revolutionary
principle, became an accepted commonplace of modern democracy.

Meanwhile William Paley, author of the once celebrated
Evidences of Christianity, had composed a reasoned series of objections which must have been highly damaging to the theory (still
substantially the theory of Locke) as commonly held in his day.
The compact between the citizens and the state, which is held to
be the ground of civil obedience, he remarks, is really twofold:

(*a*) an express compact by the primitive founders of the State, who are
supposed, . . . in the first place, to have unanimously consented to be
bound by the resolutions of the majority; that majority, in the next
place, to have fixed certain fundamental regulations; and then to have
constituted, either in one person or in an assembly, . . . a standing
legislature, to whom . . . the government was thenceforth committed.
(*b*) A *tacit* or *implied* contract, by all succeeding members of the State,
who, by accepting its protection, consent to be bound by its laws.[1]

Paley's objections to the contract theory are likewise twofold:
'that it is founded upon a supposition false in fact, and leading to
dangerous conclusions'. The first of these is the usual historical
objection that such a contract was never made; nor could it have
been made, because it is unthinkable that 'savages out of caves
and deserts' could 'deliberate and vote upon topics which the
experience and studies and refinements of civil life alone suggest'.
No government, therefore, began in contract. He concedes that
'some imitation of a social compact may have taken place at a
revolution', and that recent events in America lent some colour
to this notion, but even there the theory will not work properly.
To the argument that the original compact 'is not proposed as a
fact but as a fiction, which furnishes a commodious explication of

[1] W. Paley, *Moral and Political Philosophy* (1785), bk. vi, c. 3. Paley evidently
has in mind the systematic contractarianism of Pufendorf and his followers.
'This transaction', he adds, 'is sometimes called the *social compact*'; but it
covers Pufendorf's two contracts and intermediate settlement of the constitution.

the mutual rights and duties of sovereigns and subjects', he replies that if it is not a fact it is nothing, and can be the foundation for nothing, and that in practice its adherents treat it not as a fiction but as a reality. Paley here does less than justice to the contractarian position, which regarded the contract as a logical, if not an historical, truth.[1] Next he demolishes the tacit compact supposed to be implied by the continued residence and allegiance of succeeding generations. Here he seems to have Locke particularly in mind, and his attack is closely modelled on that of Hume, though he adds a special objection to the idea that a contract is involved in the occupation and possession of land.

Secondly, according to Paley, the contract theory is dangerous in three ways. In the first place, the supposition that there are fundamentals of the constitution established before the creation of the legislature, which the legislature may not alter, 'serves extremely to embarrass the deliberations of the legislature, and affords a dangerous pretence for disputing the authority of the laws. It was this sort of reasoning', he adds, '. . . that produced in this nation the doubt, which so much agitated the mind of men in the reign of the second Charles, whether an Act of Parliament could of right alter or limit the succession of the Crown.'[2] His second objection is in the interests not of the government but of the governed: that as the contract would bind subjects as well as rulers, a man would be obliged 'to abide by the form of government which he finds established, be it ever so absurd or inconvenient'. Lastly, the idea that 'every violation of the compact on the part of the governor releases the subject from his allegiance and dissolves the government', owing to the uncertainty of the terms of the compact and the difficulty of determining whether they have actually been violated, 'would endanger the stability of every political fabric in the world, and has in fact supplied the disaffected with a topic of seditious declamation'. The compact, therefore, being 'unfounded in its principle, and dangerous in the application', must be rejected; the duty of allegiance, according to Paley, is really grounded on

---

[1] Paley in effect confuses a fiction with a logical postulate; but he was not alone in this. Cf. Cornewall Lewis's theory (below, p. 203; also Kant's theory that the contract was an 'idea of reason', according to which we were to treat the state 'as if' it were based on contract.

[2] Here Paley seems to suggest that the Whigs themselves were deterred by their own idea of contract; but in fact the objections to the competence of Parliament to pass the Exclusion Bill came from the Tory belief in divine right. Cf. my *Fundamental Law in English Constitutional History*, c. ix.

'the Will of God as collected from expediency', and this position he proceeds to justify.

Paley's practical objections to the contract theory leave its theoretical value as an analysis of political obligation untouched, as do his arguments that it is historically untrue; while in so far he deals with it in its philosophical sense he appears to misunderstand it. But he probably did much to shake what faith remained in the old theory, and to compel those who still found something of value in the idea of contract to reshape their doctrine in order to meet his arguments.

We noticed that the Radicals found no use for the original contract, which seemed more appropriate for the defence of a balanced constitution than for the championship of popular sovereignty. An interesting example of this attitude may be seen in William Godwin's celebrated *Enquiry concerning Political Justice*.[1] He mentions three current explanations of the origins of government—that it is founded on force, on divine right, or on the social contract. The first two of these he thinks 'may easily be dismissed', but the third, 'which has been most usually maintained by the friends of equality and justice', 'demands a more careful examination'.[2] It presents various difficulties, and in the end will be found to be unsatisfactory. 'Who are the parties to this contract? For whom did they consent? for themselves only or for others? For how long a time is this contract to be considered as binding? If the consent of every individual be necessary, in what manner is that consent to be given? Is it to be tacit, or declared in express terms?'[3]

There follows a discussion of these familiar objections. The cause of equality and justice will gain little if our ancestors could barter away the independence of posterity; on the other hand, if 'the contract must be renewed in each successive generation', how in fact do I signify my consent to the existing constitution? A common answer is that acquiescence implies consent, but this might be held to justify 'the usurpation of Cromwell or the tyranny of Caligula', and Hume has shown that the peasant and the artisan really have no choice but to remain where they are and submit to the government. Locke, 'the great champion of the doctrine of an original contract', was aware of this difficulty, but his solution of it was unacceptable: it implied that mere acquiescence sufficed

---

[1] First published in 1793. I quote the corrected 3rd edition (1798).
[2] Op. cit. i. 185–7.   [3] Ibid. i. 188.

'to render a man amenable to the penal regulations of society; but that his own consent[1] is necessary to entitle him to the privileges of a citizen'.[2] Further difficulties arise when we consider the doctrine of the general will, which Rousseau derived from his version of the social contract, among them being the problem of reconciling majority-rule with the hypothesis of individual consent.[3]

Godwin follows Hume in thinking that the contract theory really rests on the notion that we are obliged to obey the government because we have promised to do so; but the binding force of an obligation can be explained without the interpolation of a promise to respect it, and Godwin added the opinion that in themselves promises are an evil, because they may make a virtuous man act from a lower instead of from the highest motive.[4] Government, he concludes, is really not a matter of compact or consent at all, but of necessity: 'it is indisputably an affair of hardship and restraint. It constitutes other men the arbitrators of my actions, and the ultimate disposers of my destiny.' Most people, if asked, would deny the existence of any compact: they never entered into any engagement, they would say, and they would repudiate the suggestion that they must obey because they have promised to do so. The real reason why men submit to government is that no real alternative is open to them: 'government in reality . . . is a question of force, and not of consent'.[5] This, however, is not to justify any kind of force. Government 'should be made as agreeable as possible to the ideas and inclinations of its subjects'; yet in spite of the best possible arrangements for consulting the wishes of the people, no government can obtain the consent of all its citizens. There will always be a minority from whom it will encounter 'a strenuous, though ineffectual, opposition'.[6]

Here speaks the born rebel. Nevertheless, many of Godwin's points are true as far as they go, and some of his objections to the contract theory, though they really say nothing new, are effective statements of the case against it. But his somewhat pessimistic disillusionment with any sort of government is a result of his concentration on only one side of a complex problem, and there is more to be said in favour of the principles of the contractarians, if not of their method of stating them, than Godwin admitted or perceived.

---

[1] Signified, it will be remembered, by the inheritance of property: cf. above, p. 138.   [2] Op. cit. i. 190.   [3] Ibid. i. 192–3.
[4] Ibid. i. 194–7.   [5] Ibid. i. 224–5.   [6] Ibid. i. 226.

That the theory had not yet been entirely demolished is evident from the fact that a series of writers for more than half a century to come still thought it necessary to clear the ground of its ruins before erecting their own political systems. Thus Richard Whately, subsequently Archbishop of Dublin, alluded to the contract in a university sermon on 'The Christian Duty of Obedience to Rulers',[1] and surmised that it probably arose (in defiance of the plain lesson of his text, which consisted of the injunctions of St. Peter to submit oneself to every ordinance of man, and of St. Paul not to resist the powers that be) because many men's minds were revolted by the extravagant claims of 'ferocious monsters' who abused their power, like Nero or Caligula. Refusing to believe that it could be sacrilege to resist such tyrants, men either rejected the Apostles' authority altogether, or interpreted it with unwarranted laxity. But 'since the governors cannot be expected to detect and proclaim their own faults', this necessarily meant that the people themselves were left 'sole judges of the existence and amount of misconduct in their rulers', and so 'the ultimate result of the doctrine' is simply 'that the people are bound to obey the magistrate as long as they think proper—a doctrine which, if acted upon, would expose all the world to the horrors of anarchy, till a ruler should be found, not only faultless, but able to convince his subjects that he was so'. The popularity of the contract theory could be attributed largely, in Dr. Whately's opinion, to the 'misrepresentation and the perversion of the opposite doctrine' that men must obey their rulers. The truth is that 'the governor is bound to make a good use of his power, no less than his subjects are to obey him: and he is accountable to God for so doing; but not to them: for if this merely conditional right to obedience be once admitted, it . . . must destroy all government whatever'. The real need was for moderation; resistance was in great measure provoked by unwise and unjustifiable encroachments, but it was also carried to an unwarrantable excess by ambitious and turbulent men.

A more lengthy and thorough examination and refutation of the contract theory is to be found in Austin's *Lectures on Jurisprudence*.[2] The doctrine that every government arises through the people's consent is wrongly expressed if it is maintained, as is implied by

---

[1] Preached on 30 January 1821; published in *Five Sermons on several occasions preached before the University of Oxford* (Oxford, 1823).

[2] 1832; Lect. vi (5th edn., 1885), pp. 299–326.

the contract theory, that 'the inchoate subjects of every inchoate government *promise* to render it obedience'; besides this, it would be preferable to speak of an original 'covenant' or 'convention' rather than 'contract', because 'every convention, agreement or pact is not a contract properly so called: though every contract properly so called is a convention, agreement or pact'.[1] The theory as imagined by different writers, he continues, has various forms and purposes, but it generally involves three stages: (*a*) a union of the future members of the community (*pactum unionis*), (*b*) a joint determination of the constitution (*pactum constitutionis* or *ordinationis*), (*c*) mutual promises between government and subjects (*pactum subjectionis*). Finally, all this is held to be binding on subsequent members of the same community. This is clearly the formal contractarian system of the Pufendorf–Wolff school, though Austin maintains that only the third stage is properly a convention, the others being merely introductory to it.

Austin's objections to the contract theory add little to the arguments of previous writers such as Bentham or Paley, and are based largely on utilitarian grounds. In the first place, the hypothesis of a contract is needless as an explanation of the rights and duties of government, because these can be sufficiently accounted for by referring them 'to their apparent and obvious fountains; namely the law of God, positive law, and positive morality', the index to the first and third of which is the principle of utility. It is not only needless but worse than needless, because it could not have produced the effects attributed to it: it could not bind either original or succeeding sovereigns or subjects either legally, religiously, or morally. Not legally, because there cannot have been a legal contract before the existence of the sovereign who creates the positive law from which a contract derives its efficacy, and not religiously or morally, because religious and moral obligation are derived not from the pact but from the laws of God and morality.[2]

Secondly, the contract is not only needless and worse than needless but also a fiction, because in actual fact no societies originated in this way; and an impossible fiction, because the meaning of the proceedings involved would have been unintelligible to the persons concerned, unless we are to suppose 'that the society about to be formed is composed entirely of adult members ... of sane mind, and even of much sagacity and much judgement,

---

[1] On this point see above, p. 5.
[2] This is just the utilitarian argument over again.

and that . . . they also are . . . familiar . . . with political and ethical science'. The attempt to identify the coronation oath with the original contract has nothing to commend it, nor is the position improved by watering down the contract to a 'tacit' covenant. Even if not expressed in words, the intention must be the same as in an express covenant, and it is just this which could not have existed among the original members of 'an inchoate society'. The fundamental error of the theory, finally, is that it falsely supposes a necessary connexion between covenant and duty, whereas in reality there are duties which have no basis in convention at all, while there are conventions and promises (such as immoral or illegal bargains) which do not create duties. Even if there had been an original contract, therefore, it would not necessarily bind either sovereign or subjects.

Little was left standing of the old-fashioned idea that the contract had been an actual fact, even a fact of which all records had perished, when Sir G. Cornewall Lewis[1] advanced further reasons against what he called 'the fictitious theory of the social contract'— a theory which he attributed to Blackstone, and according to which, though no contract was ever actually made, 'yet it is implied, or may be assumed to exist'. In this he seems to identify an implication with a fiction, but he explains that he is not dealing with 'common language', in which 'a thing is said to be implied when it follows from another by a certain inference', but with the technical phraseology of English law. Here, he explains, 'implication has a different meaning, and is nearly equivalent with fiction. Where a thing is presumed to exist under circumstances in which it might probably exist, though it has not existed, or (what comes to the same) is not proved to have existed, there is said to be an implication of law as to its existence.' Thus there may be an implied contract (e.g. an implied promise to pay for something) although no actual contract or promise to pay was made, the meaning being that the legal consequences are the same as if it had been made. Accordingly, he argues, the social contract theory cannot find support either in the common or in the legal sense of implication. It cannot be an inference from the existence of government, because governments may exist without a previous convention. 'Nor can it be considered as a legal fiction; for a legal fiction is a supposition avowedly false, but treated as if it were true, for the imagined convenience of administering the law. A legal fiction

[1] *The Use and Abuse of some Political Terms* (1832; new edn. 1877), pp. 147–50.

without the sanction of law is a mere absurdity', and so we are involved again in the familiar objection that we cannot treat as the foundation of law something which derives its own force from the law.

This is an ingenious argument, but it seems to me unsound. In saying that a contract cannot be inferred from the existence of government because governments may exist without a *previous* convention, he is really confusing historical and logical priority; and it does not appear that an implied contract in the legal sense, such as an implied promise to pay, is a legal fiction because it is something which is not actually proved in the trial of a case. The whole point, surely, is not that the implied contract is a fiction, imagined for the sake of convenience, but that the legal conse-quences are the same (i.e. the buyer must pay), because a real obligation to pay (which is a contractual obligation) can be incurred without the execution of a formal contract, or even a verbal promise to pay. In any case, no one would maintain nowadays that the basis of government is a technical legal contract, and whatever objections this theory may be open to, criticisms based merely on the construction of legal phraseology will not affect it.[1]

Belief in the social contract as an historical fact, then, was practically extinct long before the matter was clinched by the publication in 1861 of Maine's *Ancient Law*, though his proof that the development of society has been 'from status to contract', and that the legal contract is of comparatively late appearance in the history of civilization, was no more relevant to the refutation of the basic principles which the contract theory was an attempt to express than the scepticism of less enlightened historical critics. But even if those principles survived, the whole atmosphere of the middle of the nineteenth century was hostile to contractarianism. Darwinism and biological metaphors tended to oust the mechanistic interpretation of politics associated with the contract, and not only corroborated the historical arguments that society had grown instead of being made, but also, with the doctrine of the sacrifice of indi-viduals on behalf of the species, seemed to play into the hands of the authoritarian theory of the omnicompetent state. Herbert Spencer, indeed, attempted (without much success) to combine

---

[1] Cf. above, pp. 5, 6. What English lawyers call a 'constructive' or 'implied' contract corresponds to the 'quasi-contract' of Roman Law (e.g. the obligation to repay money paid in error, on which cf. below, pp. 226 ff.), and is discussed in R. M. Jackson, *History of Quasi-Contract in English Law* (Cambridge, 1936).

individualism and evolution,[1] but most of those who clung to individualism were utilitarians, and followed Bentham in abandoning the contract.

We have confined ourselves mainly to English writers, but the same tendencies were visible abroad. As we shall see in the next chapter, a number of nineteenth-century French writers tried to retain or revive the contract theory, and echoes of contractarian phraseology continued to be heard from time to time in the political arena.[2] But in France, as in England, the scientific and biological approach to politics influenced writers like Renan, while the Positivist school of Comte and his followers, with its cult of Humanity rather than of the individual, was equally hostile to the contract theory. The political atmosphere of the Second Empire was unfavourable to libertarian principles, and the constitution of the Third Republic was based more on practical bargains and concessions than theoretical principles. Even the revolutionists had by now left the contract and all it stood for far behind, for its traditional role had been as a defence of the rights of individuals against the government, but the effect of revolutionary tradition was to allow more and more power to the state. Nothing must stand in the way of the will of the sovereign people, and it did not seem to matter if men lost some of their liberty as individuals provided that they gained more power as citizens. This had been Rousseau's doctrine, and to the same source, reinforced by the practice and slogans of the Revolution, may be traced the tendency in France to equate liberty with equality, or at any rate to acquiesce in a great deal of interference in private affairs by government officials or the police, so long as one's neighbour was treated in the same way.[3] If the political radicals thus rejected contractarian thought, social revolutionaries[4] were even less receptive of it, and soon followed Marx in preaching a communist dictatorship based on a kind of inverted Hegelianism.

---

[1] See below, p. 213.

[2] After the Bourbon restoration, for example, liberal politicians disliked Louis XVIII's claim that his Charter had been granted (*octroyée*) to his subjects by the free exercise of his royal power. They would have preferred it to be regarded as a genuine contract between the king and his people. Cf. also the remark, many years later, of P. Lissagaray, author of the *History of the Commune of 1871*, on the communard manifesto of 19 April, that 'thousands of mutes and blind are not fitted to conclude a social pact' (c. xvi; Eng. trans. (1902), p. 201).

[3] Cf. R. Soltau, *French Political Thought in the Nineteenth Century* (1931), pp. xxi, xxvii.

[4] With one or two exceptions, e.g. Proudhon (cf. below, p. 219).

In central Europe the failure of the revolutionary movements of 1848, followed by the rapid advance of the Prussian State under the guidance of Bismarck, spelt the eclipse of liberalism, at any rate as an independent and effective force; while the ardent nationalism which accompanied it, whether triumphant, as in Germany, where the teaching of Fichte and Hegel came to hold the field, or stifled, as in parts of Austria-Hungary, turned out to be the ruthless enemy of individualism. German professors no longer upheld the sanctity of natural law; not to mention the extravagances of Treitschke or Nietzsche, writers like Bluntschli were arguing that the social contract was unhistorical, illogical, because it assumed as prior to the state what is only conceivable as its product, and also practically dangerous.[1] To Jellinek, half a century later, the great objection to the contract theory was that it assumed the existence of rights independent of any social organization, and this was simply 'ein naives ὕστερον πρότερον'.[2]

It is not surprising that the only countries where the idea of contract still showed some signs of vitality in the late nineteenth century were those with democratic governments. In America, which remained a stronghold of *laissez-faire* individualism, the contract lingered for a long time, though its main stream was diverted into a new and local channel;[3] of European countries, it was only in England and France that some attempts were made to rehabilitate it as the theoretical basis of the state. None of these can be regarded as entirely successful; some, indeed, were remarkably futile, but they are worth some attention, if only for the light they throw on the central problem of political philosophy.

[1] K. Bluntschli, *Theory of the State* (1852), bk. iv, c. 9. At the same time he conceded that there was an element of truth in the contract theory, viz. that, as opposed to the theory which regards the state as purely a product of nature, it emphasized the truth that the form of the state can be influenced and determined by human will.

[2] G. Jellinek, *Allgemeine Staatslehre* (Berlin, 1900), p. 191.

[3] See Chap. XIV, below.

XIII

SURVIVALS AND REVIVALS IN THE NINETEENTH CENTURY

WHILE the Benthamite Utilitarianism, which was popular in England in the early nineteenth century, rejected the social contract, and other writers from Hume onwards had done their best to discredit it, there were a few who still sought, by suitable modifications and adaptations, to preserve it as an element in their political philosophy. One of the most eminent and interesting of these was Coleridge, whose thought is particularly worth attention because it went closer to the heart of what the contract theory stood for than the relatively superficial arguments, both for and against it, of some of his contemporaries.[1] Coleridge admitted without hesitation that if the 'original social contract' were meant as 'an actual historical occurrence in the first ages of the world', whether in the form of a covenant between men to associate together, or in the form 'in which a multitude ... entered into a compact with a few, the one to be governed and the other to govern under certain conditions', it was 'a pure fiction'. Moreover it could not explain the origin of political obligation, because unless our ancestors were already under its impulsion they would not have been capable of making an original contract. Social obligation, in fact, can be referred, without any contract, to the duty 'to act for the general good'. Not only, therefore, is the original contract 'incapable of historic proof as a fact'; it is also 'senseless as a theory'.[2]

The *original* social contract, therefore, can and must be jettisoned completely, but Coleridge propounds instead 'the idea of an ever-originating social contract' as 'a very natural and significant mode of expressing the reciprocal duties of subject and sovereign'. Just as 'the continuation of the world may be represented as an act of continued creation', so the social contract in this sense is 'a means of simplifying to our apprehension the ever-continuing causes of

---

[1] On Coleridge's political thought cf. A. Cobban, *Edmund Burke and the Revolt against the Eighteenth Century* (1929), pp. 180–1.

[2] S. T. Coleridge, *On the Constitution of Church and State* (1839), pp. 13–15. The same argument is stated more briefly in *The Friend*, § 1 ('Principles of Political Knowledge'), Essay ii (4th edn., 1844), i. 234 ff.

social union', for 'if there be any difference between a government and a band of robbers, an act of consent must be supposed on the part of the people governed'.[1] It is this which 'constitutes the whole ground of the difference between subject and serf, between a commonwealth and a slave-plantation'. Behind this difference again lies the difference between a person—a responsible being, capable of moral freedom—and a thing, which 'may be used altogether and merely as a means to an end'.[2]

This 'ever-originating contract' Coleridge sees in the constitution, about which, he suggests, many people have wrong views. It should not be equated with any particular law, such as the Bill of Rights, nor even with 'the body of our laws'. It is rather 'an idea, arising out of the idea of a State', and 'our whole history from Alfred onwards demonstrates the continued influence of such an idea, or ultimate aim, on the minds of our forefathers in their characters and functions as public men'. It was this idea which inspired their efforts in resisting some forms of government and endeavouring to establish others, and we can rightly speak of this idea 'as actually existing, that is, as a principle, existing in the only way in which a principle can exist—in the minds and consciences of the persons whose duties it prescribes and whose rights it determines. . . . In the same sense that the sciences of arithmetic and of geometry, that mind, that life itself, have reality, the Constitution has real existence, and does not the less exist in reality because it both is and exists as an idea.'[3]

This is not the place to discuss the German idealist metaphysics by which Coleridge's thought was obviously influenced. This kind of philosophy is out of fashion nowadays, but that must not blind us to the importance of the principle he was insisting on—the need to recognize an ethical basis for the state. A community cannot be held together by force and fear alone; or if it can, it is not a state. Conquerors themselves recognize this when they demand an oath of fealty from the people they have conquered, as though the people were subjects, not slaves, 'for who would think of administering an oath to a gang of slaves? But what can make the difference between slave and subject if not the existence of an implied contract in the one case and not in the other? . . . Where fear alone is

---

[1] *The Friend*, i. 235, 236. The allusion, of course, is to St. Augustine's famous query: 'Remota justitia, quid sunt regna nisi magna latrocinia?' (*De Civitate Dei*, iv. 4).   [2] *Church and State*, pp. 15, 16.
[3] Ibid., pp. 17–19.

relied on, as in a slave ship, the chains that bind the poor victims must be material chains.'

Coleridge therefore rejected the doctrine of Hobbes. According to Hobbes, 'laws without the sword are but bits of parchment',[1] but even if this were true, Coleridge replies, 'without the laws the sword is but a piece of iron'.[2] In reality the only sound foundation of government is not fear but men's sense of duty. A government is only secure when men obey it because they believe that it is right to do so, and this they will only do when they are convinced that the aims and motives of the government are good. A government which satisfies these conditions will be obeyed willingly and with consent, because men will recognize that it has a moral right to impose on its citizens the obligations necessitated by the pursuit of these ends. This consent is a present and continuing consent, and, though not an historical event, is not a mere supposition or fiction, but a reality, which can be symbolized or represented by the idea of a contract. In thus associating the contract with the implications of constitutional government, Coleridge was developing an idea which we have already met in Burke and other writers. It has been propounded again in recent years by Sir Ernest Barker, and we may perhaps leave it for the moment and return to it after completing our survey of the history of contractarian thought.[3]

A similar idea, but in a somewhat different and less subtle form, appears in the moral and political philosophy of Dr. Whewell,[4] who, after a distinguished career as a mathematician and scientist, was Master of Trinity College, Cambridge, in the middle years of the nineteenth century. He steered a middle course between the theory which represented government as 'an external fact'—the divine right of kings and the derivation of political authority from the patriarchal system—and the opposite theory which, basing government on the will of the governed, ascribed the institution of the state to the social contract. Two principles are involved in government, he points out, a principle of order and a principle of freedom, and no theory that emphasizes one of these principles at the expense of the other is adequate to actual circumstances.[5]

---

[1] What Hobbes actually said was that 'covenants without the sword are but words and breadth', but the meaning is the same. Coleridge's version may recall the German Chancellor Bethmann-Hollweg's famous allusion in 1914 to the treaty guaranteeing Belgian neutrality as 'a scrap of paper'.

[2] *The Friend*, i. 232–3.   [3] Cf. below, p. 250.

[4] W. Whewell, *The Elements of Morality* (1845), bk. v (*Polity*), cc. 4–6 (vol. ii, pp. 187–220).   [5] Op. cit., §§ 869–76.

There have never been governments which were always un-questioningly obeyed, nor on the other hand can one maintain that the rules which any individual obeys are the product of his own will. There may be 'some approximation' to this state of affairs 'when men have freely combined to found a new and independent colony', but even there individuals do not have everything their own way. Man's condition, in fact, is largely the result of circum-stances external to his own will, and Whewell accordingly agrees with the critics of the contract theory that to found government on a contract to which each individual is a party is a 'groundless and inapplicable fiction'. There are also objections, he considers, to the suggestion that by continuing to live under a government a man has given tacit consent to the contract by which it was estab-lished.[1]

As an historical theory, then, the doctrine of contract has nothing to commend it, but in spite of this 'it may be a convenient form for the expression of Moral Truths'.[2] This is only so, however, according to Whewell, if the social contract is regarded as some-thing unique, to be distinguished from any ordinary contract between individuals; for it must be remembered that a govern-ment has rights which cannot be derived from any contract between its subjects.[3] 'These rights are articles in the Social Contract', but 'it is not because it is *A Contract*, but because it is THE SOCIAL CONTRACT, that the Foundation Deed of Human Society contains these Covenants.'[4] What then, are the terms of this unique con-tract? Whewell alludes to the use made of the contract theory at the deposition of James II, but he suggests that a disadvantage of this is that it makes one of the parties judge in their own cause; and while there are occasions when resistance to government is justified, the phrase 'original contract' is useless as a practical guide in such circumstances.[5] More recently the phrase had occurred in the preambles to various codes of national law, and particularly in the prefaces to the constitutions of a number of the American States.[6] 'In these States the terms of the social contract . . . are to be found in the Constitution', and the same principle can be applied universally. In any state, then, the social contract is embodied in its constitution, 'that is, in the collection of the

---

[1] Op. cit., §§ 882–3.   [2] § 886.

[3] The instances he gives are the right to the national territory, the right of making war, inflicting capital punishment, and imposing oaths.

[4] § 887.   [5] §§ 888, 890, 895.

[6] Whewell quotes several of these: cf. Chap. XIV, below.

Fundamental Rules and Maxims of Rights, and especially of Political Rights. For that the Constitution of any country has not been authoritatively promulgated in a compendious written form, but is to be gathered from various Sources, in various forms, does not alter the nature of its obligation. If the Social Contract of New England be its Constitution, the Social Contract of Old England must be its Constitution, . . . the Common Understanding by which the Laws of Order and Freedom are bound together.'[1] It is in this sense, he urges, that the social contract has in fact been understood in this country, even in times of resistance and revolution.[2]

Whewell then turns to Paley's arguments against the contract theory. To the objection that the social contract is not a fact he replies that nevertheless, like other conceptions appealed to by moral and political writers (e.g. the idea that governors are trustees for the benefit of the governed, 'though no Deed of Trust was ever executed'), it may be a valuable moral reality.[3] But there is also a sense in which it is indeed a fact. The aggregate of laws and maxims which compose the constitution are a fact, although they grew up piecemeal, and the social contract is not the less a fact because it is not a single historical fact: other contracts, incidentally, are often the result of long negotiations in the course of which the parties abate the pretensions originally put forward.[4] An advantage of the doctrine, owing to the sacredness of contractual obligation, is that it 'harmonizes well with the love and reverence for the constitution which are among our duties', and which great statesmen and lawyers from Fortescue and Coke to Blackstone and Burke have always felt and expressed. Paley, who based political obligation on expediency, is rebuked for not admitting the 'moral sacredness' of the constitution, and for speaking with contempt of those who ascribe to it 'a kind of transcendental authority or mysterious sanctity'.[5] It cannot be maintained that the social contract theory is 'captious and unsafe'; it is certainly no more so than any other doctrine which 'recognizes Civil Liberty as an important object'. The Commons managers in the Sacheverell trial, and Burke who quoted them with approval, were no up-

---

[1] § 899. [2] § 902.
[3] § 908. In this sense it would resemble the contract in Coleridge, and in Kant.
[4] § 909. This analogy with ordinary contracts is hardly convincing, for apart from the express distinction drawn by Whewell himself between the social contract and other contracts, the preliminary negotiations must conclude in a definite legal contract which alone will be legally binding. [5] § 912.

holders of sedition; far more seditious, in fact, were the principles of the French Revolution, that power belongs to the numerical majority of the people, with which Burke contrasted the doctrine.[1]

In thus identifying the social contract with the historical constitution of the country, and at the same time basing on it an almost conservative doctrine, Whewell undoubtedly avoided many of the fallacies to which contractarians were generally prone, but his doctrine is more superficial than Coleridge's, and his contract, though distinguished from ordinary contracts between individuals, is more literal: it is not only 'a moral reality' but 'a fact'. Yet surely, even if we grant that a constitution has contractual implications (which is debatable), we must insist that in a literal sense the English constitution is not a contract at all. No rigid distinction can be drawn in England between constitutional and other laws, and though there have been contractarian writers who went so far as to describe all laws as contracts,[2] no English lawyer could agree with them. They did so, in fact, in the light of a particular theory, and to apply this to the English constitution is to beg the question. If by the social contract Whewell really meant the historical constitution, it would be much better simply to call it so; if, on the other hand, he means that there is a really contractual element in political obligation, this is something quite different from the actual constitution of any particular state.[3] Whewell probably derived his theory from ideas current in the United States, and found some corroboration of it in Burke, and possibly in Coleridge, but it is doubtful if his exposition added anything of value to theirs.

In the light of the principle of utility, which made 'the greatest happiness of the greatest number' the guide to life, public and private, Bentham and his followers had abandoned both the social contract and natural rights, although the inconsistency between this altruistic conclusion and the psychological hedonism from which he started[4] was partly concealed by his maxim that 'every

---

[1] Op. cit., §§ 915 ff.   [2] e.g. Salamonius; cf. p. 47, above.

[3] All Whewell gives us by way of supporting his theory is a vague identification of the constitution with a 'common understanding' (§ 899).

[4] 'Nature', according to Bentham, 'has placed mankind under the governance of two sovereign masters, pain and pleasure. It is for them alone to point out what we ought to do, as well as to determine what we shall do. On the one hand the standard of right and wrong, on the other hand the chain of causes and effects, are fastened to their throne. They govern us in all we say, in all we think: every effort we make to throw off their subjection will serve but to demonstrate and confirm it.' (*Introd. to the Principles of Morals and Legislation*, ad init.) This conjunction of pointing out what we ought to do and

one is the best judge of his own happiness'.[1] In practice, therefore, utilitarianism was individualist, and maintained that the state should interfere as little as possible with the liberty of its citizens. J. S. Mill, it is true, in order to safeguard the rights of individuals, was prepared to advocate a very considerable control of their conduct by the government, but his fundamental principle was that every individual should enjoy as much liberty as was consistent with an equal enjoyment of liberty by every one else, and that state action should be confined to preventing individuals from behaving in such a way as to impede the liberty of others.

This individualist theory of the state reached its climax in England in Herbert Spencer, though he inconsistently and unsuccessfully attempted to combine it with the idea, borrowed from biological science, that society is an organism subject to evolution. The goal towards which humanity was developing, according to Spencer, was a condition of 'final anarchy',[2] in which there would be no need for government interference of any kind; and even in the meantime he advocated the 'right to ignore the State'—the right of any citizen at will to be relieved of his civic duties in return for the surrender of the protection of the state, or, as he puts it, 'to adopt a condition of voluntary outlawry' or 'civil non-conformity'.[3] At the same time he attacked Rousseau's theory of the social contract on several grounds, though his root objection to it seems to have been that it led to submission to 'legislative control'.[4] Later on he reverts to the hypothesis of the social contract, to reject it once more, because 'men did not deliberately establish political arrangements, but grew into them unconsciously'.[5] Yet it soon appears that Spencer objected only to the idea that the state originated in a formal and explicit contract, for he maintained that the state is formed voluntarily for mutual protection, and 'citizen-

determining that we shall in fact do it is itself inconsistent, apart from the further inconsistency of telling us that what we ought to aim at is not our own pleasure but that of the greatest number.

[1] Cf. A. V. Dicey, *Law and Public Opinion in England*, pp. 146 ff.

[2] On this see E. Barker, *Political Thought in England from Spencer to the Present Day* (1915), pp. 92 ff.   [3] H. Spencer, *Social Statics* (1851), c. xix.

[4] Ibid., c. xviii, § 4. His objections, in effect, are (1) such a contract was never made in fact, but on the contrary 'under the earliest social forms, whether savage, patriarchal or feudal, obedience to authority was given *unconditionally*'. (His choice of feudalism is unfortunate, for if ever there was conditional allegiance it was in feudal times.) (2) Even if such a contract were made, it has been so constantly broken since that it could no longer be valid. (3) Even if it survived it could only bind those who made it, and not their descendants in perpetuity.

[5] Ibid., c. xxi. § 2.

ship then being willingly assumed, we must inquire what agreement is thereby tacitly entered into between the State and its members'.[1]

In Spencer, then, as in so many of his predecessors, individualism led inevitably to the contract theory of political obligation, and, as we shall see, he ended by openly advocating the other logical concomitant of his principles—the doctrine of natural rights. If in this he was more consistent than the utilitarians, he made up for it by inconsistency in other ways. In his last book, *The Man versus the State*, in spite of his contractarianism, he remarks that the misdeeds of legislators (i.e. their ill-conceived efforts to interfere too much in the lives of individuals) 'have their root in the error that society is a manufacture; whereas it is a growth'.[2] But these echoes of his earlier biological views were becoming faint by now, and a few pages farther on we are told that while 'mere love of companionship prompts primitive men to live in groups, yet the chief prompter is experience of the advantages to be derived from co-operation'. This can only arise when 'those who join their efforts severally gain by doing so. . . . The possibility of co-operation depends on the fulfilment of contract, tacit or overt', and these contractual relations, though obscured by the 'militant' organization of contemporary governments, always remain in force, even if only partially.[3]

The Man versus the State is a huge tirade against excessive government interference and a plea for the maximum of individual liberty. The essential contractarianism of Spencer's position is clearly revealed in the chapter, already quoted, on 'The Great Political Superstition'.[4] He attacks Hobbes's version of the contract theory as an 'indefensible assumption', just as previously he had attacked Rousseau's, and for the same reason, that both led to the exaltation of the government over the individual. Then, remarking that 'the divine right of parliaments means the divine right of majorities', he proceeds to criticize, as trenchantly as Burke had done, the current idea, accepted, he says, as a self-

[1] *Social Statics*, c. xxi, § 3. Cf. c. xxii, § 1, where he describes the state as a 'joint-stock protection society'. Cf. the views of Möser, above, p. 175.

[2] *The Man versus the State* (1884), § 3, ad fin. 'Incorporated humanity', he continues, is not a 'plastic mass' which can be shaped at will, but an 'organized body'.   [3] Ibid., § 4.

[4] Ibid. ('The great political superstition of the past was the divine right of kings. The great political superstition of the present is the divine right of parliaments.')

evident truth, that a majority has powers to which no limits can be set. He quotes from an article he had published (in the *Edinburgh Review* of 1854) on 'Railway Morals and Railway Policy', in which he argued that if a private association were formed for a specific purpose, and at any time a majority of the members decided to apply the common funds for some different purpose,[1] a dissentient minority would have a right to object.

Everyone must perceive [he continues] that by uniting himself with others, no man can equitably be betrayed into acts utterly foreign to the purpose for which he joined them. . . . The general principle underlying the government of every incorporated body is, that its members contract with each other severally to submit to the will of the majority in all matters concerning the fulfilment of the objects for which they are incorporated; but in no others. To this extent only can the contract hold.

If the majority attempts to coerce the minority into undertaking some extraneous object, their action 'is nothing less than gross tyranny'.

The same principle, he argues, holds when there has been no deed of incorporation, 'and I contend that this holds of an in-corporated nation as much as of an incorporated company'. Spencer, then, maintains the extreme contractarian view which regards the state as nothing more than a large partnership (*societas*) of individuals, though in reply to the objection that the members of a nation were never formally incorporated, nor were the purposes for which their union was formed ever specified, he admits that 'the hypothesis of a social contract, either under the shape assumed by Hobbes or under the shape assumed by Rousseau, is baseless', as also is 'the assumption that such a contract would bind the posterity of those who formed it'. Nevertheless, he proceeds, 'if, dismissing all thought of any hypothetical agreement to co-operate heretofore made, we ask what would be the agreement into which citizens would now enter with practical unanimity, we get a sufficiently clear answer; and with it a sufficiently clear justifica-tion for the rule of the majority inside a certain sphere, but not outside that sphere'.[2] Spencer is thus defending in effect the idea

[1] The ingenious examples he suggests are if a book-club devoted itself to rifle-practice, or a philanthropic society to anti-popery, or a freehold land society to financing an emigration to the Australian gold-diggings.

[2] He gives instances (e.g. fixing creeds or forms of worship, fashions and qualities of clothes, or of drink, and 'many other actions which most men nowa-

of a tacit contract, and urges that though no contract was ever actually made, yet a contractual relationship is implied in the institution of government. He was led to this position, as were most contractarians, by his fundamental individualism: the question at bottom really is, as he says, whether 'the rights of the community are universally valid against the individual, or has the individual some rights which are valid against the community?', and so at last he is led to avow his belief in 'natural rights', which he proceeds to defend against their critics.

Spencer's views had a considerable influence on T. H. Huxley, at any rate in his earlier days, although even then he could not accept Spencer's anarchism, or his theory of the social organism, which he described as a contradiction in terms. 'Much as the notion of a social contract has been ridiculed,' he writes, 'it nevertheless seems to be clear enough, that all social organization whatever depends upon what is substantially a contract, whether expressed or implied, between the members of the society. No society ever was, or ever can be, really held together by force.' The relation between a slave and his master, he continues, is really contractual. If the contract were expressed it would take the following form: ' "I undertake to feed, clothe, house and not to kill, flog, or otherwise maltreat you, Quashie, if you perform a certain amount of work". Quashie, seeing no better terms to be had, accepts the bargain and goes to work accordingly.' Similarly, if I am robbed by a highwayman who presents a pistol and demands my money or my life, 'and I, preferring the latter, hand over my purse, we have virtually made a contract, and I perform one of the terms of that contract. If, nevertheless, the highwayman subsequently shoots me, every one will see that, in addition to the crimes of murder and theft, he has been guilty of a breach of contract. A despotic government therefore, though often a mere combination

days regard as of purely private concern') which he thinks most people would be unwilling to put into the hands of a majority. The kind of ends for which all men would agree to co-operate includes defensive (but not offensive) war and resistance to invasion (except for Quakers), defence against criminals (except for the criminals themselves) and also (rather vaguely) 'use of the territory they inhabit'. Spencer was over-sanguine in thinking that all men were staunch individualists like himself. Most men (certainly most women) follow the fashion of the majority in their clothes; and we do not nowadays regard it as an unwarrantable interference with individual liberty when the state controls the sale of drugs and prohibits the sale of adulterated food and drink. Admittedly there is a limit beyond which state interference becomes intolerable, and it is impossible to lay down *a priori* where such a limit lies; but in practice it is largely a question of what people are or have grown accustomed to.

of slaveholding and highway-robbery, nevertheless implies a contract between governor and governed, with voluntary submission
on the part of the latter; and *a fortiori* all other forms of government are in like case.'

A contract between any two men, he points out, implies the
restriction of the freedom of each in some particulars. The high--
wayman gives up his freedom to shoot me, on condition that I give
up my freedom to do as I like with my money: I give up my
freedom to kill Quashie, on condition that Quashie gives up his
freedom to be idle.

And the essence of every social organization, whether simple or complex, is the fact that each member voluntarily renounces his freedom in
certain directions, in return for the advantages which he expects from
association with the other members of that society. Nor are constitutions, laws, or manners, in ultimate analysis, anything but so many
expressed or implied contracts between the members of a society to do
this, or abstain from that.[1]

If Huxley's examples of contracts are valid, the implication is
that any amount of tyranny or coercion could be interpreted as
contractual, and this is surely a *reductio ad absurdum* of the whole
idea of an implied contract. Twenty years later, indeed, Huxley
had changed his mind on the subject of the social contract, and
admitted that while 'we have sadly little definite knowledge of the
manner in which polities arose, . . . if anything is certain, it is that
the notion of a contract, whether expressed or implied, is by no
means an adequate expression of the process. The most archaic
polities of which we have any definite record are either families, or
federations of families: and the most doctrinaire of political philosophers', he now tells us, 'will hardly be prepared to maintain that
the family polity was based upon contract between the *pater-
familias* and his wife and children.'[2] He traces the history of two
opposing theories of politics, one individualism, the other what for
want of a better word he calls *regimentation*:[3] neither is a satisfactory theory of government, he contends, and he suggests that
government in effect should be empirical in policy, and be guided
in its conduct and decisions by the circumstances and public
opinion of the day.

[1] T. H. Huxley, *Administrative Nihilism* (1871), published in *Method and
Results* (1893), pp. 272–4.
[2] In his *Essay on Government* (1890), published in *Method and Results*,
p. 420. 		[3] Ibid., p. 392.

All that survived of our theory in England by the later part of the nineteenth century, even in individualist circles, was thus a kind of implied or tacit contract, which was clung to as a necessary hypothesis in order to correlate government with individual liberty; but with the realization, as by Huxley, that an adequate political theory can never be founded on a one-sided individualism, even that had to be abandoned. If we turn to the few French writers of the same period who still maintained a belief in the social contract, we shall find that they too were continually driven to modify or attenuate their contractarianism in the face of attack, until at last there was hardly anything left of it.

Before examining these, however, it is worth noticing that one or two of the early communists in France, before communism had become dominated by the doctrines of Karl Marx, made use of the contract theory, and still retained, politically, the individualism of the revolutionary tradition. Étienne Cabet, for instance, defined a 'véritable Société' as a 'réunion d'hommes qui, librement et volontairement, conviennent de s'associer dans leur intérêt commun'.[1] There can be only 'société' among men, he explains, when they are free and equal and willingly consent to unite; otherwise they are not 'associés', but masters and slaves or quasi-slaves, exploiters and exploited. The common interest is the interest of them all, for it is inconceivable that men who are free and equal should voluntarily unite in the interest of only some of their number; and their common interest is 'de conserver et de garantir leurs droits naturels et d'empêcher que les plus forts ne portent atteinte aux droits des plus faibles; c'est de maintenir et de perfectionner l'Égalité naturelle'. In the light of these principles, existing nations, in which 'société' is found among the aristocrats, but not between the aristocrats and the people, or between rich and poor, are condemned as not 'véritables sociétés' at all: they have been created by conquest, and not 'par une convention expresse'.[2]

This is little more than an echo of common revolutionary doctrine, but the idea of contract took a more original shape in the mind of Proudhon. He starts from a position of extreme individualism, according to which 'l'association est un lien qui répugne

---

[1] E. Cabet, *Voyage en Icarie* (2nd edn., Paris, 1842), p. 554. Cabet was largely influenced by Babeuf, who, as we have seen (p. 177, above), also thought in contractual terms.

[2] Ibid., p. 555.

naturellement à la liberté, et auquel on ne consent à se soumettre qu'autant qu'on y trouve une indemnité suffisante': all 'utopies sociétaires', therefore, can be met by this 'règle pratique: Ce n'est jamais que malgré lui, et parce qu'il ne peut faire autrement, que l'homme s'associe.'[1] The 'contrat d'association', therefore, cannot become 'la loi universelle', because it only applies under certain conditions, and its disadvantages increase much more rapidly than its advantages: moreover, the 'solidarité' which it creates is limited to 'ce qui concerne les affaires de la société'; apart from that, men remain 'insolidaires'.[2]

Rousseau, therefore, misunderstood the social contract, and his principles lead not to liberty but to the subordination of the workers to a capitalist tyranny.[3] The true *contrat social*, in fact, which should increase every man's liberty and well-being, is to be distinguished, according to Proudhon, from the *contrat de société*, with which it has nothing in common. Among the many 'rapports' defined and regulated by the social contract Rousseau saw only 'les rapports politiques', and so suppressed the fundamental elements of the contract, and occupied himself with secondary ones, while liberty was lost in the process.[4] The true *contrat social* is not 'l'accord du citoyen avec le gouvernement' but 'l'accord de l'homme avec l'homme, accord duquel doit résulter ce que nous appelons la société'.[5] It is equivalent to *justice commutative*;[6] it is the act whereby two or more individuals 'conviennent d'organiser entre eux . . . cette puissance industrielle que nous avons appelée *l'échange*'. It is essentially synallagmatic, reciprocal.[7]

This is not the place to discuss Proudhon's purely economic ideas, or the attempt of his followers to realize by a Bank of Exchange, in which notes were to be issued against produce handed in, his idea that society should rest on a basis of equality and reciprocity of service. According to Proudhon his commutative contract not only 'laisse le contractant libre, il ajoute à sa liberté; non seulement il lui laisse l'intégralité de ses biens, il ajoute à sa

---

[1] P. J. Proudhon, *Idée Générale de la Révolution au XIXᵉ Siècle* (Paris, 1851), p. 89.   [2] pp. 90, 92.

[3] pp. 124, 128 ff., 133.   [4] Op. cit., p. 127.

[5] Proudhon obviously misinterprets Rousseau here, for Rousseau expressly repudiated the contract between government and citizens, and, as far as the parties to it were concerned, his contract in fact was just what Proudhon proposed to substitute for it.

[6] p. 123. Cf. p. 124, where the contrat is called *la convention commutative*, and p. 127, where *le contrat social* is said to be 'de l'essence du contrat commutatif'.   [7] p. 125.

propriété'.[1] It must be 'librement débattu, individuellement consenti, signé, *manu propria*, par tous ceux qui y participent'. Otherwise it will be only 'une conspiration contre la liberté et le bien-être des individus les plus ignorants, les plus faibles et les plus nombreux'.[2] But while even more Utopian than Rousseau's, Proudhon's contract, for all its individualist appearance, involves just as complete a surrender by the individual of his personal independence; for it is 'l'acte suprême par lequel chaque citoyen engage à la société son amour, son intelligence, son travail, ses services, ses produits, ses biens; en retour de l'affection, des idées, travaux, produits, services et biens de ses semblables'.[3] In the absence of coercion such an ideal would seem to involve a degree of unselfishness and public spirit seldom attained by men; but apart from the novelty of its content and its consequent unpracticalness, the principle underlying Proudhon's contract does not differ fundamentally from that of the regular political contractarians.

We return to more normal channels with the philosopher Renouvier, who had been a revolutionary in 1848, but in later life adopted a view modified to some extent by the influence of idealism. 'La convention sociale', he tells us, must not be understood 'comme réelle historiquement, mais comme supposée en vertu de la raison qui la conçoit et qui travaille incessamment à la dégager des faits. Elle est donnée d'une manière implicite . . .; elle se formule plus ou moins imparfaitement à travers toutes sortes de voies d'habitude et de contrainte acquise ou renouvelée.' The contract is thus an 'idea of reason', as in Kant, but it is more than this: it is not an hypothesis by which we can explain political obligation 'as if' it were founded on contract, but is real in fact as well, since it is implicit in social relationships.[4] Renouvier goes farther still, and in a guarded form upholds the idea of natural rights. For since 'la puissance sociale' may fail to protect the rights of each citizen against his neighbours, and act unjustly, certain rights must be reserved against society itself. Therefore 'il faut ajouter à la fiction et à la réalité du contrat social cette autre fiction et cette autre réalité de la conservation stipulée de droits personnels, individuels'. These must include a right to act, 'dans une mesure quelconque', either without or against society, and to

---

[1] Op. cit., p. 127.   [2] p. 126.   [3] p. 125.
[4] Ch. Renouvier, *Science de la Morale* (Paris, 1869), i. 471. Cf. p. 383: 'Le contrat social est une fiction si l'on veut, mais qui a son équivalent réel dans la nature des choses.'

modify its conditions when necessary.[1] In a hesitant way Renouvier thus resembled Herbert Spencer, but his ideas were inadequately thought out, and one can hardly rest satisfied with this notion that the social contract and its accompanying natural rights are at the same time both fictitious and real.

A more thorough attempt to combine what truth there was in contractarian thought with current ideas that seemed to conflict with it was made by Alfred Fouillée, who, like Spencer, tried to reconcile the individualism associated with the social contract with the theory borrowed from contemporary biology, according to which society was to be explained as a social organism.[2] To the objection of Bluntschli, Maine, and others that the social contract is unhistorical he answers, rightly enough, that their criticism is due to a misunderstanding, since the social contract theory is not properly concerned with the past of the state; though we might not all agree with his further dictum that its proper subject is what the state can, and ought to, become.[3] Even historically, he declares, the theory is not so false as its critics assert, for it expresses a real tendency of humanity.[4] It is true that we are born, in spite of ourselves, into a formed society, but even so, according to Fouillée, the contract is not ruled out. When we come of age, 'nous adhérons par nos actes mêmes au contrat social en vivant au sein de l'État sous les lois communes de l'État'. This (which reminds us of the theory of Locke[5]) is no mere juristic quasi-contract,[6] 'c'est un contrat réel dont le "signe juridique" est l'action au lieu d'être une parole ou une signature'. Fouillée thus ranges himself, in a modified form, with those who regard the state as based on a real but tacit contract. Indeed, his contract is not even tacit, for he holds that in a constitutional country, particularly one in which there is universal suffrage, the exercise of the vote amounts to a solemn renewal of the social contract.[7]

This seems rather dubious language, but he is on a sounder footing when he asserts that 'le droit' is the proper standpoint from which to appreciate the contractual position. Political philosophy is concerned with right, not with historical fact; the philo-

---

[1] Ibid. This presumably involves a justification of revolution under certain circumstances.

[2] A. Fouillée, *La Science Sociale Contemporaine* (Paris, 1880), p. 2.

[3] Ibid., pp. 5–6.   [4] Ibid., p. 7.

[5] Cf. above, p. 138.

[6] Such, e.g., as the payment in error by someone of a sum not due; cf. below, p. 226.   [7] Op. cit., p. 11.

sophical right of property, for example, would not be established by an historical recital of all the thefts, robberies, and conquests in which property actually originated.[1] Bluntschli objects that individuals by contract could create only *droit privé*, but not *droit public*: individuals possess private property which they can dispose of by contract; but their contracts cannot have a political object unless there already exists a community superior to the individual, since a political object is not the property of individuals, but the public good of the community. This is dismissed as the objection of a jurist. For even if the individual can dispose by contract only of his private fortune, after all, asks Fouillée, is it not this which is involved in the constitution and government of the state? Is it not my fortune, my property, my liberty which is affected by the laws? Bluntschli, in fact, like all Germans under the influence of Hegel, regards the state as possessing a personality different from that of its component citizens, and having rights of its own opposed to theirs. But this is a mythological attitude to the state, and its danger, as he truly says, is that it leads to imperialism, *Grosspolitik*, war, and conquest.[2]

As against this, Fouillée stoutly defends what he calls the *État de Droit* or *Rechtstaat*,[3] whose object is to safeguard the rights and increase the capacities of its citizens.[4] At the same time he does not agree that the function of the state is confined to the mere maintenance of security—the *laissez-faire* conception popular among English individualists, to which Bluntschli objects that it suppresses public life for the sake of private profit, and makes the state a mere means to the gratification of individual selfishness.[5] This idea, says Fouillée, belittles the conception of the *Rechtstaat*. For if a man has rights, we cannot say that he has them solely as a private individual, and even if we admit that the whole object of the state is the protection of rights, it may yet be also the protector of social life, which is the milieu in which these rights are exercised. The true *Rechtstaat*, then, is not solely a judge or a policeman at the service of the individual: it embraces public life

[1] A. Fouillée, op. cit., p. 12.

[2] pp. 21, 23, 25, 39. Fouillée is not strictly fair to the Hegelians, in attributing to them the exaltation of a state which has rights *opposed* to the rights of its citizens, for they would identify the 'real' interests (and therefore rights) of the citizens with the state.

[3] He reverts, in fact, to the seventeenth- and eighteenth-century *naturrechtlich* theory of the state.   [4] p. 32.

[5] p. 33. On pp. 48–52 he refers specially to the theories of H. Spencer, which he censures for their exaggerated individualism.

too, and is educational and civilizing. Fichte, says Bluntschli, began as an individualist, but ended as a socialist. True, but this is not inconsistent with the social contract theory; it may quite well be a consequence of it.[1] In fact, declares Fouillée, the contract, 'entendu dans toute son extension, doit être l'idée directrice de la société moderne'.[2]

He then examines the rival theory of the naturalistic school and their idea of the 'social organism',[3] until at length we reach his solution of the problem of the state: 'L'Organisme contractuel, conciliation des idées de contrat et d'organisme.'[4] Suppose the various organs of the human body were conscious of their functions, but accepted the necessity of their organic coexistence, and continued to fulfil their functions voluntarily instead of automatically; would the body be any the less an organism? You may say that this would mean the dissolution of the body, for each conscious organ could separate itself from the others, and revolt, like the members against the belly in the fable. But, replies Fouillée, you are here making two presuppositions: (a) that the organs are self-sufficient, (b) that they are not properly aware of the necessity for their mutual co-operation. But (a) they are not self-sufficient, and (b) we supposed that they were aware of this necessity. How then could they separate themselves, were they free to do so? In a state, do all the functionaries simultaneously abandon their functions, though they are at liberty to retire? There may be crises, strikes, and revolutions in a state, but they correspond to crises and illnesses in the living body. The organic bond of the state, which seems so loose when one considers an isolated individual, is assured by the statistical law of averages, and in a lesser degree the same is probably true of the organic bond in an animal. One must avoid the error of supposing that a free contract or convention means an arbitrary one. As a matter of fact, the presence of consciousness and will does not make a social organism less organic than an animal organism, but it adds a new bond and gives it additional solidity.

This synthesis of organism and contract enables us, Fouillée continues, to accept and put in their proper place the truths embodied in the principal theories about the nature of life and of society, and *inter alia* the conceptions of organic life and of mechanism.[5]

---

[1] Cf. the position reached on an individualist basis by J. S. Mill in his *Liberty*.   [2] Fouillée, op. cit., p. 55.
[3] pp. 74 ff.   [4] p. 111.   [5] pp. 112–15.

For these two opposing political theories, social organism and contract, both contain some truth, though neither is true alone. The one appears to reduce society to deterministic laws, the other to the free play of human will and thought: the one is always talking of gradual evolution, the other seems to hope that liberty will somehow create a new world. Push the former to extremes, and the result is a kind of conservatism, almost amounting to immobility: push the latter to its extreme, and you have revolutionary principles. The truth lies between (but not midway between) the two, in a kind of left-centre position.[1]

In working out this theory Fouillée says much that is worth saying, and his criticism of the two extreme views to which he was opposed is often acute and sound. Yet I doubt whether his solution of the conflict between them achieves all that he claims for it, or whether the phrase 'contractual organism' is anything more than a phrase. For whatever be the relationship between the members of political society, it is not a real legal contract; nor is society a real organism like a living individual body. To call society an organism is to use a metaphor or an analogy; so also to call it contractual is to borrow a metaphor or analogy from the legal relationship between individuals. One metaphor emphasizes the solidarity of society at the expense of the individuality of its members; the other emphasizes their separate identity at the expense of what they owe to their life in common. Neither is adequate by itself because it is incomplete; for after all no analogy can be expected to correspond at every point, or it would not be an analogy but an identity. In some respects society is like an organism, in others like a contract; but if neither metaphor fits exactly, do we really make them fit by mixing them?

In 1896 the French politician Léon Bourgeois published a book entitled *Solidarité*, in which he attempted to reconcile the conflict between *laissez-faire* principles and the need for state intervention in economic life. There is no such thing as the state itself, he maintained; the only real beings are individuals, and they are the only real subjects and objects of rights and duties. Yet between men there arises a natural solidarity which is a scientific fact, and which, if not the origin, is at any rate the determining factor in modern social morality.[2] As a political theory Bourgeois's ideas

---

[1] A. Fouillée, op. cit., p. 392.

[2] L. Bourgeois, *Solidarité* (Paris, 1896). Cf. p. 89: 'L'État... n'est pas un être isolé ayant en dehors des individus qui le composent une existence réelle, et

were nothing but a shallow eclecticism borrowed largely from Fouillée, but he seems to have had a remarkable influence on contemporary intellectual life in France, so much so that *Solidarité* has been described as the dominant philosophy of French republicanism till well after the end of the First World War.[1] In the course of this work Bourgeois remarked that the mutual exchange of services 'est la matière du quasi-contrat d'association qui lie tous les hommes'.[2] He derived the phrase 'quasi-contract' from Fouillée, who used it[3] to denote the tacit but voluntary adhesion to a community which its members signify by their continued presence in it. Fouillée had expressly said that this was something more than the juristic quasi-contract, and Bourgeois probably meant to convey by it no more than that the relationship between the individual members of the state, though not really a contract, was like a contract. But his possibly unguarded remark gave rise to a novel theory, which, far-fetched as it was, is of some interest as having fanned one of the last expiring flickers of contractarianism in modern political discussion.

The dispute began with a short article by A. Darlu, in which he reviewed Bourgeois's book, and condemned his doctrine as nothing but an extreme form of individualism, logically ending in anarchy, and in fact contradictory to the thesis of solidarity which Bourgeois himself had based upon it. The real explanation, according to Darlu, of the solidarity of society, including both the bonds which unite men living together, and the solidarity of the past with the present and future generations, is that society has its own reality; that society is truly an organism, though not necessarily an animal organism, and that social duty, therefore, while different from the inescapable heredity which binds the animal to its species, is not a mere contract of exchange or association of business men. In fact neither biology nor economics can provide an adequate account of the almost mystic bond which unites citizens to their country, and men to humanity.[4]

pouvant être le sujet des droits particuliers et supérieurs opposables au droit des hommes. Ce n'est pas donc entre l'homme et l'état ou la société que repose le problème du droit et du devoir; c'est entre les hommes eux-mêmes, mais entre les hommes conçus comme associés à une œuvre commune, et obligés les uns envers les autres par la nécessité d'un but commun.'

[1] Cf. J. A. Scott, *Republican Ideas and the Liberal Tradition in France* (New York, 1951), pp. 159 ff.

[2] Ibid., p. 138.   [3] Cf. above, p. 221.

[4] A. Darlu, 'La Solidarité', in *Revue de Métaphysique et de Morale* (1897), pp. 120–6.

Charles Andler, in an article written in reply to this,[1] contended that Darlu had missed the real significance of Bourgeois's theory, namely the disappearance of the distinction between public and private right. Most political writers have in effect personified the state,[2] but Bourgeois was unique in entirely denying the existence of the state as such. Though they are united together, only individuals really exist, by his theory, the bond of their relationship being a quasi-contract. Bourgeois himself apparently had not realized the full significance of this concept; but Andler proceeds to subject it to closer analysis, and reveals how fruitful it can be as an explanation of social relationships.

The quasi-contract, he points out, is a concept of Roman Law, and includes, according to Justinian's Code, various obligations formed without any express agreement between either party. Among a number of examples which he cites is that of persons responsible for the administration of other people's affairs (e.g. the captain of a ship, the foreman of a factory, the manager of a joint-stock company), who are sometimes obliged, without precise orders, to undertake engagements which will bind their masters. Again, if several persons own property in common, the decision of the proprietors present at a meeting summoned for the purpose (e.g. a shareholders' meeting) will bind absentees; another instance is that of a sum of money which was not due being paid in error, when *ipso facto* an obligation arises for the payee to repay the money.

Legally obligations such as these do not rest on contract, Andler continues, for often no express agreement could be made, and the Romans held that they arose out of the nature of things, either from utility or from equity, and therefore, though not contracts, they were binding like contracts, *quasi ex contractu*. They resemble contracts, not in the causes which render them valid, but in their legal effect. Now the private quasi-contract and the social community have this point in common, that they both represent a solidarity not expressly agreed to, and one of the errors of the social contract theory is therefore avoided by the theory of the quasi-

---

[1] Ch. Andler, 'Du Quasi-Contrat Social et de M. Léon Bourgeois', in *Revue de Métaphysique et de Morale* (1897), pp. 521–30.

[2] Apart from the theories of Hegelians or biologists, most contractarians even, it will be remembered, had conceived that the social contract produced a corporate personality of some sort or other which then stood over against individual citizens. Even an extreme individualist like Spencer spoke of the rights which men had against the state, thereby attributing to the state a real existence.

contract. Bourgeois, however, did not explain how social solidarity is actually created by the quasi-contracts of individuals, and Andler accordingly devotes some pages to demonstrating that all the obligations of public life can be explained on this basis.

Modern division of labour, he suggests, is nothing but a continous administration of the affairs of all by each. Every man therefore owes a debt to all living men, by reason of and in proportion to the services they all render to him. This exchange of services, as Bourgeois had said, is the matter of the quasi-contract of association which binds all men together, and the object of social legislation is the equitable redistribution of the services exchanged. Are not these genuine quasi-contracts, Andler asks, such as that which involves the repayment of money not rightly due? Further, in order that this debt of each to all, and of one class to others, may be repaid, there must be an arrangement by which the administration of the affairs of all the individuals in the community is put into the hands of an administrator who shall administer them simultaneously. This simultaneous and equitable administration of the interests of all is what is called government, and in this respect men in society are like the members of a joint-stock company when they choose a board of directors. Here, then, is a new quasi-contract, between individuals and those of their number who form the government, and its content corresponds exactly with affairs of state.

Besides the debts, material and intellectual, which each individual owes to all his contemporaries, we must consider what he owes to all the dead as well. Before we were born our ancestors administered our affairs, and we owe them a debt in respect of these services. We cannot, indeed, repay debts to the dead, but our descendants will need us in turn to perform services on their behalf. This unending quasi-contract is what we call 'le sentiment de la patrie'. So, he concludes, we have three quasi-contracts enclosed within one another—that of individuals between each other, of governors with the governed, and of living men with past and future generations—and these constitute the whole legal structure of public life.

Here, indeed, was a novel and ingenious political theory. Several previous writers had used the phrase quasi-contract as a vague concession to the objection that political relationships are not really contractual, but none had attempted a detailed analysis of the state into a congeries of the quasi-contracts actually recognized by Roman Law. But presumably this was just a clever *jeu d'esprit*, and its inadequacy in real life was amply shown in a second article by Darlu,[1] in which he also pointed out that Andler had misconstrued the Roman quasi-contract, which properly interpreted would not really bear the weight that he had laid upon it. Into the details of this refutation we need hardly enter here, for though there have been contractarians who compared the state to a joint-stock company, no one has ever seriously proposed to explain the whole fabric of the state by means of such an obscure and relatively unimportant juristic concept as the Roman quasi-contract. Whatever truth there was in the contract theory, or whatever validity it might still retain in the light of modern thought, it could hardly be rescued from extinction by being diverted into this bypath.

[1] A. Darlu, 'Encore quelques Réflexions sur le Quasi-contrat Social', in *Revue de Métaphysique et de Morale* (1898), pp. 113–22.

XIV

THE CONTRACT IN AMERICAN THOUGHT

WE have seen in Chapter VII that contractarian ideas were widely held in the Puritan colonies in New England in the seventeenth century. They were reinforced by the writings of Locke, which had a considerable influence in America, and it was a common belief there in the eighteenth century that the people possessed certain natural rights, that governments owed their power to the consent of the governed, and that consequently the people could revolt against oppressive rulers. The struggle for independence gave a new impetus to this type of thought, which found expression in numerous publications of the time, and was reflected in the Declaration of Independence itself. The social contract was not usually interpreted as literally as it was by Thomas Paine, who drew a fanciful picture of early settlers assembling round a tree to debate and make regulations for their future government, which later, as the settlement grew, came to be in the hands of elected representatives;[1] but it was a constant factor in political discussions in America.

In Rhode Island, for example, it was maintained that liberty was man's greatest blessing, though it was admitted that absolute liberty was incompatible with any kind of government. 'The safety resulting from society, and the advantage of just and equal laws, hath caused men to forego some part of their natural liberty and submit to government. This appears to be the most rational account of its beginning; although, it must be confessed, mankind have by no means been agreed about it.' But none could dispute that the British constitution was founded by compact, and established by the consent of the people. 'By this most beneficent compact, British subjects are to be governed only agreeably to laws to which themselves have some way consented; and are not to be compelled to part with their property, but as it is called for by the authority of the laws.' On these grounds (supplemented by quotations from Thucydides on the relations between Corinth, Corcyra, and Epidamnus, and other authorities, in Greek history and elsewhere, to show that the rights of colonies were equal to

[1] T. Paine, *Common Sense* (1771), *ad init.*

those of the mother country) was based an argument for colonial immunity from the stamp-duties and other grievances.[1]

The direct influence of Locke is well shown in an essay by Samuel Adams, written in 1771 in opposition to Hutchinson's Anglophile *History of Massachusetts*. After quoting Locke's theory with approval, Adams remarks that 'our historian, before he asserted so peremptorily that the ancestors of this colony, as colonists, were subject to the control of the parent state, should have first made it appear that by positive engagement, or express promise or compact, they had thus bound themselves'. Locke had defended the right of the subjects of any country to sever their connexion with it and 'incorporate into any other commonwealth, or begin a new one *in vacuis locis*': it was just this that the American colonists had done, and the parent state therefore had no jurisdiction over them.[2]

Locke was also probably the source of the famous 'self-evident truths' enunciated in the opening paragraphs of the Declaration of Independence (4 July 1776): 'That all men are created equal, that they are endowed by their Creator with certain unalienable rights, that among these are Life, Liberty and the pursuit of Happiness. That to secure these rights, Governments are instituted among Men, deriving their just powers from the consent of the governed . . .', and that the people have a right to alter or abolish a government which 'becomes destructive of these ends', or to institute a new government in its place. This Declaration involves the contract theory only by implication, but the Virginian Declaration of Rights which preceded it (12 June 1776) is closer both to Locke and to the contract theory, while incidentally it directly repudiates the Hobbesian version of the contract:

I. That all men are by nature equally free and independent, and have certain inherent rights, of which, when they enter into a state of society, they cannot by any compact deprive or divest their posterity; namely, the enjoyment of life and liberty, with the means of acquiring and possessing property, and pursuing and obtaining happiness and safety.

II. That all power is vested in, and consequently derived from, the people; that magistrates are their trustees and servants, and at all times amenable to them.[3]

[1] 'The Rights of Colonies Examined' (Providence, R.I., 1764), in *Rhode Island Records*, vi. 416.

[2] Quoted in W. V. Wells, *Life of Samuel Adams* (Boston, Mass., 1865), i. 428, 429.

[3] Both these Declarations of Rights are printed in the Appendix to D. G. Ritchie, *Natural Rights*.

The prevalence of contractarian ideas in the United States at this time is well illustrated by reference to the actual constitutions of the component states of the Union. The constitution of New Jersey (1776),[1] for instance, declares:

Whereas all the constitutional authority ever possessed by the kings of Great Britain over these colonies, or their other dominions, was, by compact, derived from the people, and held of them for the common interest of the whole society; allegiance and protection are, in the nature of things, reciprocal ties, each equally depending on the other, and liable to be dissolved by the others being refused or withdrawn.

George III had refused protection, and therefore no longer had any civil authority. Two other early constitutions imply or refer to the same theory. The Virginia Declaration has already been quoted, and in the same year (1776) Maryland declared 'that all government of right originates from the people, is founded in compact only, and instituted solely for the good of the whole'. The constitution of Massachusetts (1780) echoes the same theme: 'The body-politic is formed by a voluntary association of individuals; it is a social compact by which the whole people covenants with each citizen and each citizen with the whole people that all shall be governed by certain laws for the common good.' The same is true in effect of New Hampshire (1784), though the actual phrase 'social compact' does not occur there. Several states, though not mentioning the contract, refer to men's natural (or inherent) and inalienable rights,[2] and sometimes we find a reference to both natural rights and the social contract, the latter being virtually identified with the constitution itself.[3] Thus in Kentucky (1792) it was declared 'that all men, when they form a social compact, are equal', while several states adopted a formula, practically identical in each case, which stated that in order 'that the general, great, and essential principles of liberty and free goverment may be recognized and established, we declare: that all free men, when they form a social compact, are equal in rights . . .', &c.[4]

[1] For this and other constitutions see B. P. Poore, *The Federal and State Constitutions . . . of the U.S.* (Washington, D.C., 1877).

[2] e.g. Delaware (1776), Pennsylvania (1776), Vermont (1777), Tennessee (1796), Ohio (1802), Indiana (1816), Maine (1820), Iowa (1846), Wisconsin (1848), California (1849), Kansas (1855), Nevada (1864), Nebraska (1866–7). North and South Carolina, whose original constitutions (1776) mentioned neither social contract nor natural rights, included natural rights in later revisions.　　　[3] Cf. Chipman's theory, below, p. 232.

[4] Words to this effect occur in Mississippi (1817), Connecticut (1818), Alabama (1819), Arkansas (1836), Florida (1838), Texas (1845), and Oregon (1857).

With the successful conclusion of the revolt against Great Britain, American political writers continued to develop the same basic principles as had served them well in the revolutionary period, while adapting them to the new requirements of an epoch of settled government. Thus Chipman, while maintaining that it cannot be denied that 'the savage state is a state of nature to man', also declared that 'a state of improvement is not opposed to a state of nature' and that man has 'an appetite for society'.[1] Almost all writers, he continued, European and American, had held that 'man, on entering into civil society, of necessity sacrifices a part of his natural liberty'.[2] But 'the revolution in America has opened new avenues to the science of government'. No distinction should be drawn, he argued, between natural and civil liberty, because man as a naturally sociable being has no right (and therefore no liberty, which means a right to act) to pursue his own interest or happiness to the exclusion of that of his fellow men.[3]

According to Chipman, the idea 'that men, on entering into society, give up a part of their rights' arose from, or at any rate is supported by, the legal notion that a 'consideration' is necessary for the validity of any contract; the political contract, therefore, involved the surrender of certain rights 'as a consideration for the security of the remainder'. This was 'a point of great consequence', he continued, 'while government was supposed to depend on a compact, not between the individuals of a people, but between the people and the rulers'. But the idea of a contract with the government has since been discarded, and it is now held that 'government is produced by the individuals entering into a compact among themselves for that purpose'. With this form of contract we need not look for any consideration for the duty of obeying the laws, which can be based directly on 'the inviolable obligation arising from the laws of social nature'. Man's rights, in fact, are not 'exclusively and independently in himself. They arise in society and are relative to it. Antecedently to that state, they could only exist potentially.'[4]

---

[1] N. Chipman, *Sketches of the Principles of Government* (Rutland, Vt., 1793), pp. 22, 33.

[2] Ibid., p. 70. He mentions Locke, Beccaria, and Blackstone, and quotes a *Letter from the Convention for forming the Federal Constitution to the President of Congress*, 17 Sept. 1787, in which it is said that 'Individuals entering into society must give up a share of liberty to preserve the rest', the practical difficulty being to decide where to draw the line between rights to be sacrificed and rights to be retained.

[3] Chipman, op. cit., pp. 74, 75. On the distinction between natural and civil liberty cf. the ideas of Winthrop, above, p. 88.   [4] pp. 110, 111.

This is an ingenious attempt to reconcile the idea of contract with the truth that there cannot be rights except in society; but in reality, if no consideration was necessary, neither was a contract. Chipman's contract, in fact, like the political contracts of many other writers, was tacit or implicit rather than explicit and historical, for he admits that 'few governments, ancient or modern, have been constituted by an actual compact among the people'. What happened, rather, was that power was conferred blindly on one or a few individuals, or assumed by fraud or violence, or allowed in the course of ages to accumulate in the hands of certain families. 'Whenever men happen in society,' in fact, 'they naturally and from an unavoidable necessity . . . fall into some kind of government.'[1]

It will be observed that Chipman's contract, while not a contract between government and people, was not strictly a social contract proper, but (like Locke's) was the method by which men, already social and living in a kind of society, collectively erected a government. This, he considered, was the principle applicable to the democratic constitution of the United States. Whatever may have happened in the infancy of mankind, it is now, 'in every free and enlightened nation, admitted as fundamental, that all legitimate government originates in the free consent of the people: that to produce a rightful government, the people, among themselves, must enter into a mutual compact for that end'. But it was not necessary, he considered, in order that the compact should be valid, that everybody should consent to every article of it. Since men are naturally social beings, it is 'a principle of natural law' that 'upon a fair discussion' the minority shall be bound by the decision of the majority if they choose to remain in the society.[2]

Enshrined as it was in the state constitutions, the contract theory lingered on as an accepted element in American political theory, at any rate in certain regions, until after the middle of the nineteenth century, but in course of time it gradually lost ground. This was partly due to the growth of the spirit of nationalism, evoked by the struggle over secession, and strengthened by the Federal victory in the Civil War, especially since the contract theory had come to be associated with the doctrine of state rights.[3]

[1] pp. 113, 115.
[2] p. 116. Why the principle of majority-decision is a 'principle of natural law' is not explained; actually Chipman only reconciles it with the contractual principle by recourse to what amounts to the tacit contract theory.
[3] Cf. next page.

Belief in the social contract was also undermined, however, by the publication of such works as the *Manual of Political Ethics* (1838-9) by a German emigrant named Francis Lieber, in which the whole individualist theory with its apparatus of natural rights and social contract was attacked in the light of German idealist philosophy. This never found a really congenial soil in a country whose traditions of the pioneers, *laissez-faire* and individual self-help, were fostered in their natural home on the frontier; yet Lieber's writing made a deep impression on American political thought, and with the growing realization that the social contract was unhistorical it came to be generally abandoned. It took some years, however, for this change of view to make itself felt in the constitutions of some of the less enlightened states, and in some it was not until their constitutions were revised in 1865 and later years that the social compact was omitted from them.[1]

Meanwhile the contract theory had branched out into a new and characteristically American form,[2] and played an important part in the controversy about the rights of the states against the federal government, which finally culminated in the Civil War. An early stage of this can be seen in a speech delivered by James Wilson in November 1787 at a convention which met in Pennsylvania to consider the federal constitution. Here he alluded to 'federal liberty' as something distinct from 'civil liberty', which was 'natural liberty itself, divested only of that part which, placed in the government, produces more good and happiness to the community than if it had remained in the individual. . . . When a single government is instituted', he explained, 'the individuals of which it is composed surrender to it a part of their natural independence, which they before enjoyed as men.' In like manner, 'when a confederate republic is instituted, the communities of which it is composed surrender to it a part of their political independence, which they before enjoyed as states. The principles which directed, in the former case, what part of the natural liberty of the man

---

[1] Thus in 1865 the constitution of Florida was amended to read: 'That all freemen, when they form a government, have certain inherent and indefeasible rights', &c. In Arkansas the phrase about the social contract was repeated in the constitution of 1864 (though with 'all men' for 'all freemen'), but was omitted in 1868 and later revisions. In Texas the social contract recurred even as late as 1876.

[2] It was not strictly speaking new, for it had been foreshadowed by Althusius, but it is very unlikely that American politicians owed anything to him. Their theories were developed largely from the idea that the American constitution was itself a compact.

ought to be given up, and what part ought to be retained, will give similar directions in the latter case. The states should resign to the national government that part, and that part only, of their political liberty, which, placed in that government, will produce more good to the whole, than if it had remained in the several states.'[1]

A similar standpoint was taken in the Kentucky Resolutions drafted by Jefferson in November 1798 in protest against the Alien Act and Sedition Act recently passed by Congress. Here we read that 'the several states composing the United States of America are not united on the principle of unlimited submission to their general government, but that by compact under the style and title of the Constitution for the United States . . . they constituted a general government for special purposes. . . .' Much the same theory was put forward a month later in the Resolutions drafted by James Madison for the Virginia Assembly, which declared:

that it views the powers of the Federal Government as resulting from the compact to which the states are parties, as limited by the plain sense and intention of the instrument constituting that compact [and] as no further valid than they are authorized by the grants enumerated in that compact.[2]

Madison, who was a member of the committee which reported on these resolutions in 1800, made the comment that if the states in their sovereign capacity were 'parties to the constitutional compact', it would necessarily follow 'that there can be no tribunal above their authority to decide . . . whether the compact made by them be violated', and that consequently 'they must themselves decide, in the last resort, such questions as may be of sufficient magnitude to require their interposition'. It is clear, however, that he viewed this prospect with considerable misgiving, and he insisted at some length that this right ought not to be exercised by the states hastily or in doubtful or unimportant cases.[3]

From this point forward the state-rights controversy developed (as far as the contract was concerned) round two questions: first,

[1] J. Wilson, *Works* (Chicago, 1896), i. 539.
[2] Both sets of Resolutions are printed in R. Birley, *Speeches and Documents in American History* (Oxford, 1944), i. 239, 246.
[3] J. Madison, *Works* (New York, 1906), vi. 349. A similarly conservative view was expressed by Madison in a contribution to *The Federalist* in 1788 (no. 43): 'The forms of government under which the compact was entered into should be substantially maintained.'

whether the federal constitution was a compact or not; second, if it was, whether the states had a right to secede, or whether, once formed, the federation must be maintained intact.[1] The whole question received a thorough examination at the hands of Joseph Story.[2] What is the constitution, he asks; is it a treaty, convention, league, contract, or compact? If so, who are the parties to it? A vigorous assertion of the contractarian view had been put forward by H. St. George Tucker in his *Commentaries on Blackstone* (published in 1803), where he maintained that the constitution 'is an original, written, federal and social compact, freely, voluntarily and solemnly entered into by the several states, and ratified by the people thereof respectively; whereby the several states, and the people thereof, respectively have bound themselves to each other, and to the federal government of the United States, and by which the federal government is bound to the several states and to every citizen of the United States'.

There was justification for each epithet which Tucker had employed; it was federal, because it was between states; to some extent also it was social, because individuals had entered into agreement with each other; it was original, because there had been a break with the old colonial connexions and a fresh start had been made; it was undeniably written; it was also freely entered into and ratified. Yet, as we shall see, Story refused to accept Tucker's conclusions.[3] Nevertheless there were other authorities who had supported the contractarian point of view: Jefferson, for example, had said that the states 'entered into a compact which is called the Constitution of the United States, by which they agreed to unite

[1] This latter question clearly involved the same point as that discussed within the sphere of the state by medieval theorists: whether the people by the *lex regia* had made a total or only a conditional surrender of their powers.

[2] J. Story, *Commentaries on the Constitution of the U.S.* (Boston, 1833), vol. i, c. iii, §§ 306–72. It is outside my purpose here to attempt to narrate the history of the state-rights question, but it is worth observing that the position taken up by Story was not original, but had been substantially foreshadowed by the judgement of Chief Justice John Marshall in *McCulloch* v. *Maryland* in 1819. 'The government of the Union, then,' he declared, 'is emphatically and truly a government of the people. In form and substance it emanates from them. Its powers are granted by them, and are to be exercised directly on them, and for their benefit.' As Professor Morison remarks, 'here is the classic definition of national sovereignty, cutting the whole ground of the state rights theory from underneath'. (S. E. Morison, *History of the U.S.* i. 316–17.)

[3] Tucker had argued that the right to secede was a natural right of which 'no force or compact can deprive the people of any state, whenever they see the necessity and possess the power to do it'. (Quoted in C. E. Merriam, *Hist. Amer. Pol. Theories* (New York, 1903), p. 266.)

in a single government'[1] for specific purposes; and many traces of it could be found in the public debates in the state legislatures and in congress at different times.[2]

The implications of this theory, however, according to Story, were that the constitution was a mere treaty or convention between the states, with no obligatory force over a state except what that state itself chose to accept. Each state could judge for itself the nature and extent of its obligations, independently of how the federal government or any other state interpreted them, and each state would have the power to withdraw and dissolve the connexion at will. Not all these views were avowed, but this was the tendency,[3] and, Story maintained, it was wholly inconsistent with the intentions of those who framed the constitution, for they never meant to place the dissolution of the government in the hands of a single state.

He then enters upon a general discussion of the meaning of compact and its relation to the doctrine that government is founded on consent, and, after a survey of the views of Locke and Burke, quotes with approval the theory of Blackstone that compact is not an historical fact but an implication of the state, in the sense that the community protects its citizens on condition that they obey its laws. This was the meaning of the preamble to the constitution of Massachusetts, and it was this which Chief Justice Jay had in-

[1] On Jefferson's views see Merriam, op. cit., p. 148, and V. L. Parrington, *The Romantic Revolution in America* (*Main Currents in American Thought*, vol. ii), pp. 11-12, and *The Colonial Mind* (id., vol. i) (New York, 1927), pp. 333-4. In opposition to Burke, who had argued that the English constitution was settled once and for all in 1689, and could not be altered without the consent of both parties to the contract, Paine had urged that fundamental laws must be reaffirmed by each generation, and could at any time be remade by the general body of the people. Jefferson in effect adopted Paine's view, and maintained that 'no society can make a perpetual constitution or even a perpetual law'. The consent of the governed, which was the only legitimate foundation for government, had been assured for Americans in the first place by the Revolution; it could be assured for the future by periodical renewals of the agreement. 'In this suggestive theory of the terminable nature of compact', as Parrington remarks, 'is to be found the philosophical origin of the later doctrine of states rights.'

[2] Story quotes the resolution proposed in the Virginia Legislature in 1798, to the effect that the powers of the federal government resulted from the compact to which the states were parties. The original form of the resolution had read 'states alone', but there was some dispute whether the people were not also parties, and the word 'alone' was therefore struck out. Similar views were expressed in the same year in Kentucky, in South Carolina in 1830, and elsewhere.

[3] He cites the Kentucky resolutions of 1798 and the Virginia tariff resolutions of 1829.

tended to convey in his judgement in *Chisholm* v. *The State of Georgia*, when he declared that 'the constitution of the United States is . . . a compact made by the people of the United States, to govern themselves as to general objects in a certain manner'. Generally and theoretically, then, the foundation of states may be said to rest on social compact or contract, i.e. the 'solemn, express or implied consent of the individuals composing them'; in practice, nevertheless, the doctrine requires qualification, for many individuals never did and never could consent, and in fact the majority has often coerced the minority. Even if we admit, in this restricted sense, the contractual origin of civil society, it does not follow that every individual can throw off the government when he likes. Citizens have duties of allegiance and obedience, and the true view of a state constitution is that in it the people ordain and establish laws for the government of themselves and their posterity. A constitution, in fact, is a fundamental law and basis of government; it 'is no farther to be deemed a compact, than it is a matter of consent by the people, binding them to obedience by its requisitions'.[1]

The same principle, Story continues, applies to the federal constitution of the United States. There is nothing on the face of it to say that it is a compact. On the contrary, the preamble declares

[1] In his Oration on 4 July 1831 John Quincy Adams had said that the constitution of Massachusetts was a social compact, and also that the 'Declaration of Independence was a social compact, by which the whole people covenanted with each citizen of the united colonies, and each citizen with the whole people, that the united colonies were, and of right ought to be, free and independent states'. But, according to Story, when Adams called the constitution a compact he meant 'no more than that it is a voluntary and solemn consent of the people to adopt it as a form of government, and not a treaty obligation to be abrogated at will by a single state'. Cf. the remarks of Andrew Jackson in his Message to Congress in 1833: without inquiring closely into the exact nature of the compact, he maintained that if it were a compact it must 'possess the obligations incident to a compact'. No party could dissolve the association without 'acknowledging the correlative right in the remainder to decide whether that dissolution can be permitted consistently with the general happiness'. (Quoted in C. E. Merriam, *Hist. Amer. Pol. Theories*, p. 264). Cf. also Jackson's Proclamation to the people of South Carolina in December 1832, repudiating their claim to nullify an Act of Congress: 'The Constitution of the United States then forms a *government*, not a league; and whether it be formed by compact between the States, or in any other manner, its character is the same. It is a government in which all the people are represented, which operates directly on the people individually, not upon the States. . . . But each State having parted with so many powers as to constitute, jointly with the other States, a single nation, cannot, from that period, possess any right to secede, because such secession does not break a league but destroys the unity of a nation.' (Quoted in S. E. Morison, *History of the U.S.* (Oxford, 1927), i. 399, note.)

not that the people of one state contract with the people of another, but that the people of the United States *ordain* and *establish* the constitution. Confederacy and compact are mentioned only in connexion with foreign powers, with which no state is authorized to enter into relations without the consent of Congress. The constitution, in fact, as its sixth article declares, lays down the supreme law of the land. When it was drawn up, its opponents objected to it for the very reason that it was a *government of individuals* and not a confederation of the states; again, when this subject was discussed, as it often was, in the state conventions summoned to ratify the constitution, the opponents of the constitution criticized it on the ground that it established a consolidated government instead of a confederation, while its supporters did not deny that its object was the creation of a national government, and not a mere league or treaty.

Story's conclusion, accordingly, was that the constitution was not a compact between parties, to last only as long as each of them wished, but a government, ordained and established by the whole people. Even if it were a compact, it certainly was not a compact between the state governments. The state governments were set up to govern their respective states, and had no power to contract with others or to delegate powers for establishing a new government over their own people. It was a gratuitous assumption, therefore, to say that the constitution was a compact to which the states were parties; the language of the constitution itself declared that it was ordained and established by *the people of the United States*, and not by the governments of the several states, or even by the people of the several states. It followed, therefore, that there was no warrant for the inferences drawn from the assumption that the constitution was a compact. And even if the constitution were a compact between the states, one state alone could not interpret it exclusively. If a question of secession arose, the consent of all would be necessary.

Story's *Commentaries* were published at a time when the state-rights question had recently been brought to a practical issue by the refusal of South Carolina to accept a national tariff which conflicted with the property interests of its slave-owning planters. In the interests of slavery John C. Calhoun and his followers in South Carolina repudiated the doctrine of natural rights and boldly upheld an inequalitarian theory of society. Government was not superimposed by a social contract on a pre-civil state of nature, but man was naturally social and political. Yet, somewhat inconsistently with this, Calhoun maintained that though government was indispensable, the minority (of white men) was not necessarily bound to acquiesce in the tyranny of the majority. Applying this view to the position of the states, he urged that the south need not submit to the will of the majority in the north, for the states were sovereign and had never abandoned their sovereignty. Though he had rejected the social contract as an explanation of the relationship of individuals to the government, he thus used its offshoot, the constitutional compact, as the basis of his claim for state-rights.

What Calhoun proposed was not secession but the doctrine known as nullification, according to which any one of the sovereign states in a state convention could determine whether a given Act of Congress was constitutional or not, and if it was found unconstitutional, take steps to prevent its enforcement within the territory of the state. By this doctrine, which found expression in a document called the Exposition of 1828, Calhoun hoped both to safeguard the interests of South Carolina and at the same time to preserve the Union.[1] This claim for nullification by a single state, however, was going a long way beyond the Kentucky and Virginia Resolutions of 1798, which proposed only collective resistance by the states, and it was clear that unless the federal government was prepared to give way, it would be bound, if pressed, to lead to secession and disunion.

In accordance with these views Calhoun moved several resolutions in the Senate (21 January 1833), two of which were as follows: '1. That the people of the several states composing these United States are united as parties to a constitutional compact, to which the people of each state acceded as a separate sovereign community, each binding itself by its own particular ratification; and that the Union, of which the said compact is the bond, is a union between the states ratifying the same. 2. That the people of the several states thus united by the constitutional compact, in forming that instrument, and in creating a general government . . .', delegated to it certain specified powers, retaining the residuary powers for themselves; that the federal government was not the final

[1] See Morison, op. cit., i. 384–401, and C. E. Merriam, *Hist. Amer. Pol. Theories*, pp. 201, 269 ff. Cf. also Calhoun's *Address on the Relations which the States and the General Government bear to each other* (26 July 1831), in *Works* (ed. Crallé, New York, 1860), vi. 60. On Calhoun's doctrines and general circumstances see also D. F. Houston, *Critical Study of Nullification in South Carolina* (Harvard Hist. Studies, vol. iii), pp. 82 ff.

judge of the extent of its powers, but 'as in all cases of compact among sovereign parties, without any common judge, each has an equal right to judge for itself, as well of the infraction as of the mode and measure of redress'.

Calhoun's speech in favour of these resolutions was met by a reply from Daniel Webster, which revealed his cleverness in debate, even if it went no deeper than the rather verbal and legalistic arguments of Story, on which it was closely based.[1] What did Calhoun mean, Webster asked, by a 'constitutional compact'? The American frame of government was distinctly called a constitution: it could not, therefore, be a compact between sovereigns, like a league or treaty between England and France. Calhoun, he proceeded,

seeks . . . to compromise the matter, and to sink all the substantial sense of the word, while he retains a resemblance of its sound. He introduces a new word of his own, viz. *compact*,[2] as importing the principal idea, and designed to play the principal part, and degrades *constitution* into an insignificant, idle epithet. . . . Sir, I must say to the honourable gentleman, that, in our American political grammar, CONSTITUTION is a noun substantive, . . . and it is not to lose its importance and dignity, it is not to be turned into a poor, ambiguous, senseless, unmeaning adjective, for the purpose of accommodating any new set of political notions. Sir, we reject his new rules of syntax altogether. We will not give up our forms of speech to the grammarians of the school of nullification. By the constitution we mean not a 'constitutional compact', but, simply and directly, the Constitution, the fundamental law.

Webster then scored another neat point by fastening on the word 'accede'. This word, he declared, 'not found either in the constitution itself or in the ratification of it by any one of the states, has been chosen for use here, doubtless not without a well-considered

---

[1] D. Webster, *Writings and Speeches* (Boston, 1903), vi. 181–238. Parrington points out (*The Romantic Revolution in America*, p. 311) that Webster and Story were friends, and Webster spoke a month after Story's *Commentaries* were finished, so that there is little doubt whence Webster derived his arguments.

[2] Webster was going much too far in saying that the word compact as applied to the American constitution was *new*, and in defending himself against Webster's attack (26 Feb. 1833) Calhoun had no difficulty in showing that it had often been used before, e.g. in the conventions in Massachusetts and Virginia; he was even able to refute Webster out of his own mouth, for in a speech in the Senate on 26 January 1830 Webster had himself used the phrase 'constitutional compact'. The word 'accede' also, Calhoun continued, had the authority of Jefferson; it occurred in the Kentucky Resolutions, and had furthermore been used by Washington himself of the admission of North Carolina to the Union. (J. C. Calhoun, *Works* (ed. Crallé), ii. 268, 276.)

purpose. The natural converse of *accession* is *secession*; and therefore, when it is stated that the people of the states acceded to the
union, it may be more plausibly argued that they may secede
from it'. The American people, however, 'do not say that they
accede to a league, but they declare that they *ordain and establish*
a Constitution', and the language used by their conventions was
'that they *ratified the Constitution*'. The constitution, then, is not
a compact; it sets up a government, and the doctrine of nullification and secession by individual states must be repudiated. The
whole object of the union had been to supersede the revolutionary
confederation by a regular government which was intended to be
perpetual, and if amendment of the constitution became necessary,
the constitution itself provided the proper machinery for the
purpose.

We need not here pursue the whole story of the state-rights
question in American history; but although the practical outcome
of the Civil War was to destroy the possibility of secession, there
was much more to be said in favour of the contractual theory of
the federation than was perceived by either Story or Webster.
Story's argument, as Parrington has pointed out, was very superficial, and all he did was to assert dogmatically 'that the phrase
"We the people of the United States" must be understood in its
simple literal sense, and that thus interpreted the Constitution is
seen to derive immediately from the individual citizens acting in
their sovereign capacity, without the intermediation of the state
governments. The dispute long waged furiously about this point,
and Story's analysis touches only the fringe of the argument.'[1]
Webster's argument also, stripped of its verbal debating points,
amounted to the same thing, with the additional contention that
the constitution, once established, was irrevocable and final. This
last, as Parrington remarks, was no more than an application to
America of Burke's doctrine that the British constitution had been
immutably established by the compact of 1688; and, though
tenuous in Burke, 'as applied by Webster to the interpretation of
a written document it is extraordinarily plausible to the legal
mind'.[2]

Controversialists like Story and Webster could see no third
alternative between a mere treaty or league between independent
states and the unitary supremacy of a centralized national govern-

[1] V. L. Parrington, *The Romantic Revolution in America*, p. 303.
[2] Ibid., p. 311.

ment; but in truth a federal government was something new which could not be made to fit either of these two categories exactly: it had some of the attributes of both, though all the attributes of neither alone. It is not surprising, perhaps, considering the magnitude of the issues at stake, that this theoretical question of the nature of a federation could not be discussed impartially in America; nor need we wonder, seeing that a federation was an experiment of which statesmen as yet had little experience, if American writers failed to realize that it could not be forced into categories which really suited only the unitary type of state.

Though rejected in its native country by the arbitrament of war, the contractual theory of federation (which, if its historical origin may be found in Althusius, was for practical purposes the gift of the United States to modern political theory) has since proved useful as a juristic instrument to be applied to the numerous federations of various sorts which are now to be found all over the world, and notably in the British Commonwealth. The social contract has long been discarded as an explanation of the allegiance of individual subjects to their government, but where the component units of a federation are not individuals but communities with separate governments, which may have been in existence before the union was made, there is no question of pre-social and therefore unhistorical natural rights. In this new guise the contract theory, unencumbered by the objections to which it was open in its parent form, is freely employed by constitutional lawyers.[1] This, however, though an offshoot from the social contract, forms a subject by itself, and cannot be more than mentioned here.

[1] Cf. A. V. Dicey, *The Law of the Constitution* (9th edn.), p. 146, on a contract as the constitutional basis of a federation, and D. L. Keir and F. H. Lawson, *Cases in Constitutional Law* (4th edn., Oxford, 1954), p. 481: '. . . a federal constitution embodies in effect an agreement between contracting parties'. This theory, according to which there is something of a treaty element in a federal constitution, is of course incompatible with the strict Austinian theory, and in a narrow legal sense a constitution such as that established in Canada by the British North America Act of 1867 could be regarded as simply the creation of the sovereign Imperial Parliament. But since the Statute of Westminster (1931), which provides (§ 4) that no Act of the Imperial Parliament shall extend to a Dominion unless its enactment has been requested or consented to by that Dominion, the Austinian theory of sovereignty has really lost all meaning even in a strictly legal sense in regard to the modern British Commonwealth, and it has long been realized that Austin's doctrine is useless as a key to its real political nature.

XV

CONCLUSION

WE have now reached the end of the history of the social contract theory, and it has been suggested more than once that, though open to serious objections, and inadequate by itself as an explanation of the state, it nevertheless contains some elements of value. It would indeed be surprising if a theory which had commanded such widespread support for so many centuries were wholly worthless. The end of this book is hardly the place to embark on the construction of a complete political philosophy, but we must at least attempt to disentangle the truth that lies concealed beneath the apparatus of the contract, and decide what justification there really was for the support the theory has received.

The contract theory in each of its forms has usually had two purposes; on the one hand it is an historical account of the origin of government, or of the state, or of society itself; on the other hand it is a theory of political obligation, to explain the nature and limits of the duty of allegiance owed by subjects to the state, and of the right on the part of the state or its government to control the lives of its citizens. There is no need to dwell further on the first of these two purposes, for as an historical theory the contract has now long been discredited, and its more recent adherents have wisely confined themselves to the claim that a contract is the philosophical basis of the state. This claim itself has taken various forms. It may be argued, as by Kant, that the contract, though historically a fiction, is valid as an 'idea of reason'; and this, we saw, meant that political rights and duties should be ordered 'as if' political obligation were founded on a contract, although really it is not. This theory was doubtless intended as a guarantee of justice and a safeguard against oppression; but it seems to reduce the contract to a merely pragmatic reality, and we may wonder whether in that case it retains much value or efficacy.

Or there is Fouillée's theory, who, like Kant, admitted that many existing states govern tyrannically, and believed that contract ought to be the basis of government. Fouillée's contract, however, unlike Kant's, was to be real not in idea only but in fact; but while he abandoned the theory that a contract had been made in the past, he projected it instead into the future, suggesting that the contract could be realized in practice by establishing a democratic constitution with universal suffrage.[1] But little is gained and much confusion may arise from the really quite groundless identification of representative institutions with contract, and if what is really meant is that democracy should be the goal of political evolution, it would be much better to say so directly without misleading allusions to the social contract.

More often, however, and perhaps more defensibly, it is argued that while the state is obviously not the product of any formal or express contract, yet political obligation is essentially contractual; or, if it be objected that the word 'contract' has a legal connotation which is inadmissible, that the mutual relationship of citizens is sufficiently analogous to contract to justify the use of the word in some metaphorical or qualified sense. A member of a state is aware that in return for the security, protection, and opportunity for development afforded him by political organization, he is bound to obey the laws, pay the taxes, and share the risks of defence, while the state recognizes that if it makes these claims on its members it must in return provide the benefits that they can rightly expect of it. The rights and duties of the state and its citizens, in other words, are reciprocal, and the recognition of this reciprocity constitutes a relationship which by analogy can be called a social contract. This kind of theory may, as in Herbert Spencer, be associated with an extreme individualism which seeks to reduce the claims of the state to a minimum; but there is no logical reason why the claims of the state or of individuals should be fixed at any particular level, and in principle the contract theory is compatible with a far more reasonable attitude than Spencer's to the duties of citizenship and the functions of the state.

A good example of this kind of qualified contract theory may be found in Nettleship.

The conception of an original contract upon which society is based [he writes] is, emphatically, unhistorical (in some writers, who have used it, it is avowedly fictitious), but it has been not the less influential. It is one of the most striking examples of the reflexion of an idea into the past to give it apparent solidity and concreteness. . . . It is based upon a very important fact, that every civilized community, perhaps any real community, requires, in order that it may exist at all, a mutual recognition of rights on the part of its members, which is a tacit contract. It becomes unhistorical if one goes on to say that at a certain period in the world's history people met together and said, Let us come to an understanding, and make society on the basis of contract. This has never taken place, but the potency of the idea lies not in the fictitious historical account it gives of the matter, but in the real present truth it expresses.'[1]

Farther on he repeats his belief in 'the truth that the existence of society does in the last resort depend on a mutual understanding; all the institutions of the state and of society are forms of mutual understanding, and, as they are emphatically creations of man, there is no reason why he should not dispense with them if he wished. If the theory of contract is understood in this sense, it is not profitable to dismiss it by saying it is unhistorical. That does not invalidate the fact, for it is a fact, that society is based upon contract.' It is equally true, he continues, 'that the existence of society implies that the individual members of it agree to sacrifice a part of their individuality, or to sacrifice a part of their rights, if we call what a man *can* do his rights'.[2]

What a man *can* do, however, can only be called his rights in the peculiar sense which Hobbes gave to that word, and it is entirely fictitious to suggest that men could dispense with the institutions of society if they wished. Nettleship, in fact, rightly rejects the extreme individualism which such a contention would involve,[3] and his fundamental position, though his statement of it is not altogether consistent, really approximates to that of T. H. Green. For if an agreement to dissolve society and return to a 'state of nature' is ruled out as not a practical possibility, his remark that the institutions of the state are 'forms of mutual understanding' amounts in the end to no more than the foundation of government on consent, in the sense in which Green argued that 'will, not force, is the basis of the State'.[4] Apart from this, it will be observed

---

[1] R. L. Nettleship, *Lectures on the Republic of Plato* (2nd edn., 1901), pp. 52, 53. [2] Ibid., p. 55.

[3] 'Two people cannot live and work together', he points out, 'without surrendering something which they would do if separate, for joint action is not the same as separate action.' But it is absurd, he continues, to represent 'the results of this mutual understanding not only as conventional but as *merely* conventional, contrasting them with something natural which has a deeper authority'. A 'natural' man in this sense would only be 'himself *minus* everything that he is by convention, and that means *minus* everything in him which the existence of society implies. Such a "natural" man does not exist.' (Ibid., pp. 55, 56.)

[4] T. H. Green, *Principles of Political Obligation*, §§ 80–136. Green himself is really, though perhaps unconsciously, admitting a contractual element into his

that Nettleship equates his 'mutual recognition of rights' with a 'tacit contract', and this is a formula that we have often met with in tracing the history of the contract theory. Alternatively, we have sometimes read that there is an implied contract in membership of the state, and that political obligation is implicitly though not explicitly contractual. Both of these formulae, however, are open to the objection that the recognition of reciprocal obligations, which, it is argued, is involved in the structure of society, is not in fact a contract; but if we say that there is a tacit or implied contract, we must mean, if we mean anything precise at all, that what is understood or implied is a genuine contract.

This was Coleridge's contention when he pleaded eloquently for 'the idea of an ever-originating contract', not as a fiction or a supposition 'as if', but as a means of expressing the real and abiding ethical foundation of society—the element of right or justice which distinguishes a political community from a band of robbers or a gang of slaves. This ethical element Coleridge associated with the principle of consent, the link being the idea of moral freedom. The citizen differs from the slave in that the community the citizen belongs to recognizes his personality—treats him as an end, and not merely as a means, in the Kantian terminology Coleridge inherited—and he, in return for and in exercise of the moral freedom thus granted and guaranteed him, willingly accepts the obligations his citizenship involves. The consent thus implied in the continued adhesion of citizens to the community further involves a constitutional form of government, and the reality of the constitution itself is seen by Coleridge in terms of 'an idea', really existing in the minds of men, and corresponding with the 'idea' of the contract itself.

Many of these elements in themselves are valuable and important—an ethical foundation for political obligation, a mutual recognition on the part of government and citizens of reciprocal rights and duties, political liberty, and a voluntary element, or consent, in the structure of the state, which therefore must be a constitutional structure. What may be questioned, however, is whether it is wise to identify all these elements, connected though they are, under the label of a contract, in however qualified a sense. To do so undoubtedly involves serious risks of loose thinking, as may be seen from the variety of phrases—tacit contract,

political thought in so far as he maintains that rights depend for their existence on recognition by society.

implied contract, quasi-contract, and so on—by which different writers have tried to express themselves. Aware that political obligation does not rest on a legal contract properly so called, they clung to the belief that nevertheless there was some kind of contractual element in the composition of the state, and so they attached to the word 'contract' some vaguely qualifying epithet. If we could dismiss from our minds the technical meaning of quasi-contract in Roman Law, and the elaborate and rather absurd erection that was built on Léon Bourgeois's use of it,[1] we might perhaps be inclined to feel that quasi-contract was the least objectionable of the possible alternative phrases, for it at any rate avoids confusing implication and analogy. Its attractiveness, however, is insidious by the very reason of its vagueness, and we ought really to define it more exactly. If we attempt to do this, I think we shall be forced to admit that what we really mean is not that political obligation implies a contract properly so called, but that it involves a relationship which resembles or is analogous to contract in some respects but not in others.[2] In other words, it has some features in common with contract, but others which are not contractual at all. If the phrase 'social contract' is to be retained, therefore, it had probably best be interpreted as an abbreviation for the idea that political obligation involves a relationship analogous to contract.

This, I think, is the maximum that can be conceded to the contract theory. Whether even this is tenable remains to be considered, but before pursuing this inquiry any further let us pause a moment to examine briefly the associated question of natural rights. The social contract theory has often been attacked on account of its association with this idea, and contractarians have sometimes held that not only the state but society itself is a contractual union of unrelated individuals, each claiming the enjoyment of certain rights which belong to him as a man. We are not considering here the historical idea that society was ever actually formed in such a way out of such elements, though we may notice in passing that the objection that society is not an artificial construction but a natural growth can only carry weight against the contract theory in its historical sense. History apart, however, it

---

[1] Cf. above, pp. 225 ff.

[2] Similarly, if we say that society is an organism, we are using another analogy which also is appropriate in some respects but not in others. To some extent these two analogies supply each other's deficiencies, and it will be remembered that Fouillée proposed to combine them (above, p. 223).

may be held that if society, as it is, is subjected to a logical analysis into its component parts, those parts will be found to be right-possessing individuals mutually related in a manner analogous to contract. One objection to natural rights as ordinarily understood is that if any man possesses rights, he must possess them against or in relation to somebody else; that it is therefore meaningless to attribute rights to isolated individuals, and that in fact rights necessarily involve society. But if you admit this, it is argued, why drag in a social contract to explain society and guarantee your rights, seeing that unless society already existed there could be no rights to guarantee? This argument, however, while it has point if directed against the theory that society originates in contract, does not refute the contractual origin of government or the state. At the same time it really introduces the historical factor once more, which we have agreed to disregard; in a logical analysis, on the other hand, there is no question of pre-social or pre-political natural rights or the *creation* of society or the state, for we never supposed that the individual units existed or had rights independently.

Another common objection to the idea of natural rights is its vagueness or indefiniteness. Who is to decide what are and what are not natural rights? Or are men simply to claim as their rights what they happen to desire? To qualify as a natural right a claim must indeed be a valid claim: it must be validated, that is, by some standard outside the claimant's own beliefs. Historically such a standard was supplied by natural law, with which natural rights were long associated, and their position may indeed be precarious without its support. In the last century, Hobbesian–Austinian notions of law combined with historical and idealist theories of the state to discredit natural law and the whole nexus of ideas connected with it; but more recently there has been a perceptible reaction against this attitude, both to law and to the state.[1]

Recent political trends have lent fresh meaning to old battles for toleration, whether political or religious, and even the rights of man are becoming intellectually respectable again. We need not mind admitting that the historical and idealist schools of political thought in the nineteenth century were needed in their day, if only as a corrective to the exaggerated individualism and artificiality

[1] Cf. C. G. Haines, *The Revival of Natural Law Concepts* (Cambridge, Mass., 1930), and A. P. d'Entrèves, *Natural Law* (London, 1951).

of the outlook they combated. We may admit, too, that their teaching could 'ennoble the individual and lift him above self-centred concern in his own immediate life',[1] that a one-sided individualism is inadequate as an explanation of the varied manifestations of social life, and that the liberal or *laissez-faire* theory of the state, which reduces its functions to the mere protection of life and property, is not only insufficient but unworkable. Yet the practical consequences of totalitarianism, which is what the opposite alternative leads to when exaggerated, are dangerous and repulsive. It may involve a virtual deification of the nation, or the folk, or the race (perhaps quite mythical in reality), which so engulfs and enslaves the individual that he loses all independence of mind and action; while in the international sphere the state may be led to cast aside all considerations of law and morality and embark on a naked career of aggression and conquest. 'Individualism is often used as a word of reproach,' as Sir Ernest Barker has remarked, 'but it is good to see simple shapes of "men as trees, walking", and to think in simple terms of human persons. . . . If we hold that individual personality is the one intrinsic value of human life, we shall have no very great reason to fling stones at a theory which rested on a similar basis.'[2] We can fully agree with the idealists that it is only in society that rights can have any meaning or individual personality develop its potentialities, but with these qualifications we may well feel that there is more to be said for the natural rights of individuals than their critics have allowed.

Sir Ernest Barker goes farther than this, and still stands up for the validity of the contract, suitably redefined, as an element in a modern political theory. Over twenty years ago he declared that 'there is still a case to be made for the view that the State, as distinct from Society, is a legal association which fundamentally rests on the presuppositions of contract'.[3] More recently he has expounded his theory at greater length, first in the Introduction to his edition, entitled *Social Contract*, of some of the works of Locke, Hume, and Rousseau,[4] and later in his *Principles of Social and Political Theory*.[5] The gist of his doctrine is to admit, first of

---

[1] E. Barker, Introduction to his translation of Gierke's *Nat. Law*, p. xvii.

[2] i.e. the theory of natural law; ibid. and p. xlix.

[3] Ibid., p. xlix.

[4] In 'World's Classics' (Oxford, 1947). This introduction was subsequently included, as Essay iv, in the second edition (Oxford, 1951) of *Essays on Government*.   [5] (Oxford, 1951), pp. 188–92.

all, that both the historic forms of the contract—the social contract proper and the contract of government—must be abandoned, the social contract because it is false in principle, the contract of government because it is unnecessary. The social contract is false because '*Society* is not constituted, and never was constituted, on any basis of contract. Society is an all-purposes association . . . which transcends the notion of law, and has grown and exists of itself'. And there is no need nowadays for a contract of government 'by which one part of the State, called ruler or rulers, has covenanted with another, called the subjects'.[1] In the past, when governments, consisting of kings and their ministers, stood apart from and in obvious contrast to their subjects, it was natural and useful to think in terms of a contract which defined the relations between them. But in the modern constitutional state, where all are united under the terms of the constitution, which defines the rights and duties of government and citizens alike, such a governmental contract is superfluous.

Yet, Sir Ernest believes, we can still retain the contract in the shape of a 'political contract'. The state, as distinct from society, 'is a legal association, constituted by the action of its members in making a constitution', and so the constitution itself may be regarded, like a memorandum of association, as 'the articles of a contract which constitutes the State'. A constitution is, indeed, only created by an act of contract, 'at a point of time', after a revolution, or where a federation is established, and historically, he admits, most states have not arisen 'in the climate of contract'. They have been 'formed and developed by a variety of factors: the bond of kinship uniting, or supposed to unite, a people or group of peoples . . ., the bond of neighbourhood joining the residents of some definite area in a common system of economic and social relations . . .', and so on. But even in a state like Great Britain, where the formation of the constitution has been not a single act but an historical process 'along a line of time', the same principle holds good, for if a written constitution is plainly contractual, an unwritten one is no less so. We must recognize, Sir Ernest insists, that nowadays the modern western state, whatever its origin or history, 'lives and has its being in a climate of contract, and of all the concomitants of contract: mutual concession, mutual toleration, mutual discussion, and general give and take'.

The theory thus persuasively elaborated is not essentially a

---

[1] *Social Contract*, pp. xv, xvi.

new one. It will be remembered, for instance, that Whewell also identified the contract with the constitution, and we have met with a number of other writers who, with varying degrees of clearness, worked along the same lines. Can we then preserve the contract theory in this latest sense of the 'political contract'? One cannot help feeling that the motive for doing so is at bottom a sentimental one—a reluctance to part company with an historic idea which has for so long been associated with cherished political ideals. This is by no means an unworthy motive, and if we retained the contract in our everyday political vocabulary it might be a salutary reminder of our debts to the past. For it is undeniable that in the course of its history, for all its faults and errors and inadequacies, and the wrong uses to which it has sometimes been put, the contract theory has stood for important values. It has stood, to quote Sir Ernest Barker again, for two values in particular: 'the value of Liberty, or the idea that will, not force, is the basis of government, and the value of Justice, or the idea that right, not might, is the basis of all political society and of every system of political order'.[1] We may well sympathize with the conviction that a theory which has had such a history, and which, despite the attacks of historians, lawyers, and philosophers, has performed such notable services, is not to be abandoned if it can still fulfil a useful function. But though useful, it can hardly be maintained that the contract theory is a necessary truth about the state. It is quite possible to reject the contract and still believe in liberty and justice, and indeed to argue (as T. H. Green did)[2] that 'will, not force, is the basis of the state'. At the same time I should concur without hesitation in a number of Sir Ernest Barker's points, and in particular with the importance of the distinction between society and the legal structure of the state. The failure or refusal to distinguish the political from other aspects of society, and the consequent identification of society and the state, is undoubtedly a dangerous error which a sound political theory should avoid;[3] yet I doubt if, in spite of this distinction, we are really entitled to rest political obligation on contract.

The political and legal aspects of society—the government and laws of the state—though they do not include the whole of social

---

[1] *Social Contract*, p. vi.

[2] *Principles of Political Obligation*, §§ 80–136.

[3] Cf. R. M. MacIver, *The Modern State* (Oxford, 1926), esp. pp. 4–7, 33–45, W. Temple, *Christianity and the State* (1928), pp. 98–140, and B. Bosanquet, *The Philosophical Theory of the State*, pp. 140, 172.

life, profoundly affect its character, and may even be indispensable to its cohesion and very existence, and Sir Ernest Barker himself admits that 'there is a sense in which the State precedes Society. When the State is once there, with its scheme of law and order, it provides a general security in whose shelter social formations can easily grow. . . . From this point of view . . . the State is anterior to Society, or at any rate prior to the great bulk of the voluntary social formations which constitute Society.' In fact, he concludes, neither state nor society is prior; in historic times they 'have been concomitants, either acting in turn on the other'.[1]

This being so, can one say that men constitute the state by a political contract, but do not constitute society? Men are born into the state just as much as they are born into society, and as far as consent, or a contractual element, is concerned, most men have far more opportunity of employing it in constituting or joining voluntary societies within the state than in the political or constitutional sphere itself. Sir Ernest seems to think of the modern state as contractual in two ways, but they are really quite distinct. The state, he says, 'lives and has its being in a climate of contract, and of all the concomitants of contract'; then, secondly, its constitution is an actual political contract. As regards the first of these, I should say that the 'climate' today, with its planning, bureaucratic controls, and varying degrees of socialism, is far less one of contract than in the mid-Victorian age, when Maine could plausibly assert that progressive societies advance 'from status to contract'.[2] At the same time, no human society whatever, however arbitrarily governed, could exist without some degree of mutual give and take (which is a mark of the contractual climate). This aspect of life in a community, therefore, does not necessarily connote a constitution, though no doubt a constitution encourages it. Apart from this, however, it is hard to see what connexion there is between this vague characteristic of social life and an actual political contract supposed to be embodied, as 'articles of association', in the legal constitution. It may indeed be argued that planners and bureaucrats, existing under and deriving powers from a modern constitution, and serving to adjust the relationships between citizens (the mutual give and take) for the general good, are part of the contractual climate. But in that case, as far as individual citizens are concerned, the give and take is not voluntary

[1] *Principles of Social and Political Theory*, p. 49.
[2] H. S. Maine, *Ancient Law*, chap. v, *ad fin.*

but compulsory. This, of course, brings us to the edge of one of the perennial and notorious problems of political theory—the precise meaning or definition of 'consent' in government, with all its accompanying difficulties, the general will, majority-rule, democracy, and so on. We will not plunge into that now; but before we agree that a constitution is a contract we should, I think, beware of the mistake, to which scholarly persons are sometimes prone, of imagining that all their fellow citizens are as reflective and intellectual as they are themselves. In what real sense are Tom, Dick, and Harry (or their wives) parties to the constitutional contract which defines the legal fabric of the state? They have rights which the government protects and maintains, and duties and obligations towards the legal and political organization on which the security of their lives depends, yet after all this relationship is not really a contractual or voluntary one on their part.

There have been, of course, and are conditions and circumstances in which the terminology of contract is apposite and appropriate. Such was feudal society, for instance, and such again (as between the federating units) is a federal state. And in every community there is a reciprocity of rights and duties between its members, which in some respects sufficiently resembles the relationship established by contract as to afford some ground for using the terminology of contract as a metaphor or analogy in describing the political structure of society. But I think we must decline to say that this political or legal structure, or constitution, even when it is a definite 'written' constitution, either is or implies any actual contract, however qualified. Whether in its social, or governmental, or political form, the contract theory can only be defended, it seems to me, in a metaphorical sense, and even in this sense, though often useful, it is not essential.

The ultimate *raison d'être* for the contract theory, all through its history, has been to reconcile the apparently conflicting claims of liberty and law. The demands of government could be explained and justified, it was thought, if they were based on the consent of the governed: people would freely obey a government they had themselves created and undertaken to obey. This was a useful practical weapon in the struggle against the tyranny of absolute monarchs, but when kings have been replaced by constitutional or parliamentary governments, the contractual formula cannot be applied without notorious intellectual difficulties. When I vote for a member of parliament in a general election (or for a city councillor in a municipal election), to say that I am undertaking to obey the laws he and his colleagues are going to enact does not really describe my action. In so far as I peacefully cast my vote in accordance with the constitution, and do not conspire to overthrow it, I may perhaps, in a loose and negative sense, be said to accept or consent to the constitution, but the real purpose of constitutional machinery nowadays is not to register consent.

The great drawback to kings who claimed to rule by divine right was that, though they often admitted that they had duties to perform, they acknowledged no responsibility except to God, and there was no earthly means of calling them to account except rebellion. Constitutional government, on the other hand—representation, popular elections, and so on—provides a mechanism for ensuring that ministers, and persons put in authority under them, are responsible to the electorate for their actions. If we want a formula to express this responsibility, the metaphor of trusteeship, which Locke and others employed, seems to me preferable to that of contract, for it is free from many of the misleading associations of the contract theory.

There have always been some political theorists, from the sophists of ancient Greece to the communists and others of the present day, who have sought to explain political obligation purely in terms of a struggle for power. If we reject that, and believe that justice is not simply 'the interest of the stronger',[1] we are insisting on the primacy of a moral principle. We are implying that political obligation rests on the same basis as moral obligation, or rather that, in the last analysis, political obligation is a special kind of moral obligation. Correspondingly, the powers and functions of government rest on the same foundation, and must be exercised subject to the same conditions. Here is the ethical principle Coleridge and others strove to safeguard, but it is not impaired if we recognize that the duty of obedience to the laws can be explained, without any recourse to a social or political contract, in terms of the responsibilities and duties to our fellow men which are the necessary correlatives of their rights.[2]

[1] Cf. the theory of Thrasymachus, above, p. 10.
[2] While contract, on this view, is not necessary as the general ground of political obligation, there may of course be particular political obligations, just as there may be particular moral obligations, which are definitely contractual. Such, for example, would be the special duties which a volunteer soldier undertakes to perform when he enlists.

INDEX